DATE DUE

NOV 2 6 2012	

BRODART, CO.   Cat. No. 23-221

Abraham Lincoln, Esq.

Abraham Lincoln, Esq.

The Legal Career
of America's
Greatest President

EDITED BY
ROGER BILLINGS AND
FRANK J. WILLIAMS

THE UNIVERSITY PRESS OF KENTUCKY

Copyright © 2010 by The University Press of Kentucky

The University Press of Kentucky

Scholarly publisher for the Commonwealth,
serving Bellarmine University, Berea College, Centre College of Kentucky, Eastern
Kentucky University, The Filson Historical Society, Georgetown College,
Kentucky Historical Society, Kentucky State University, Morehead State University,
Murray State University, Northern Kentucky University, Transylvania University,
University of Kentucky, University of Louisville, and Western Kentucky University.
All rights reserved.

Editorial and Sales Offices: The University Press of Kentucky
663 South Limestone Street, Lexington, Kentucky 40508-4008
www.kentuckypress.com

14 13 12 11 10   5 4 3 2 1

Library of Congress Cataloging-in-Publication Data
Abraham Lincoln, Esq. : the legal career of America's greatest president / edited by
Roger Billings and Frank J. Williams.
     p. cm.
 Includes bibliographical references and index.
 ISBN 978-0-8131-2608-1 (hardcover : alk. paper)
 ISBN 978-0-8131-2609-8 (ebook)
 1. Lincoln, Abraham, 1809-1865—Career in law. 2. Lawyers—Illinois—Biography.
3. Presidents—United States—Biography. I. Billings, Roger D.
II. Williams, Frank J. III. Title: Abraham Lincoln, Esquire.
 E457.2.A1447 2010
 973.7092—dc22
 [B]   2010033291

This book is printed on acid-free recycled paper meeting
the requirements of the American National Standard
for Permanence in Paper for Printed Library Materials.

∞ ⊛

Manufactured in the United States of America.

Member of the Association of
American University Presses

Contents

Illustrations follow page 138

Introduction

Roger Billings and Frank J. Williams

Abraham Lincoln, Esq. features chapters by leading scholars on the professional career of Abraham Lincoln. Four chapters were first published in the "Abraham Lincoln" issue of the *Northern Kentucky Law Review* in 2009, which was supported by a grant from the Kentucky Historical Society. Another was first published in the *Journal of Illinois History* (summer 2005). Three are based on presentations for a symposium cosponsored by the New York City Bar Association and Scribes, the American Society of Legal Writers. The rest were written especially for this book.

The chapters are organized into three parts. Part One, "Evaluating Lincoln's Career," offers four authors' assessments of Lincoln's career. Harold Holzer, Brian Dirck, Mark Steiner, and Frank J. Williams are well known in the Lincoln field. Holzer is Senior Vice President for External Affairs at the Metropolitan Museum of Art in New York and a preeminent scholar who has published numerous books on Lincoln. Dirck, a professor at Anderson University, has published the recent book *Lincoln the Lawyer*. Williams is the retired Chief Justice of the Rhode Island Supreme Court. Mark Steiner, a Ph.D. in history and Professor of Law at South Texas College of Law, is author of a recent book on Lincoln, the lawyer, *An Honest Calling*.

The aim of Part Two, "The Illinois Years," is to present overlooked aspects of Lincoln's career in Illinois. The two chapters by Roger Billings on Lincoln as debtor-creditor and property lawyer reveal that the cases in those areas of Lincoln's practice were his most important sources of income. The chapter on property law discusses rare examples of chattel mortgages when they were in the early stages of development as well as the more common real estate mortgages. Billings is Professor of Law at Salmon P. Chase College of Law, Northern Kentucky University.

John Lupton and Christopher Schnell (as well as Steiner in Part One) draw on their experience working for the Lincoln Legal Papers project in Springfield, now part of *The Papers of Abraham Lincoln*. Lupton, who has devoted his entire professional career to research on Lincoln's law career, is director of History Programs with the Illinois Supreme Court Historic Preservation Commission. Schnell, formerly with the Papers project, is now pursuing further graduate studies.

Numerous books discuss Lincoln's speeches and presidential writings, but they all overlook the words Lincoln wrote solely in his capacity as a lawyer. Billings's chapter on client letters reveals Lincoln's verbal skills as he confronted ethical dilemmas. William T. Ellis and Billie J. Ellis Jr. dig further into the ethics of Lincoln's practice. Their chapter traces several facets of Lincoln's practice and provides lessons applicable to today's lawyer on how to comply with and transcend some of the most important Model Rules of Conduct. Schnell's chapter sheds light on an aspect of Lincoln's career that is generally overlooked: in central Illinois, Lincoln was essentially a Kentuckian practicing law among other Kentuckians. A great many of his clients and fellow lawyers in the Springfield area were born in Kentucky.

Part Three, "The Washington Years," offers a fresh look at Lincoln as he used his legal background during the Civil War. Mackubin Thomas Owens, who teaches at the U.S. Naval War College in Newport, Rhode Island, and William D. Pederson, who is director of the Abraham Lincoln Institute and a professor at Louisiana State University in Shreveport, discuss the legal skills Lincoln brought to constitutional and international law problems. Their chapters demonstrate clearly that Lincoln's long, arduous, and intense legal career in Illinois, along with his political career, constituted his principal schooling and prepared him for later presidential duties, including the role of commander in chief. It proved to be dynamic training.

Lincoln biographers have often concluded that his legal practice ended on the day he last visited his law office. Nothing could be further from the truth. It would be more accurate to say that the most important part of Lincoln's career as a lawyer was his presidency; there, he put to the highest use all that he had learned since his admission to the bar in 1837.

Part One

Evaluating Lincoln's Career

Reassessing Lincoln's Legal Career

Harold Holzer

At the beginning of the historic 2008 presidential campaign, an aspirant for the Democratic nomination appealingly described himself as another "tall, gangly, self-made Springfield lawyer."[1] Barack Obama's declaration hardly represented the first or only example of a politician striving to identify himself with Abraham Lincoln. But it was rare indeed—perhaps unique— because then-Senator Obama called to mind not Lincoln the orator, writer, emancipator, or union-preserving commander in chief, but Lincoln the attorney—a profession that has hardly enjoyed universal approval in recent years (or even in Lincoln's time).

One might more rationally begin this essay by talking not about Lincoln himself, but about a movie—a movie that most lawyers probably know and hate. *The Fortune Cookie* is about an ambulance chaser, played by Walter Matthau, whose name in the film is "Whiplash Willie Gingrich."

Willie's brother-in-law, Harry Hinkle, played of course by Jack Lemmon, works as a television cameraman at sports events. One Sunday, an errantly thrown football and a pass receiver crash into Harry and his camera. The next thing we know, he is in a hospital bed. But miraculously, except for some aches and pains, he's ready to go home and forget that the accident ever happened.

Enter Whiplash Willie. He tries to convince his brother-in-law to fake a serious injury so he can sue for millions. Harry is about to fall under Willie's spell, when he glimpses what is playing on TV: an old movie about that paragon of honesty, Abraham Lincoln.

Worried that his brother-in-law is falling under the TV's spell, Whiplash Willie steps in front of it and utters this classic line: "Abraham Lincoln. Great president. Lousy lawyer!"

Most good laugh lines are based on an element of truth, or at least what passes for truth at the time. And this one is no exception—*at the time.* For generations, Americans were taught that our greatest president had first been one of our most hapless attorneys.

He never finished a law book, never researched a case, seldom bothered to collect his fees, and spent most of the time in the squalid room that passed for his law office lying on a couch with his feet in the air, swapping stories with friends. It was almost as if the more mundane his law practice was made to seem, the more miraculous his rise to greatness would appear. Hagiographers could catapult him from the log cabin of his birth directly to the White House with hardly a professional rest stop in between.

Movies like the one cited above fueled the fire of this log cabin-to-White House fairy tale. In the most influential of these, John Ford's *Young Mr. Lincoln,* the future president is pretty indifferent about lawyering until an old friend's son is unjustly accused of murder.

In the film, Lincoln devotes most of the trial to insulting the prosecuting attorney, throwing punch lines at the judge, or joking with an enthralled jury.[2] But at the climactic moment, he produces a farmer's almanac that reveals that there was no moon at all on the night that the prosecution's key witness swore he saw the defendant kill the deceased from 150 yards away. Lincoln's client is acquitted. Then Lincoln refuses his fee and goes wandering off on horseback, while the music of the "Battle Hymn of the Republic" swells over the credits. So an entire generation was indoctrinated to perceive Lincoln's entire career as an attorney-at-law. As Lincoln had modestly put it himself, in notes for a law lecture he never gave: "I am not an accomplished lawyer. I find quite as much material for a lecture in those points wherein I have failed, as in those wherein I have been moderately successful."[3]

Then, suddenly, beginning in the 1960s and 1970s—in the midst of a great deal of revisionism about Lincoln—an entirely new image of his law practice suddenly began taking shape, identifying him as a ruthless and enormously successful corporate attorney. Writers in the anti-Lincoln tradition have kept the notion alive ever since.[4] In this re-perception, Lincoln seemed anything but a simple country lawyer. He was portrayed instead as one of the sharpest legal minds in the West, and unscrupulous as well. He represented the railroads in their rape of the prairie in order to build unsightly railroad tracks that despoiled the landscape, or hideous bridges that marred the beauty of our rivers. He earned gargantuan fees and even helped his corporate clients evade taxes. And according to one writer, it even seemed that Honest Abe had put one over on us with that legendary almanac, too.[5]

What he had really done, we were now informed, was hold up the wrong almanac—and trick a witness into recanting his testimony. He never actually read from it because it really did not say there was no moon that night. He was just setting a trap—maybe not unlike Whiplash Willie Gingrich.

Obviously, what the reading and thinking public was left with were two radically different understandings—if that's the right word ("misunderstandings" may be more to the point)—of what Lincoln was really like as a lawyer. The problem was that serious historians had not yet done much more to unearth the truth than had movie makers. Lincoln was an attorney for nearly a quarter of a century. Yet until 2002, when new titles on the subject began appearing after a four-decade lull, only a handful of major books were offered to assess the work that engaged Lincoln for half of his adult life, and they were hopelessly out of date.[6] Yet even in the absence of easily available raw materials, a survey conducted in 1991 counted 509 monographs and journal articles on Lincoln's legal career.[7]

Fortunately, the Lincoln Legal Papers project was completed after years of meticulous research throughout Illinois, making available to historians in one central data bank, or on a widely distributed DVD-ROM version, the complete annals of the future president's career as an attorney. More recently, a handsome, four-volume boxed edition of prime cases has appeared in print.[8] David Herbert Donald relied on the then-fresh Legal Papers archives for the chapter he wrote on the future president's legal career in his magisterial biography, *Lincoln*—the first major biographer to do so.[9] But until 2006, no complete books had been based on all this newly accumulated data about Lincoln's case-by-case career in the courthouses of Illinois. I can testify personally to the perils of proceeding with research on Lincoln's life as a lawyer in the absence of this material. Together with a colleague, I signed a contract to write such a book years ago. We never finished it—never really started. We had to return our advance on royalties. It was not one of the highlights of *my* Lincoln career, but perhaps reflected the uncertainties still afflicting this vital area of study at the time it was undertaken. Happily, future scholars fared better.

At least I could console myself that I was not the first author to be done in by the challenge. Even the earliest biographies of Lincoln—commissioned by the Republicans in 1860 to introduce the presidential candidate to the people—devoted as little attention to his profession as possible. They took pains to assure readers that Lincoln remained a man of the people even though he was a member of the bar. The trouble then, as now, is that voters did not seem to like lawyers much.

The first *Life of Abraham Lincoln* put it this way: "Lincoln does not grow rich at the law . . . though possessing a decent competence, and owing no man anything."[10] Meanwhile, an anti-Lincoln writer attacked him *based* on his life's work: "He is like any other clever, awkward, common place, humdrum lawyer . . . of a small country city."[11] So the question still remains, a century and a half after he left Springfield, Illinois—telling his junior law partner not to change the shingle outside their office because he intended to return to his practice: what was Abraham Lincoln's law practice really like? And why should we care?[12]

To answer the second question first: why should we care? The fact is, Lincoln's life as a lawyer informed nearly every aspect of his future, a future that became inseparable from the nation's future. There were the obvious benefits of legal training, of course: the law refined Lincoln's speaking style, and sharpened his powers of reasoning. This was never more evident than in his Cooper Union address, which I spent more than five years researching and writing about. This oration is so deeply researched, so closely and carefully reasoned, so full of cleverly arranged facts and arguments and calculations, that it was described even in its own time as resembling a brief to a jury.[13] But this merely skims the surface.

It was Lincoln the lawyer-president who found a way to craft an Emancipation Proclamation that would read, as he put it, not as if it were written "*from the bosom of philanthropy*,"[14] but so it would stand up to the court challenges he felt would inevitably come after the Civil War. It was Lincoln the lawyer-president who ordered the suspension of the writ of habeas corpus, telling critics who argued that his actions were unconstitutional that any good doctor would cut off a limb to save a patient . . . while only a quack would kill a patient to save a limb.[15] It was just such a Lincoln who, in a letter to editor Horace Greeley, created an argument for delaying emancipation unless it could be proved that it would sustain his battle to save the union—even though he had already written such a document, and merely tabled it until a battlefield victory could provide the public relations "bounce" to cushion the controversy it was certain to inspire.[16] This manifestation of legal logic and political genius caused editor Greeley, recipient of the letter (although it was really meant for a national audience) to throw his hands up and declare: "I can't trust your 'honest old Abe.' He is too smart for me."[17] Of course, it was Lincoln the lawyer-president who had labored to find a legal rationale to wage war in the first place, calling up the militia and ordering a blockade of Southern ports, without congressional consent.

And in one of his least acknowledged but most important decisions, it was Lincoln the lawyer-president who insisted that the 1864 presidential election go on as scheduled. Without that adherence to law and tradition, he believed, the Confederacy would in effect have defeated the democracy Lincoln was pledged to defend. No other nation in the midst of a rebellion had ever held a free election. But as Lincoln put it in remarks from the White House in response to a serenade celebrating his reelection victory: "the election was a necessity. We can not have free government without elections; and if the rebellion could force us to forego, or postpone a national election, it might fairly claim to have already conquered and ruined us. . . . What has occurred in this case, must ever recur in similar cases."[18] All these decisions—extraordinary, history-making, nation-affirming decisions—had their genesis in the Illinois law practice that consumed Lincoln for twenty-five years.

But how best to understand it? For years, it was all but impossible. The records of Lincoln's legal practice had long been scattered across Illinois, preventing a full and informed assessment. But over the past decade and a half, as noted earlier, a team of researchers plowed through these neglected records to assemble the first complete record of every legal case in which Lincoln ever participated—from the rural courthouses of his judicial circuit to the bench of the state's highest court. We do not have all the answers even yet: the research is done, but the books and analyses are just beginning. But we do have more clues than ever before.

The records show, at latest count, that Lincoln took an astounding 340 cases to the Illinois Supreme Court, and that in his prime he dominated the bar in his home county. In his final decade in practice his firm handled between 17 and 34 percent of all local cases, far outpacing rival law firms, and becoming an outstanding appellate litigator who helped make Illinois common law.[19] All told, he took some two hundred cases a year on average—as many as five thousand over the course of his career.

The jury is still out on the final statistics. But one thing the preliminary records show is that Abraham Lincoln was not the lawyer of myth—or counter-myth. He was no mere "country lawyer," and he did not operate out of a dusty village (Springfield had at least twenty-six attorneys the year of Lincoln's election to the White House).[20] Nor was he unscrupulous. He might far more accurately be called a lawyer's litigator with a greatly varied general practice, including divorce, murder, and bankruptcy (a field he dominated until Congress in 1842 repealed the federal law that had made orderly bankruptcies briefly possible). Lincoln was also the professional to whom other attorneys turned over their cases for appeal. Finally, as a lawyer who functioned simultaneously as a legislator, he not only practiced law but made law—in the courtroom as well as the state assembly—helping to shape a system of justice still in its infancy. And this is important. For Lincoln, lawyering was not only a way to make money, it was a way to make law.

When Lincoln first passed the bar, Illinois jurisprudence was still based on twenty-five-year-old legislation that declared the state's legal system to be based on "the common law of England . . . prior to the fourth year of . . . King James I." The Illinois legislature tried to fill the void, and Lincoln worked as a legislator even as he worked as a lawyer. Lincoln believed passionately in economic advancement and internal improvements—what we today call "economic development," or "stimulus funding." He drafted and supported bills designed to propel his state into the economic competition of the nineteenth century. But with so little law on the books, a new body of law could also be forged in the courts. There, common law could be made through judicial decisions, and Lincoln was actively involved in this process. He made law as he practiced law, winning cases that created new legal precedents for the country—some of which are still taught in law schools.

He certainly was not as poorly read a lawyer as legend has suggested. The size of his law office library was underestimated because his law partner, William Herndon, kept most of the volumes after Lincoln's death and, it can be argued, did not want people to think he had appropriated them.[21] (The late president's lawyer son, Robert Lincoln, was one of those who so believed.) Instead, almost in self-defense, Herndon created the image of the Lincoln who practiced law from a prone position on the office sofa, never reading "a single elementary law book through in his entire life."[22]

In fact, Lincoln read exhaustively to prepare for his cases, and wrote long, intricate briefs, the only records we have of his work from an era in which courtroom stenography was unheard of. Yes, he could also spellbind a jury. That was no myth up there on the screen in *Young Mr. Lincoln*. A lawyer who watched him in action frequently later admitted: "Any man who took Lincoln for a simple-minded man [in court] would very soon wake [up] with his back in a ditch." He was "wise as a serpent" in conducting a case, Leonard Swett conceded, expanding his animal metaphor by adding: "I have got too many scars from his blows to certify that he was harmless as a dove."[23] Juries loved his humor. In one case, *People v. Wyant,* Lincoln aided the prosecution in a murder trial involving one of the earliest invocations of the insanity defense in Illinois. Lincoln argued that the defendant was "possuming" insanity.[24] After a medical witness testified to the defendant's habit of picking bleeding sores from his head, Lincoln convulsed the courtroom with this question in cross-examination: "You say, doctor, that this man picks his head, and by that you infer that he is insane. Now, I sometimes pick my head, and . . . there may be a living, moving cause for it, and the trouble isn't all on the inside. It's only a case for fine-tooth combs."[25]

Before one too casually dismisses this text as just the kind of corny quote that argues against a new assessment of Lincoln the serious lawyer, consider this: Lincoln later came to regret prosecuting the defendant. As president, he provided for mental examinations of defendants in military courts martial for the first time.

Yes, he was a major legal voice for the expansion of the railroads in Illinois. But this was hardly based on mere avarice. Economic development was a pillar of his political philosophy, and his embrace of the railroads' cause was its natural outgrowth. He saw in the railroads an American future that united the disparate rural communities of the West. He saw them bringing prosperity and opportunity to pioneers willing to work hard for the chance to improve their lot in life. When it came to his largest railroad fee, a hefty $5,000 bill to the Illinois Central Rail Road, Lincoln had to sue his own client to collect it, and earned an extra $50 in the bargain.

But he was very much a professional. He did not turn away clients for philosophical reasons—not at the start of his legal career, anyway. In the Matson case of 1847, he even argued for a slaveowner in a fugitive slave case—and lost—arguing that slaves were perpetually "domiciled" in their home states even when they were taken to free states to "sojourn." It was actually a position he took ten years later in arguing against the Dred Scott decision: bad law had to be obeyed, but it could also be redressed in future courts, and in the legislature.

In his staunch opposition to Dred Scott, we see not only the politician who told every audience he could reach that it had been part of a conspiracy between President James Buchanan, former President Franklin Pierce, Senator Stephen A. Douglas, and Chief Justice Roger B. Taney. We also hear the lawyer—especially at Springfield in 1857: "Judicial decisions are of greater or less authority as precedents, according to circumstances. That this should be so, accords both with common sense, and the customary understanding of the legal profession."

And he went on: "If this important decision had been made by . . . unanimous concurrence . . . and without any apparent partisan bias, and in accordance with legal public expectations, and with the steady practice of the departments throughout our history" and had it not been "based on assumed historical facts which were not really true," then it might be "revolutionary to not acquiesce in it as a precedent." But "when we find it wanting in *all* these claims to the public confidence, it is not resistance, it is not factious, it is not even disrespectful, to treat it as not having yet quite established a settled doctrine for the country."[26] Here was a skilled lawyer railing at bad law that did injury to original law and defiled the founding documents. To make slavery universal and eternal, the Declaration of Independence itself, he charged, had been "assailed, and sneered at, and construed, and hawked at, and torn, till, if its framers could rise from their graves, they could not at all recognize it." And no law could supersede the original American promise—that all men are created equal.

Admittedly, Lincoln's legal career was not always so lofty. Here are some career "highlights": Fearing that he was losing a murder case, he once told a thirsty client during recess that the best place for fresh water was on the other side of the river, in a different state. The client escaped. On another occasion Lincoln urged a county government to hire him in its battle with a huge railroad over taxation. When the county refused, he went to work instead for the railroad. In that role, Lincoln saved the western railroads millions of dollars in the 1850s, arguing successfully that they should be exempted from local taxes.

Lincoln also argued and won one of the earliest known defenses of a capital crime that still divides legal experts today: the murder of an abusive husband by an abused wife. He defended a doctor in one of his state's earliest malpractice suits—arguing that a defendant whose broken legs had been set improperly after an accident had no right to expect better, because of his advanced age. He argued successfully that a client had a perfect right to shoot his political rival to death (the famous Truett murder case) because of their long-simmering feud.[27] The year was 1838, and one of the lawyers on the other side was his future political rival Stephen A. Douglas. It was difficult to get convictions in those days in blood-feud cases, plus the accused was much smaller than the victim, but Douglas must have cringed at the verdict anyway.

And in what may have been the most important case of Lincoln's entire career, Lincoln successfully defended a bridge-building company against a steamship line whose captain had crashed into a new railroad bridge, sinking the ship. Popular opinion was on the side of tradition, meaning riverboats. But Lincoln argued that railroad bridges were no longer unusual navigational hazards. He insisted that "*adjudication* must follow, and conform to, the progress of society."[28] Lincoln won the case, and established a precedent without which American economic development might have been set back fifty years. Incidentally, one lawyer who had spent much of his time arguing against the construction of railroad bridges across the Mississippi was none other than Jefferson Davis, future president of the Confederate States of America.

But was Lincoln a sellout to the railroads? Hardly. When he gave his first speech in New York at Cooper Union, it is believed that one of the people who supposedly heard him was the president of the New York Central Railroad. The next morning, legend has it, the much-impressed spectator visited Lincoln in his Manhattan hotel and offered him $10,000 a year, a fantastic salary at the time, to become his general counsel. Lincoln said no. By then he was convinced he could do more for the country, more to preserve the most precious legal tenets of all—the Declaration of Independence that declared all men created equal, and the Constitution that bound the states together in perpetuity—as president of the United States. Nine months later he was elected.

I do not suggest that this story is altogether true in all its details. In the final analysis, there is not a shred of evidence in the railroad's records, or among the reminiscences of any of the young Republican admirers who surrounded Lincoln nearly every hour of his visit to New York, that any such offer was made. As for his promising to "get back" to his wealthy benefactor, particularly the legend that he came home and struggled with the decision until he spent an entire night roaming in a grove of trees in Springfield—finally, dramatically, seeing the light of his future with the sunrise—the story implies that Lincoln believed that law was his only life goal.[29] In fact, much as Lincoln loved the law—the argumentation that made him such an effective orator and debater, the knowledge of precedents that fueled his knowledge of history, and the camaraderie that introduced him to so many future supporters (and that third element is, I think, the key)—I still believe that Lincoln became a lawyer, and then became a *successful* lawyer, because it was his means of becoming a successful politician.

Divorce, abuse, and murder cases represented to Lincoln the kind of challenge he faced when working out problems in Euclid's geometry. Convincing juries was good practice for convincing crowds of twelve hundred—or twelve thousand. Besides, the fellow lawyers he met on trains, at courthouses, and in country inns, with whom he did battle in trials, and entertained with lively stories long into the nights on the Eighth Illinois Judicial Circuit, became the nucleus of a loyal family of supporters who grew through his nurturing friendship and hearty camaraderie into a vast network of Republican loyalists pledged not only to antislavery, but to the specific elevation of Abraham Lincoln to high office. Lincoln might have become a successful lawyer without becoming a politician. But it is doubtful that he would have become a successful politician without becoming a lawyer—and then walking through the doorways of opportunity the profession presented.

Some scholars (quoting colleagues like Herndon and David Davis) have posited in recent years that Lincoln spent month after month on that judicial circuit, failing to return home to see his family on weekends the way his colleagues did, because he simply wanted to stay far away from his fiery wife and his unhappy home.[30] I believe, rather, Lincoln stayed away from home more frequently than other lawyers in order to build this expanding political network, to meet the friends of his friends, the relatives of his colleagues, to make an indelible impression, to do favors that could be called in, friendly debts that could be traded later for political loyalty at conventions and in elections. All politicians make such sacrifices. I have never been a politician, but I have been a press secretary to two of them, both excellent lawyers who became relentless politicians, and ran, variously, for U.S. senator and mayor of New York. And my family will join me in testifying to how many weekends I—and the candidates—spent away from family in 1975, 1976, and 1977 to pursue the brass ring of political success.

For the Union, and in history, Lincoln went on to become, as Frank J. Williams and other scholars have shown, a consummate lawyer in the White

House.[31] Yes, his was a rags-to-riches success story. All the years riding the circuit in winter and summer, sleeping six in a room, sometimes four in a bed, eating bad food, earning $10 fees, finally paid off with the greatest opportunity any American could enjoy.

But Lincoln had also followed the same advice he later gave to a young man who asked how to be a successful lawyer. Answered Lincoln: "Work, work, work, is the main thing." Oh yes, he also added: "Discourage . . . never stir up litigation."[32]

But he always defended and cherished his profession. As he wrote in that law lecture he never got to deliver: "There is a vague popular belief that lawyers are necessarily dishonest. I say vague, because when we consider to what extent confidence, and honors, are . . . conferred upon lawyers by the people, it appears improbable that their impression of dishonesty is very distinct and vivid. . . . Resolve to be honest at all events," he advised, "and if in your own judgment you cannot be an honest lawyer, resolve to be honest without being a lawyer."[33]

Nothing was ever more sacred to Lincoln than the rule of law. As he declared in one of his most famous early speeches: "Let reverence for the laws, be breathed by every American . . . let it be taught in schools . . . let it be written in Primmers [*sic*] . . . let it be preached from the pulpit, proclaimed in legislative halls, and enforced in courts of justice . . . let it become the *political religion* of the nation."[34]

So, with apologies to Whiplash Willie Gingrich, perhaps it is time to revise the script of *The Fortune Cookie,* and with it to revise with finality the impermanent reputation of the so-called country attorney who became America's secular saint: Abraham Lincoln—great president *and* great lawyer.

Notes

1. Reprinted in Harold Holzer, ed., *The Lincoln Anthology: Great Writers on His Life and Legacy from 1860 to Now* (New York: Library of America, 2009), 911.

2. His style before juries was described as full of "thrilling pathos" as early as 1866. See P[hoebe]. A. Hanaford, *Abraham Lincoln: His Life and Public Services* (Boston: B. B. Russell, 1866), 47.

3. Roy P. Basler, ed., *The Collected Works of Abraham Lincoln,* 8 vols. (New Brunswick, N.J.: Rutgers Univ. Press, 1953–1955), 2:81 (hereafter cited as *Collected Works of Lincoln*).

4. From the latter category see, for example, Thomas J. Di Lorenzo, *Lincoln Unmasked: What You're Not Supposed to Know about Dishonest Abe* (New York: Crown Forum, 2006), esp. 107–14.

5. See John Evangelist Walsh, *Moonlight: Abraham Lincoln and the Almanac Trial* (New York: St. Martin's, 2000). Regarding Lincoln's railroad clients, one historian concluded that partner Herndon's success in the 1857 Dalby case catapulted their firm—and thus senior partner Lincoln—into the position of the "leading practitioner of railroad law" in Illinois. See William D. Beard, "Dalby Revisited: A New Look at Lincoln's 'Most Far-Reaching Case,'" *Journal of the Abraham Lincoln Association* 20 (summer 1999): 16.

6. The new books included Allen D. Spiegel, *A. Lincoln, Esquire: A Shrewd, Sophisticated Lawyer in His Time* (Macon, Ga.: Mercer Univ. Press, 2002); Mark E. Steiner, *An Honest Calling: The Law Practice of Abraham Lincoln* (De Kalb: Northern Illinois Univ. Press, 2006); and Brian Dirck, *Lincoln the Lawyer* (Urbana: Univ. of Illinois Press, 2007). Tellingly, all were university press books—designed principally for scholarly audiences. The two early, "standard" references were published by commercial presses: Frederick Trevor Hill, *Lincoln the Lawyer* (New York: Century, 1906), and Albert A. Woldman, *Lawyer Lincoln* (Boston: Houghton Mifflin, 1936). More recently came John J. Duff, *A. Lincoln, Prairie Lawyer* (New York: Rinehart, 1960), and John P. Frank, *Lincoln as a Lawyer* (Urbana: Univ. of Illinois Press, 1961).

7. Elizabeth W. Matthews, *Lincoln as a Lawyer: An Annotated Bibliography* (Carbondale: Southern Illinois Univ. Press, 1991).

8. Daniel Stowell, ed., *The Papers of Abraham Lincoln: Legal Documents and Cases,* 4 vols. (Charlottesville, Va.: Univ. of Virginia Press, 2008).

9. David Herbert Donald, *Lincoln* (New York: Simon and Schuster, 1995), 16, 145–61.

10. W. D. Howells, *Life of Abraham Lincoln* (Columbus, Ohio: Follett, Foster, 1860), 52.

11. *New York Daily News,* October 30, 1860.

12. Jesse W. Weik, *The Real Lincoln: A Portrait* (Boston: Houghton Mifflin, 1922), 298–99.

13. See, for example, Charles C. Nott and Cephas Brainerd, eds., *The Address of the Hon. Abraham Lincoln, in vindication of the policy of the framers of the Constitution and the principles of the Republican party, Delivered at Cooper Institute, February 27, 1860* . . . (New York: George F. Nesbitt, 1860), 3.

14. *New York Times,* December 31, 1862, reprinted in LaWanda Cox, *Lincoln and Black Freedom: A Study in Presidential Leadership* (Columbia: Univ. of South Carolina Press, 1981), 13.

15. *Collected Works of Lincoln,* 6:266.

16. Ibid., 6:388–389.

17. Quoted in Stefan Lorant, *Lincoln: A Picture Story of His Life,* rev. ed. (New York: Norton, 1969), 159.

18. *Collected Works of Lincoln,* 8:101.

19. Dan W. Bannister, *Lincoln and the Supreme Court* (Springfield, Ill.: Dan W. Bannister, 1995), xiii–xiv.

20. C. S. Williams, *Williams' Springfield Directory: City Guide and Business Mirror for 1860–61* (Springfield, Ill.: Johnson, Bradford, 1860). According to the *Illinois Daily State Journal* for August 28, 1860, the directory was issued that day.

21. See James T. Hickey, "Robert Todd Lincoln and the Purely Private Letters of the Lincoln Family," in *The Collected Writings of James T. Hickey* (Springfield: Illinois State Historical Society, 1990), 162. For more on what lawyer Lincoln read to prepare for his legal career, see Dirck, *Lincoln the Lawyer,* 17–19.

22. William H. Herndon and Jesse W. Weik, *Herndon's Lincoln: The True Story of a Great Life . . . ,* 3 vols. (Chicago: Belford, Clarke, 1889), 2:337.

23. Quoted in Douglas L. Wilson and Rodney O. Davis, *Herndon's Informants: Letters, Interviews, and Statements about Abraham Lincoln* (Urbana: Univ. of Illinois Press, 1998), 636.

24. Joseph E. McDonald, quoted in Don E. Fehrenbacher and Virginia Fehrenbacher, *Recollected Words of Abraham Lincoln* (Stanford, Calif.: Stanford Univ. Press, 1996), 321, 537 n.

25. Quoted in Duff, *A. Lincoln, Prairie Lawyer,* 307.

26. *Collected Works of Lincoln,* 2:398–410, esp. 403.

27. Dirck, *Lincoln the Lawyer,* 115–16.

28. *Collected Works of Lincoln,* 2:459.

29. John W. Starr, *Lincoln and the Railroads: A Biographical Study* (New York: Dodd, Mead, 1927), 126–30.

30. Michael Burlingame, *The Inner World of Abraham Lincoln* (Urbana: Univ. of Illinois Press, 1994), 319–20.

31. Frank J. Williams, *Judging Lincoln* (Carbondale: Southern Illinois Univ. Press, 2002), esp. chapter 3, "Lincoln, Commander in Chief or 'Attorney in Chief?'" 34–59.

32. *Collected Works of Lincoln,* 4:121; 2:81.

33. Ibid., 2:82.

34. Ibid., 1:112.

Lincoln's Lessons for Lawyers

Frank J. Williams

Introduction

Abraham Lincoln is remembered as one of America's greatest leaders. In poll after poll, Lincoln is ranked as the greatest of American presidents.[1] Lincoln's life story is a large part of why he is so popular today. His rise from poor, uneducated farm boy to president of the United States represents the quintessential American tale.[2] Lincoln said of himself and his presidency: "I am a living witness that any one of your children may look to come here as my father's child has. It is in order that each of you may have through this free government which we have enjoyed, an open field and a fair chance for your industry, enterprise and intelligence. . . ."[3]

In fact, the mythology surrounding Lincoln's humble roots is so strong that a casual observer might believe that Lincoln was elected to the White House directly from a rustic log cabin.[4] Nothing could be further from the truth. Through extensive self-education, Lincoln achieved the status of a well-respected lawyer in Springfield, Illinois.[5] Moreover, Lincoln spent almost a quarter-century in the active practice of law, during which time he argued thousands of cases.[6]

Despite Lincoln's impressive legal career, the fact that Lincoln was a lawyer is probably *not* a factor in his popularity today.[7] The public's esteem for lawyers has declined precipitously since Lincoln's day.[8] Consider the popularity of lawyer jokes at present.[9] In fact, many of Lincoln's admirers pay little attention to Lincoln's years as a lawyer, choosing instead to focus on his years in the White House. But the fact remains, Lincoln was not just a great president, he was also a great lawyer. Moreover, the two facts are inseparable. Lincoln was a great president, at least in part, *because* he honed his lawyerly skills as a young man and used them in the White House.

By exploring those lawyerly traits that contributed to Lincoln's great-ness as a president, I hope to achieve dual purposes. First, we can learn something about great leadership. Equally significant for these troubled times, we can learn something about great lawyers. In writing this piece, I am taking the advice of Charles Wirken, a past president of the State Bar of Arizona, who said, "Though our judicial system isn't perfect and is subject to some abuse by lawyers and non-lawyers alike, we have earned the right to be proud of what we do. It's a wonderful profession. Stand up for it whenever you can."[10]

I will support my argument primarily through anecdotes and examples of the way Lincoln led his administration, the Civil War, and his many sub-ordinates both civilian and military. Before embarking on this discussion, it bears remembering, as I have argued elsewhere, that Lincoln's ultimate ambition was always political.[11] Lincoln's skills as a lawyer were invaluable in supporting his political ambitions, and those political ambitions were always primary for Lincoln.[12]

The Traits of a Good Lawyer

The traits that a good lawyer will possess are not mysterious. Judges, lawyers, and their clients observe those traits every day in courtrooms, boardrooms, and law offices. I have compiled a short list of traits based primarily on my personal experience as a lawyer and a judge. Someone else would almost certainly compile a different list of words to express the same underlying virtues. The point I am making with this list is simply that a good lawyer will, through training and by his or her very nature, consistently act in ac-cordance with the values and principles of the profession. In my experience, the following list captures the most significant virtues necessary for living out those principles. They are: (1) Honesty; (2) Industriousness; (3) Meticu-lousness; (4) Confidence; (5) Rhetorical Skill; (6) Courage; (7) Zealousness; (8) Persistence; (9) Fair-Mindedness; (10) Humility.

I argue that Abraham Lincoln possessed all of the aforementioned vir-tues, and he developed a reliance on these virtues in his everyday practice of law, and later as president and commander in chief.[13] It is worthwhile at this stage to note that this list of attributes might just as easily describe any successful leader. This fact is not altogether surprising. As James Casner put it in his property law textbook, "It is an observable fact that through some combination of chromosomes and professional training lawyers tend to come to the top of the barrel in the shaking and jolting of competition for authority."[14] Abraham Lincoln is a specific example of a more general phenomenon, namely that good lawyers make good leaders.

Lawyer and President

HONESTY

[R]esolve to be honest at all events; and if in your own judgment you cannot be an honest lawyer, resolve to be honest without being a lawyer.[15]

Lincoln was well known for his honesty and integrity, hence the stereotype "Honest Abe." As Lincoln expressed in one of his now famous debates with Stephen A. Douglas, his approach to honesty was not complicated: "I do not state a thing and say I know it, when I do not."[16] Even in his straightforward approach to the world, Lincoln knew that honesty was in the details, an understanding he expressed in that same debate: "I mean to put a case no stronger than the truth will allow."[17] Lincoln espoused a personal and professional philosophy that was based in forthrightness, and his legal career is replete with examples of this philosophy at work.[18]

For example, Lincoln often traveled throughout central Illinois on the Eighth Judicial Circuit, arguing in various county courthouses.[19] Lincoln and another attorney, Leonard Swett, were appointed to defend a man indicted for murder.[20] Although the defendant did not have the means to retain a lawyer, he had friends who managed to raise $100 for his defense.[21] Swett accepted the money and handed half of it to Lincoln.[22] When Lincoln and Swett consulted the defendant, Lincoln became convinced that the defendant was guilty.[23] He tried to convince Swett that the only way to save the defendant was to have him plead guilty and appeal to the court for leniency.[24] Swett, a rather talented criminal lawyer, would not agree to Lincoln's suggestion, so the case came to trial.[25]

During the trial, Lincoln did not participate.[26] He took no further part in it than to make an occasional suggestion to Swett in the course of the examination of witnesses.[27] Ultimately, the defendant was acquitted on technical grounds, largely due to Swett's skillful lawyering.[28] When the jury rendered its verdict, Lincoln reached over Swett's shoulder, with the $50 in hand, saying: "Here, Swett, take this money. It is yours. You earned it, not I."[29]

Lincoln was proud of his reputation for honest dealing. He told a story, for instance, about a widow who had lost her cow when it was struck by a train.[30] The woman hired Lincoln to represent her and to bring suit against the railroad for damages.[31] Before Lincoln could commence the suit, the railroad company approached him with an unsavory proposition.[32] If he would refuse to represent the widow, the railroad promised to remunerate him handsomely.[33] Perhaps even more significant, the company promised to give him legal work connected with the railroad.[34] Lincoln was not impressed. Not only did he take the case despite the pressure, he won it.[35]

Lincoln's honesty should not be taken for that of a simpleton. Lincoln knew that the world was full of competing interests, and he understood the necessity of choosing between those interests. One story in particular, the case of Melissa Goings, illustrates Lincoln's savvy.

Lincoln defended Melissa Goings against a charge of murder.[36] She was accused of killing her husband, and the trial was proceeding poorly for Mrs. Goings.[37] During the trial, Lincoln asked for a recess to confer with his client, and subsequently led the defendant from the courtroom.[38] When court reconvened, Mrs. Goings could not be found.[39] Lincoln himself was accused of advising her to flee, a charge he vehemently denied.[40] He explained, however, that the defendant had asked him where she could get a drink of water, and he had pointed out that Tennessee had darn good water.[41] Apparently Mrs. Goings agreed, for she was never seen again in Illinois.[42]

Lincoln understood that honesty is complicated in the practice of law. Even so, the Goings story does not involve deception or the violation of any code of ethics, which did not exist at that time. Lincoln was forthright in his dealings with the court, but we must realize that concepts of ethics shift over time like sand. As he so eloquently stated, "resolve to be honest at all events; and if in your own judgment you cannot be an honest lawyer, resolve to be honest without being a lawyer."[43] Lincoln's reputation for honest fair-dealing served him well as a lawyer and imbued him with a reputation that he took with him to Washington.

INDUSTRIOUSNESS

Leave nothing for to-morrow which can be done to-day.[44]

Hard work is what it takes to succeed in any endeavor. This is true in the legal profession, and surely it is no less true for a president. Lincoln could not have risen to greatness without a good, honest work ethic, which he gained first as a prairie laborer and then as a prairie lawyer.

There is little more, if anything, that I can add to this subject. Lincoln put it quite directly: "The leading rule for the lawyer, as for the man of every calling, is diligence. Leave nothing for to-morrow which can be done to-day. Never let your correspondence fall behind. Whatever piece of business you have in hand, before stopping, do all the labor pertaining to it which can then be done."[45] This is an apt description of what Lincoln called "the drudgery of the law."[46] Being a lawyer is hard work.

Of course, being president is hard work as well. As president, Lincoln put his ideals into practice. For instance, Lincoln had nearly boundless energy for keeping track of events at the war front. "During particularly active days, Lincoln might send a dozen or more messages to generals in the field, and as a battle unfolded he would often spend the night reading message traffic describing it."[47] At times, Lincoln practically moved into the telegraph office.[48]

No greater tribute exists to Lincoln's industriousness than the *Collected Works of Abraham Lincoln,* edited by Roy P. Basler.[49] In his fifty-six years of life, Lincoln produced an enormous quantity of correspondence and speeches, enough to fill eight volumes and two supplemental volumes.[50] Of course, each letter and each draft of every speech was written by hand. There is no doubt that Lincoln took to heart his own advice concerning diligence.

METICULOUSNESS

[N]o good thing has been, or can be enjoyed by us without having first cost labor.[51]

Meticulousness, like industriousness, involves the day-to-day drudgery with which all professionals must contend. Lawyers in particular must have the ability to focus on detail and accuracy in their professional activities. Lincoln was particularly meticulous in his writing, often producing multiple drafts over several days.[52]

Lincoln's meticulous writing was probably a reflection of his slow and steady way of thinking. Lincoln said of himself, "I am slow to learn and slow to forget." He said, "[M]y mind is like a piece of steel, very hard to scratch anything on it and almost impossible after you get it there to rub it out."[53] What Lincoln described as mental slowness might well be considered meticulousness.

Lincoln brought his attention to detail with him to the White House. He rarely gave extemporaneous speeches, preferring instead to write his speeches out in draft form so that he could pore over the language.[54] This was true with his voluminous correspondence as well. Lincoln understood both the power and the danger of communication, as any good lawyer should. Lincoln's meticulous nature gave us such masterpieces as the Gettysburg Address and the Second Inaugural Address. His speeches and letters are the best kind of literature.

CONFIDENCE

> He who does something at the head of one Regiment, will eclipse him who does nothing at the head of a hundred.[55]

Lincoln was active as both a politician and a lawyer during his years in Illinois, allowing him to develop confidence as a leader.[56] Lincoln practiced his craft before judges and juries in countless cases all around the Illinois Eighth Judicial Circuit.[57] Like any successful trial lawyer, he had to express command and confidence in his arguments before the judge and jury. The ability to make decisions on one's feet and with confidence is a key trait of any successful lawyer in the courtroom, and all accounts are that Lincoln mastered the art. In the words of Leonard Swett, "Any man who took Lincoln for a simple-minded man . . . would very soon wake up with his back in a ditch."[58]

During his time in the White House, Lincoln constantly was faced with hard decisions. As chief executive, he sat atop a large, complex, and often conflict-ridden political organization that was charged with enforcing the law during a nationwide rebellion. As commander in chief, Lincoln sat atop a likewise large, complex, and often conflicted military organization charged with defeating an army composed entirely of fellow countrymen. He could not have functioned in either role without a great deal of confidence, and the ability to project that confidence to his subordinates and his critics around the country.

As a military leader, Lincoln showed a willingness to make hard decisions based on his own assessments. Occasionally he even felt it was necessary to disregard his professional military advisors. Both General Winfield Scott, who headed the Army, and General Irvin McDowell, Lincoln's field commander, advised against fighting the first battle of Manassas on the ground that more time was required for disciplining and drilling the troops.[59] The public, however, clamored for action, and Lincoln, always in tune with political necessity, overruled the generals.[60] The battle was fought, but with disastrous result.[61] Not daunted, the following night Lincoln prepared a detailed plan of strategy. He knew the political necessity of action, and he had the confidence to push on, even in the face of often terrible losses.

As the war developed, Lincoln became even more concerned with questions of strategy. He was greatly troubled by his inability to stir into action General George B. McClellan, the commander of the Army of the Potomac.[62] The ever serious commander in chief went so far as to educate himself on military strategy. The autodidact read Henry W. Halleck's translation of Jomini[63] and held long conversations with officers on the art of war.[64] In December 1861, he presented an elaborate memorandum to McClellan, which asked technical questions and made suggestions about an advance.[65] The over-confident McClellan returned it with penciled replies and a note rejecting all the suggestions.[66]

Lincoln could bear McClellan's diffidence no more, and he replaced him with Ambrose E. Burnside late in 1862 when he could not get McClellan to advance after the battle of Antietam.[67] McClellan was very popular among his troops and later ran against Lincoln in the 1864 presidential election.[68] Lincoln knew that McClellan could make a formidable political enemy, but he also knew that McClellan was not capable of taking the steps needed to win the war. Lincoln's confidence in his own understanding of military strategy allowed him to make the decision to relieve McClellan.

RHETORICAL SKILL

[T]hat government of the people, by the people, for the people, shall not perish from the earth.[69]

The ability to express ideas clearly and convincingly is essential to good lawyering. Likewise, a president must possess the ability to persuade the people, the Congress, and his subordinates through both written and spoken language. In this regard, Lincoln's eloquence and humor is legendary, and his words speak for themselves.

When Abraham Lincoln spoke about the issue of equality, for instance, he did it with passion and conviction: "Let us discard all this quibbling about this man and the other man, this race and that race and the other race being inferior, and therefore they must be placed in an inferior position. Let us discard all these things and unite as one people throughout this land, until we shall once more stand up declaring that all men are created equal."[70] Lincoln had the power to express the idea of universal liberty with both logic and beauty. "When we were the political slaves of King George, and wanted to be free, we called the maxim that 'all men are created equal' a self-evident truth, but now when we have grown fat, and have lost all dread of being slaves ourselves, we have become so greedy to be *masters* that we call the same maxim 'a self-evident lie.'"[71]

In debates with his longtime rival Stephen A. Douglas, Lincoln honed his skills as a worthy adversary in the art of debate.[72] Moreover, he learned to connect with an audience on a human level: "nobody has ever expected me to be President. In my poor, lean, lank face nobody has ever seen that any cabbages were sprouting out."[73]

Lincoln understood the power of simple language and metaphor, and he often used it humorously to great effect. For instance, in responding to a letter from the dilatory General McClellan after Antietam, Lincoln said, "I have just read your dispatch about sore tongued and fatigued horses. Will you pardon me for asking what the horses of your army have done since the battle of Antietam that fatigue anything?"[74] In another famous incident, General Joseph Hooker sent a dispatch to the president datelined "Headquarters in the Saddle."[75] Lincoln quipped, "The trouble with Hooker is that he has got his headquarters where his hindquarters ought to be."[76]

Lincoln knew how to joke about serious issues as well. Judge George W. Shaw says that during the Lincoln-Douglas debates, Lincoln would sometimes exclaim: "They tell me that if the Republicans prevail, slavery will be abolished, and whites will marry and form a mongrel race. Now, I have a sister-in-law down in Kentucky, and if any one can show me that if Fremont is elected she will have to marry a negro, I will vote against

Fremont, and if that isn't an argument ad hominem it is an argument ad womanum."[77]

Likewise, Lincoln could be self-deprecating with his humor. A popular story involves Judge Joseph Baldwin, a Southerner who sought permission to cross into Virginia during the war to visit his family. Lincoln told Judge Baldwin to apply to General Halleck or to Secretary of War Stanton. Judge Baldwin replied that his request had already been denied by both Halleck and Stanton. Lincoln replied, with a smile, "I can do nothing; for you must know that I have very little influence with this Administration."[78]

Lincoln often used his rhetorical skill to communicate with the people during the crisis. On the way to Washington to be inaugurated, Lincoln stopped along the way and made speeches in many towns and cities.[79] In Lawrenceburg, Indiana, he displayed his skill as a speechmaker: "I have been selected to fill an important office for a brief period, and am now, in your eyes, invested with an influence which will soon pass away; but should my Administration prove to be a very wicked one, or what is more probable, a very foolish one, if you, the people, are but true to yourselves and to the Constitution, there is but little harm I can do, *thank God!*"[80]

He was equally eloquent in his messages to Congress during the long crisis: "If there ever could be a proper time for mere catch arguments, that time surely is not now. In times like the present, men should utter nothing for which they would not willingly be responsible through time and eternity."[81] Lincoln expressed great ideas and passion in simple language. His words were filled with both power and substance, a trait we often find missing in the empty political rhetoric so often associated with contemporary politics.

I would be remiss if I did not mention the now famous Gettysburg Address. Lincoln's two-minute, 272-word address to a crowd gathered on the occasion of the dedication of a cemetery at the site of the great battle at Gettysburg is the most famous speech by any American president.[82] The speech expresses the greatest ideals of the nation in the sparest and most eloquent terms: "It is rather for us to be here dedicated to the great task remaining before us—that from these honored dead we take increased devotion to that cause for which they here gave the last full measure of devotion—that we here highly resolve that these dead shall not have died in vain—that this nation shall have a new birth of freedom—and that this

Government of the people, by the people, for the people, shall not perish from the earth."[83]

COURAGE

... until every drop of blood drawn with the lash shall be paid by another drawn with the sword.[84]

Courage is a difficult quality to define. To quote a famous U.S. Supreme Court decision, "I know it when I see it."[85] At its most basic level, courage is the willingness to act or to refuse to act in the face of potential harm to oneself or others. Whether it involves advancing unpopular ideas or facing danger on the battlefield, courage is a key ingredient in greatness. This is true for lawyers, and it is true for presidents.

As an attorney, Lincoln showed political courage when he was called upon to defend progress in 1857.[86] At that time, transportation technology was at a crossroads—old riverboat technology was pitted against new railroad technology, and bridge building was a big piece of the new railroad system. Whenever entrenched power faces a challenge from an upstart, there is danger in advocating for the upstart. Legal careers and reputations can be made and lost in the struggle for progress.

It was in this context that the Rock Island Bridge Company hired Lincoln as lead counsel to defend it in the case of *Hurd v. Rock Island Bridge Co.,* in which a riverboat, the *Effie Afton,* smacked into an abutment of the railroad bridge that crossed the Mississippi River, setting the bridge afire.[87] Lincoln tried the case before the U.S. Circuit Court in Chicago, and rested on a central, key point: the steamboat's crew was to blame for the accident, not the Rock Island Bridge Company—and surely not railroads in general.[88] Ultimately, Lincoln won the case by a hung jury, and the case was never retried.[89] This de facto victory effectively advanced the cause of commerce in the United States, with both railroad and river transportation, ensuring that both would become the country's major modes of transportation.

As president during a civil war, Lincoln faced almost daily opportunities to display his courage. Lincoln's evolving stand on the issue of emancipation, however, stands out by far as the most impressive example of his courage as president. Lincoln believed from the very beginning of his political career that the institution of slavery opposed the principles and vision embodied in the Declaration of Independence. Initially, however, he was primarily opposed to the expansion of slavery into the newly emerging Western territories. As a candidate in 1860, Lincoln did not run as an abolitionist, but rather as a compromise candidate seeking to limit the expansion of slavery.[90] Even so, his views on slavery were controversial, and he was attacked by both Northerners and Southerners for his views.

During the Civil War, slavery quickly became a central issue as Lincoln and his administration contemplated what to do about the millions of slaves living in the South and in loyal border states. Over time, however, Lincoln became convinced that the union could not survive with slavery. Undeterred by the earlier criticism he had faced, Lincoln issued a preliminary proclamation on September 22, 1862—effective January 1, 1863—giving freedom to black slaves and changing the war's aim from reunion to reunion and freedom for the blacks.[91]

Consider for a moment the courage it took to issue this executive proclamation freeing slaves in the Southern states, a move that was widely unpopular in both the North and the South and, almost unheard of, changed the war's objective in the middle of the conflict. Lincoln explained his motivation directly in his second inaugural address, delivered March 4, 1865: "Fondly do we hope—fervently do we pray—that this mighty scourge of war may speedily pass away. Yet, if God wills that it continue, until all the wealth piled by the bond-man's two hundred and fifty years of unrequited toil shall be sunk, and until every drop of blood drawn with the lash shall be paid by another drawn with the sword, as was said three thousand years ago, so still must be said 'the judgments of the Lord, are true and righteous altogether.'"[92] Lincoln stood before the American people and spoke truth to power, laying the suffering and pain of the Civil War at the doorstep of America itself. Nothing could be more courageous.

Lincoln's dedication to the cause of ending slavery did not cease with the Emancipation Proclamation. Lincoln recognized that his executive proclamation was susceptible to a constitutional challenge, and further that the chief justice of the United States, Roger Taney, was hostile toward his position on slavery.[93] Lincoln understood that the only permanent solution to the problem of slavery was a constitutional amendment to end slavery. In another act of great courage, Lincoln risked his reelection to advocate such an amendment. At the 1864 Republican nominating convention in Baltimore, Lincoln insisted on a plank calling for an amendment to end slavery permanently throughout the union.[94] Lincoln ran on that platform, and ultimately helped advocate for the passage of the Thirteenth Amendment, which ended slavery forever.[95]

ZEALOUSNESS

Are all the laws, but one, to go unexecuted, and the government itself to go to pieces, lest that one be violated?[96]

Zealousness is the energy it takes to put principle into practice. Principles are of little use without the necessary zeal to make a change. It is often stated that lawyers must be zealous advocates, which simply means that they must argue with passion and strength. Presidents, if they are to be great, must do the same. President Lincoln was zealous in many ways during his tenure, but his zeal is best exemplified in the actions he took to secure the union during the early days of the Civil War.[97]

Throughout his presidency, Lincoln asserted an expansive view of the president's independent authority based on the commander in chief clause of the Constitution[98] and on the duty to "take care that the laws be faithfully executed."[99] In the ten weeks between the outbreak at Fort Sumter and the convening of Congress in special session on July 4, 1861, Lincoln employed these clauses to sanction measures whose extraordinary magnitude suggests dictatorship to some.

In that ten-week interval, Lincoln added 23,000 men to the regular army and 18,000 to the navy,[100] called 40,000 volunteers for three years' service,[101] summoned the state militias into a ninety-day volunteer force,[102] paid $2 million from the treasury's unappropriated funds for purposes unauthorized by Congress,[103] closed the Post Office to "treasonable correspondence,"[104] imposed a blockade on Southern ports,[105] suspended the writ of habeas corpus along the railroad from Washington to Philadelphia, and caused the arrest and military detention of persons "who were represented to him" as engaging in or contemplating "treasonable practices."[106] He later instituted conscription, the first federal draft in U.S. history, when voluntary recruiting broke down[107] and extended the suspension of the habeas corpus privilege nationwide for persons "guilty of any disloyal practice"[108]—but this time with Congress's approval. Lincoln did not intend to fight a rebellion with a powder puff.

PERSISTENCE

[T]he promise being made, must be kept.[109]

Persistence brings zealous action to fruition. A short burst of zealous action is often too little when faced with a problem of any great magnitude. Great lawyers are persistent, and so are great presidents. One illuminating example was Lincoln's persistence in pushing his army to fight during the darkest days of the Civil War.

Several presidents have faced major crises either in bringing their field generals to engage in battle or in keeping them within bounds, not simply on the battlefield but within the framework of constitutional government. General McClellan, the most lagging of field generals, was a great trial to Lincoln in both spheres. Bold in his strategic conceptions, McClellan nevertheless dreaded the actual execution of his plans.[110] A repetitive pattern for him was to demand more reinforcements after overestimating the enemy's strength and depreciating his own.[111] He was a wonderfully imaginative procrastinator. If McClellan had Robert E. Lee at a disadvantage, he almost invariably failed to exploit it. He must wait, McClellan would report to his impatient superiors in Washington, until the Potomac rose, to be sure that Lee would not recross it; he must finish drilling new recruits, reorganize his forces, and procure more shoes, uniforms, blankets, and camp equipment.[112]

McClellan compensated for battlefield inaction by spending his idle time pouring his irrepressible arrogance into his letters, including one to Lincoln on July 7, 1862, pointing out that it was high time the government established a civil and military policy to cover the full canvass of the nation's troubles and "generously" informing the president what precisely that policy should be.[113] McClellan's reticence became more than a simple irritation, especially after his refusal to pursue General Lee after the Union victory at Antietam.[114] Had McClellan chosen to pursue Lee's fleeing forces, he could have decimated the Southern army, clinching victory for the Union.[115] Lincoln worked mightily, as his secretary John Nicolay put it, at "poking sharp sticks under little Mac's ribs."[116]

After serious deliberation, Lincoln relieved McClellan on November 5, 1862, and appointed General Ambrose E. Burnside in his place.[117] Upon reading the president's order, McClellan exclaimed, "Alas for my poor country."[118] Some among his officers even urged him to disobey the presidential order.[119] McClellan later wrote that he could easily have marched his troops into Washington and taken possession of the government.[120] If so, it would have been the first successful forward movement of the war! Instead, McClellan turned over the command of his 120,000 men in an elaborate ceremony.[121] But this was by no means the last encounter between McClellan and Lincoln. In 1864, two years after his removal, McClellan met Lincoln on new terrain—as the Democratic nominee for the presidency.[122] He lost *that* battle too.[123]

Perhaps Lincoln's greatest persistence was in defending the Emancipation Proclamation in the face of strong opposition. That opposition was particularly intense during the campaign for reelection in 1864, when neither Lincoln nor his closest advisors were confident that he would be reelected.[124] Lincoln understood that persistent support of his decision to liberate Southern slaves was vital, so he stood behind his decision. In a letter to James C. Conkling, which Lincoln asked Conkling to read before a large pro-Union gathering in Springfield, Illinois, Lincoln made his case: "I thought that whatever negroes can be got to do as soldiers, leaves just so much less for white soldiers to do, in saving the Union. Does it appear otherwise to you? But negroes, like other people, act upon motives. Why should they do any thing for us, if we will do nothing for them? If they stake their lives for us, they must be prompted by the strongest motive—even the promise of freedom. And the promise being made, must be kept."[125]

Lincoln set his sights on victory, and he saw the Emancipation Proclamation as a key piece of the plan to achieve his goal. He also knew that once the proclamation was made, it could never be rescinded.

FAIR-MINDEDNESS

As a peace-maker the lawyer has a superior opportunity of being a good man. There will still be business enough.[126]

As an attorney, Lincoln was able to strike a balance between zealous advocacy for his clients and a good sense of civility and professional courtesy.[127]

One of his colleagues, when discussing Lincoln's courtroom demeanor, explained that "[Lincoln] never misstated evidence, but stated clearly and fairly and squarely his opponent's case."[128] Indeed, as author Brian Dirck noted in *Lincoln the Lawyer*, "no one seems to have ever accused [Lincoln] of being an unethical attorney."[129]

Lincoln met with a potential client who was soliciting his legal expertise. After hearing the facts of the case, Lincoln replied:

> Yes, there is no reasonable doubt but that I can gain your case for you; I can set a whole neighborhood at loggerheads; I can distress a widowed mother and her six fatherless children, and thereby get for you six hundred dollars which you seem to have a legal claim to; but which rightfully belongs, it appears to me, as much to the woman and her children as it does to you. You must remember some things that are legally right are not morally right. I shall not take your case—but I will give you a little advice for which I will charge you nothing. You seem to be a sprightly, energetic man, I would advise you to try your hand at making six hundred dollars in some other way.[130]

Lincoln believed in alternative dispute resolution before that term was ever coined. He was a great advocate of settlement without litigation, and he tried whenever possible to pursue mediation or negotiated settlements.[131] Lincoln stated, "Discourage litigation. Persuade your neighbors to compromise whenever you can. Point out to them how the nominal winner is often a real loser—in fees, expenses, in waste of time. As a peace-maker the lawyer has a superior opportunity of being a good man."[132]

Over the course of his legal career, Lincoln handled several slander suits, many of which contained accusations against women of adultery or fornication.[133] An illustration of one of Lincoln's typical slander cases involved a woman by the name of Eliza Cabot, who complained that Francis Regnier wrongly accused her of fornication.[134] Lincoln represented Ms. Cabot and "delivered a 'denunciation' of Regnier that was 'as bitter a Philippic as ever uttered.'"[135] Lincoln ultimately secured a verdict of $1,600 for Ms. Cabot.[136] In these matters, Lincoln was involved heavily in maintaining community reputations and relationships; he played the role of mediator in order to restore peace to the neighborhood and keep the charges out of the courtroom.[137]

As commander in chief, Lincoln carefully reviewed the death sentences of sleeping sentinels, homesick Union soldiers, and deserters, which he called his "leg cases."[138] In all of these instances, Lincoln acted as final judge and pardoned many of the soldiers.[139] Although merciful in these types of cases, he was likely to sustain sentences for slave traders, those convicted of robbery, and those who committed sexual offenses.[140]

Lincoln also displayed his fair-mindedness after the Sioux uprising in Minnesota that killed hundreds of white settlers in 1862.[141] The military court had sentenced 303 Sioux to death.[142] These cases came before Lincoln to review as final judge.[143] Yet, despite great pressure to approve these verdicts, Lincoln ordered that the complete records of the trials be sent to him.[144] Working deliberately, Lincoln reviewed each case individually.[145] Even though he was in the midst of administering the government during the Civil War, Lincoln carefully worked through the transcripts for a month to sort out those who were guilty of serious crimes.[146] Ultimately, Lincoln commuted the sentences of 265 defendants, and only thirty-eight of the original 303 were executed.[147] Although Lincoln was criticized for this act of clemency, he responded: "I could not afford to hang men for votes."[148]

Lincoln was likewise fair-minded in his attitudes toward free African Americans. He was under a great deal of pressure from both sides on the issue of whether to allow African Americans to serve in the armed forces.[149] Having weighed the options, Lincoln came to a sensible conclusion. To a critic of emancipation, Lincoln wrote, "Why should they [the black soldier and sailor] do anything for us, if we will do nothing for them?"[150] In the end, over 200,000 black soldiers and sailors served in the Union army and navy.[151]

HUMILITY

Now, the undertaking being a success, the honor is all yours.[152]

It is difficult to overstate the significance of humility for great lawyers and great leaders alike. Great leaders pass along the credit where credit is due. Great lawyers recognize their weaknesses and work around them. Humility allows both great lawyers and great leaders to recognize their mistakes and move on.

Lincoln's short military career in the Illinois militia likely played a key role in helping develop his humility.[153] Indeed, Lincoln often joked about his brief military career, which was comprised of three months' service with several ragtag militia companies in the Black Hawk War.[154] Lincoln humorously said that his military experience during that war involved "a good many bloody struggles with the m[o]squitoes."[155]

After he was elected a captain by his New Salem friends, Lincoln inspired more humor than gallantry as a leader.[156] Once, when marching his company toward a narrow gate, he forgot the proper command to form his troops in a single column so they could advance. "Halt!" Lincoln finally shouted. "This company is dismissed for two minutes, when it will form again on the other side of the gate."[157] In another incident, Lincoln fired his weapon in camp, a clear violation of regulations. As punishment, his sword was confiscated and he was forced to wear a wooden sword.[158]

But thirty years later he remembered his election as captain of his company as "a success which gave me more pleasure than any I have had since."[159] Lincoln was a civilian by habit, experience, and vision. Yet his background served him well when he led the citizen soldiers who fought in the Civil War.

Lincoln himself laid no claim to military genius and frankly admitted that his interference with his commanders was partly the result of their sheepishness and ineptitude, and partly the result of political pressure.[160] As capable commanders emerged, Lincoln interfered less and less. He became less inclined personally to direct the strategy of the various campaigns, but he became more insistent upon generals who could work out a plan of campaign and fight.[161] When they did their jobs, Lincoln was happy to pass along the credit.

In some sense, Lincoln's humility guided him through some of the hardest decisions of his presidency. Some of Lincoln's acts as commander in chief may have been questionable, some unwise, and others of doubtful constitutionality, but in retrospect it seems clear that he was, in each instance, motivated not by any thought of personal aggrandizement but by his desire to save the union.

Lincoln's style of leadership reflected his humility. I have heard it described aptly thus, "Surround yourself with talented people and let them not only do their jobs but also take credit for a job well done."[162] This is the ultimate expression of humility in leadership, to give credit where credit is due. Lincoln understood the importance of this simple maxim. He often expressed his humility and gratefulness directly to his subordinates. Lincoln said to Sherman after the general's successful Georgia campaign, "When you were about leaving Atlanta for the Atlantic coast, I was *anxious,* if not fearful; but feeling that you were the better judge, and remembering that 'nothing risked, nothing gained' I did not interfere. Now, the undertaking being a success, the honor is all yours; for I believe none of us went farther than to acquiesce."[163]

When it comes to political leadership, Lincoln demonstrated that humility was a fundamental aspect of effective leadership in times of conflict and crisis. Recently, Doris Kearns Goodwin pointed out in her book *Team of Rivals* that good leadership sometimes requires bringing in your political enemies. Goodwin argues that "Lincoln's political genius [is] revealed through his extraordinary array of personal qualities that enabled him to form friendships with men who had previously opposed him; to repair injured feelings that, left untended, might have escalated into permanent hostility; to assume responsibility for the failures of subordinates; to share credit with ease; and to learn from mistakes."[164] Lincoln chose to include political rivals in his cabinet, including William H. Seward as secretary of state, Salmon P. Chase as secretary of the treasury, and Edwin M. Stanton as secretary of war, because, he said, "[t]hese were the strongest men. I had no right to deprive the country of their services." Through his humility, Lincoln was willing and able to concede that his political rivals were the best men for the jobs.

Conclusion

Author John J. Duff notes in *A. Lincoln, Prairie Lawyer:* "[Lincoln's] intellectual integrity; his capacity for analysis and balanced decision; his practical, hard-headed approach to legal problems; his ability to strip away trivia and get to the heart of a matter; his sensitive consideration of others and his profound insight into the deep recesses of the human mind and heart, coupled with the gift of expressing himself in plain and pointed and unequivocal language, were precisely the essentials for success on the bench—in Lincoln's or any other day."[165] Duff is referring to the same lawyerly traits that helped Lincoln guide the country through the Civil War and guide himself into history as a great leader.

I cannot, in all fairness, leave this topic without recognizing Lincoln's uniqueness. I do not suggest in this article that anyone can become Lincoln.

The traits I have discussed here are those that every good lawyer must possess, but Lincoln had something more. Put simply, Lincoln is still great today because he is remembered as a truly good person, especially through his writings. General Robert E. Lee conceded this fact, even in defeat, saying "I surrendered as much to Lincoln's goodness as I did to Grant's armies."[166] This "goodness" cannot be reduced to any simple list of attributes, it just is. As Charles Wirken said in his article, which I quoted at the beginning of this one, "a trial lawyer named Abraham Lincoln gave us not only his courageous leadership in such forms as the Emancipation Proclamation, but also his life, during the most divisive period in our country's history."[167] I could not put it better myself.

Notes

This essay was originally published in slightly different form in the *Northern Kentucky Law Review* 36, no. 2, and is reprinted here by permission.

1. Godfrey Sperling, "Rating Our Presidents," *Christian Sci. Monitor,* June 14, 2005, at 9. See generally the American Flag Foundation, "Historical Bios: Abraham Lincoln," http://www.americanflagfoundation.org/content/ educationalresources_historicalbios.cfm; Lydian Saad, "Lincoln Resumes Position as Americans' Top-Rated President," *Gallup Poll Briefing,* February 19, 2007, at 72–73 (surveying year to year the top presidents whom the American public regard as the "greatest"), available at http://www.gallup.com/poll/26608/ Lincoln-Resumes-Position-Americans-TopRated-President.aspx.

2. American Flag Foundation, "Historical Bios: Abraham Lincoln," http:// www.americanflagfoundation.org/content/educationalresources_historicalbios .cfm.

3. Speech to One Hundred and Sixty-sixth Ohio Regiment (August 22, 1864), in 7 *Collected Works of Abraham Lincoln* 512 (Roy P. Basler, ed., 1953) [hereafter cited as *Collected Works*], available at http://quod.lib.umich.edu/l/ lincoln/. Professor Gabor Boritt described Lincoln's economic philosophy as an affirmation of the "right to rise" (Gabor S. Boritt, "The Right to Rise," in *The Public and the Private Lincoln: Contemporary Perspectives* 57–70 [Cullon Davis et al., eds., Southern Illinois Univ. Press, 1979]).

4. Lincoln's campaign for the presidency in 1860 did much to encourage the myth.

5. See, for example, Brian R. Dirck, *Lincoln the Lawyer* 25–31 (Univ. of Illinois Press, 2007) (describing Lincoln's entry into the practice of law).

6. Ibid. at xi ("[H]e held national elected office for 1981 days, which constituted approximately ten percent of his entire life; he was a licensed, active attorney for 8,552 days, or about 40 percent of his life."); Herbert Mitgang, "Heritage of Lincoln, the Lawyer," *N.Y. Times*, February 11, 1988, at C29, available at http://query.nytimes.com/gst/fullpage.html?res=940DE0D8123EF932 A25751C0A96E948260.

7. See, for example, Marc Galanter, *Lowering the Bar: Lawyer Jokes and Legal Culture* 3–5 (Univ. of Wisconsin Press, 2005).

8. Ibid.

9. Entire books have been written on this subject. See, for example, ibid. at 3 ("Few who are exposed to American media and popular culture of recent decades will have missed the eruption of a great frenzy of joking about lawyers.").

10. Charles Wirken, "It's a Wonderful Profession—Let's Defend It!," 41 *Ariz. Att'y* 6, 6 (January 2005).

11. Frank J. Williams, "Abraham Lincoln: Commander in Chief or 'Attorney in Chief'?," in *Judging Lincoln* 36–37 (Southern Illinois Univ. Press, 2002) ("Lincoln did not practice law and then become a politician. Not only was he a politician first; he was always both a politician and a lawyer simultaneously.").

12. Ibid. at 34.

13. Brian Dirck's book *Lincoln the Lawyer* is a good resource for those interested in Lincoln's legal career. See generally Dirck, *supra* note 5. See also John J. Duff, *A. Lincoln, Prairie Lawyer* (Rinehart, 1960); John P. Frank, *Lincoln as a Lawyer* (Americana House, 1991).

14. David C. Hardesty Jr., "Leading Lawyers: An Essay on Why Lawyers Lead in America," 10 *W. Va. Law.* 26 (1997).

15. Fragment: Notes for a Law Lecture (July 1, 1850?), in 2 *Collected Works, supra* note 3, at 82.

16. Third Debate with Stephen A. Douglas at Jonesboro, Illinois (September 15, 1858), in 3 *Collected Works, supra* note 3, at 126.

17. Ibid.

18. Dirck, *supra* note 5, at 3 ("Here was truly—in fact, unbelievably—'an honest lawyer' who separated himself from the pettifogging legalisms of the courtroom by displaying folksy charm and down-home common sense.").

19. Frank, *supra* note 13, at 18–19.

20. Lambert Tree, "Side-Lights on Lincoln," 81 *Century Illustrated Monthly Mag.* 592 (1911).

21. Ibid.

22. Ibid.

23. Ibid.

24. Ibid.

25. Ibid.

26. Ibid.

27. Ibid.

28. Ibid.

29. Ibid.

30. Ida Minerva Tarbell, *Boy Scouts' Life of Lincoln* 87 (Macmillan, 1921).

31. Ibid.

32. Ibid.

33. Ibid.

34. Ibid.

35. Ibid.

36. Duff, *supra* note 13, at 348.

37. Ibid.

38. Ibid. at 349.

39. Ibid.

40. Ibid.

41. Ibid.

42. Ibid. at 348–50.

43. Fragment: Notes for a Law Lecture (July 1, 1850?), in 2 *Collected Works, supra* note 3, at 82.

44. Ibid.

45. Ibid.

46. Ibid.

47. Eliot A. Cohen, *Supreme Command: Soldiers, Statesmen, and Leadership in Wartime* 28 (Anchor, 2003).

48. Ibid. at 28.

49. See *Collected Works, supra* note 3.

50. Ibid.

51. Fragments of a Tariff Discussion (December 1, 1847), in 1 *Collected Works, supra* note 3, at 412.

52. Edward Steers Jr., *Lincoln Legends: Myths, Hoaxes, and Confabulations Associated with Our Greatest President* 112 (Univ. Press of Kentucky, 2007) ("Lincoln was a meticulous writer who took great care with his words whether giving a formal speech or writing a letter.").

53. Dirck, *supra* note 5, at 20.

54. See Steers, *supra* note 52, at 112.

55. Abraham Lincoln to David Hunter (December 31, 1861), in 5 *Collected Works, supra* note 3, at 85.

56. Williams, *supra* note 11, at 37.

57. Frank, *supra* note 13, at 18–23.

58. David Herbert Donald, *Lincoln* 149 (Simon and Schuster, 1995).

59. James M. McPherson, *Tried by War: Abraham Lincoln as Commander in Chief* 29–31 (Penguin Press, 2008).

60. Ibid. at 31.

61. Ibid. at 31–33. See also Donald, *supra* note 58, at 307–8.

62. Doris Kearns Goodwin, *Team of Rivals: The Political Genius of Abraham Lincoln* 479 (Simon and Schuster, 2005).

63. Henry Wager Halleck, *Elements of Military Art and Science* (New York: D. Appleton and Co., 1861). Jomini refers to Henri de Jomini.

64. Cohen, *supra* note 47, at 42; see also Frank J. Williams, "Abraham Lincoln and the Changing Role of Commander in Chief," in *Lincoln Reshapes the Presidency* 13 (Charles M. Hubbard, ed., Mercer Univ. Press, 2003).

65. Memorandum to George B. McClellan on Potomac Campaign (December 1, 1861), in 5 *Collected Works, supra* note 3, at 34–35.

66. Ibid. (see annotations).

67. William Lee Miller, *President Lincoln: The Duty of a Statesman* 190 (Knopf, 2008).

68. Ibid. at 170.

69. Address Delivered at the Dedication of the Cemetery at Gettysburg (November 19, 1863), in 7 *Collected Works, supra* note 3, at 23 (all the prior drafts by Lincoln contain this language).

70. Speech at Chicago, Illinois (July 10, 1858), in 2 *Collected Works, supra* note 3, at 484–502.

71. Abraham Lincoln to George Robertson (August 15, 1855), in 2 *Collected Works, supra* note 3, at 317–19.

72. Donald, *supra* note 58, at 224.

73. Speech in Springfield, Illinois (July 17, 1858), in 2 *Collected Works, supra* note 3, at 504–21.

74. Abraham Lincoln to George B. McClellan (October 24, 1862), in 5 *Collected Works, supra* note 3, at 474.

75. Clifton Fadiman and Andre Bernard, *Bartlett's Book of Anecdotes,* 347 (Little, Brown, 2000).

76. Ibid.

77. *Abe Lincoln's Legacy of Laughter: Humorous Stories by and about Abraham Lincoln* 108 (Paul M. Zall, ed., Univ. of Tennessee Press, 2007).

78. Ibid. at 43.

79. Speeches En Route from Springfield to Washington, D.C., in 4 *Collected Works, supra* note 3, at 190–246.

80. Remarks at Lawrenceburg, Indiana (February 12, 1861), in 4 *Collected Works, supra* note 3, at 197.

81. Annual Message to Congress (December 1, 1862), in 5 *Collected Works, supra* note 3, at 535.

82. Address Delivered at the Dedication of the Cemetery at Gettysburg (November 19, 1863), in 7 *Collected Works, supra* note 3, at 17–23.

83. Ibid. at 23.

84. Second Inaugural Address (March 4, 1865), in 8 *Collected Works, supra* note 3, at 333.

85. *Jacobellis v. State of Ohio*, 378 U.S. 184, 197 (1964) (Stewart, J., concurring).

86. Dirck, *supra* note 5, at 96–97; see also Duff, *supra* note 13, at 332–45.

87. Ibid.

88. Ibid.

89. Ibid. at 97.

90. LaWanda Cox, *Lincoln and Black Freedom* 5 (Univ. of South Carolina Press, 1994) ("In championing a moderate program of denying slavery expansion in the territories rather than joining with abolitionists in calling for a more immediate solution, Lincoln did not disguise his immoderate goal.").

91. Preliminary Emancipation Proclamation (September 22, 1862), in 5 *Collected Works, supra* note 3, at 433–36.

92. Second Inaugural Address (March 4, 1865), in 8 *Collected Works, supra* note 3, at 333.

93. Goodwin, *supra* note 62, at 686–87.

94. John C. Waugh, *Reelecting Lincoln: The Battle for the 1864 Presidency* 6 (Crown, 1997).

95. Frank J. Williams, "The End of Slavery: Lincoln and the Thirteenth Amendment—What Did He Know and When Did He Know It?," in *Lincoln Reshapes the Presidency* 13 (Charles M. Hubbard, ed., Mercer Univ. Press, 2003) (an in-depth discussion of Lincoln's role in the passage of the Thirteenth Amendment).

96. Message to Congress in Special Session (July 4, 1861), in 4 *Collected Works, supra* note 3, at 421–41.

97. I have written more extensively on this subject elsewhere. See Frank J. Williams, Nicole J. Dulude, and Kimberly A. Tracey, "Still a Frightening Unknown: Achieving a Constitutional Balance between Civil Liberties and National Security during the War on Terror," 12 *Roger Williams U. L. Rev.* 675, 684–87 (2007).

98. *U.S. Const.* Art. II, § 2.

99. *U.S. Const.* Art. II, § 3.

100. Henry J. Raymond, *The Life and Public Services of Abraham Lincoln* at 181 (University of Michigan Library, 2005), available at http://name.umdl .umich.edu/AAX3271.0001.001.

101. Proclamation Calling for 42,034 Volunteers (May 3, 1861), in 4 *Collected Works, supra* note 3, at 354–55.

102. Proclamation Calling Militia and Convening Congress (April 15, 1861), in 4 *Collected Works, supra* note 3, at 332–33.

103. Raymond, *supra* note 100, at 380.

104. Ibid.

105. Proclamation of Blockade (April 19, 1861), in 4 *Collected Works, supra* note 3, at 338–39; Proclamation of Blockade (April 27, 1861), in 4 *Collected Works, supra* note 3, at 346–47.

106. James G. Randall, *Constitutional Problems under Lincoln* 33–41 (Univ. of Illinois Press, 1964) (1951).

107. Ibid. at 37.

108. Proclamation Suspending the Writ of Habeas Corpus (September 24, 1862), in 4 *Collected Works, supra* note 3, at 438.

109. Abraham Lincoln to James C. Conkling (August 26, 1863), in 6 *Collected Works, supra* note 3, at 409.

110. Miller, *supra* note 67, at 186–88.

111. Ibid.

112. Ibid. at 186–92.

113. George B. McClellan, *The Civil War Papers of George B. McClellan: Selected Correspondence, 1860–1865* 344–45 (Ticknor and Fields, 1989).

114. Miller, *supra* note 67, at 186–87.

115. Ibid.

116. John Nicolay to John Hay, October 26, 1862, John G. Nicolay Papers, Library of Congress, Washington, D.C.

117. Miller, *supra* note 67, at 190.

118. McClellan, *supra* note 113, at 520.

119. Goodwin, *supra* note 62, at 484–86.

120. Ibid.

121. Ibid.

122. Ibid. at 654.

123. Ibid.

124. Donald, *supra* note 58, at 456–57.

125. Abraham Lincoln to James C. Conkling (August 26, 1863) in 6 *Collected Works, supra* note 3, at 409.

126. Fragment: Notes for a Law Lecture (July 1, 1850?), in 2 *Collected Works, supra* note 3, at 81.

127. Dirck, *supra* note 5, at 43.

128. Ibid.

129. See ibid. at 146.

130. Ward H. Lamon, *The Life of Abraham Lincoln: From His Birth to His Inauguration as President* 317 (James R. Osgood, 1872).

131. Frank, *supra* note 13, at 4.

132. Fragment: Notes for a Law Lecture (July 1, 1850?), in 2 *Collected Works, supra* note 3, at 81–82.

133. Dirck, *supra* note 5, at 113.

134. Mark E. Steiner, *An Honest Calling* 87 (Northern Illinois Univ. Press, 2006).

135. Ibid.

136. Ibid. at 88.

137. Ibid. at 87–88.

138. William Lee Miller, "Lincoln's Pardons and What They Mean," in *Lincoln Reshapes the Presidency* 101 (Charles M. Hubbard, ed., Mercer Univ. Press, 2003).

139. Ibid.

140. Ibid. at 107.

141. Ibid. at 108–9.

142. Ibid. at 109.

143. Ibid.

144. Ibid.

145. See Donald, *supra* note 58, at 394.

146. Ibid.

147. Miller, *supra* note 138, at 109–10.

148. Ibid. at 110.

149. Donald, *supra* note 58, at 429–31.

150. Abraham Lincoln to James C. Conkling (August 26, 1863), in 6 *Collected Works, supra* note 3, at 409.

151. Donald, *supra* note 58, at 429–31.

152. Abraham Lincoln to William T. Sherman (December 26, 1864), in 8 *Collected Works, supra* note 3, at 181.

153. Cohen, *supra* note 47, at 19.

154. Ibid.

155. Speech in U.S. House of Representatives on the Presidential Question (July 27, 1848), in 1 *Collected Works, supra* note 3, at 510.

156. Donald, *supra* note 58, at 45.

157. Francis Fisher Browne, *The Every-Day Life of Abraham Lincoln* 107 (Univ. of Nebraska Press, 1995).

158. Paul M. Angle, *The Lincoln Reader* 44 (Da Capo, 1990).

159. Abraham Lincoln to Jesse W. Fell, Enclosing Autobiography (December 20, 1859), in 3 *Collected Works, supra* note 3, at 512.

160. Donald T. Phillips, *Lincoln on Leadership* 103 (Warner Books, 1992).

161. Ibid. at 104.

162. Craig Gargotta, "A Tough Act to Follow," *Fed. Law.* 5, 8 (October 2003).

163. Abraham Lincoln to William T. Sherman (December 26, 1864), in 8 *Collected Works, supra* note 3, at 181.

164. Goodwin, *supra* note 62, at xvii.

165. Duff, *supra* note 13, at 301.

166. Jay Winik, "Abraham Lincoln," in *Presidential Leadership* 86 (James Taranto and Leonard Leo, eds., Free Press, 2005).

167. Wirken, *supra* note 10.

Does Lawyer Lincoln Matter?

Mark E. Steiner

Lincoln's Image as a Lawyer

An opinion poll a few years back revealed that Abraham Lincoln was one of the five most admired lawyers in America.[1] Lincoln's status probably has more to do with how Americans view Lincoln the president than what they actually know about Lincoln the lawyer. The lawyer in popular biographies, movies, and children's books is a virtuous and heroic lawyer.[2] Early biographers, aware of the distrust and hostility toward lawyers, glossed over Lincoln's law practice. These writers were content with somewhat superficial depictions of Lincoln as a virtuous, heroic country lawyer. The treatment of Lincoln's law practice improved somewhat with the professionalization of history in the twentieth century, but, until recently, Lincoln biographers have tended to write about the same handful of cases. Historians' lack of interest in his law career, their apparent belief that their lack of legal training precluded study of Lincoln's law practice, and the inaccessibility of documents had stymied a thorough examination of the law practice.[3]

Lawyers, on the other hand, have written a lot about lawyer Lincoln.[4] Lawyers have wanted to use the image of Lincoln to clean up their own. They have been invested in an image of Lincoln as a country lawyer who is above the fray and who seeks justice only. Lawyer Lincoln has become even more popular with the advent of alternative dispute resolution, as lawyers and law professors often turn to Lincoln's advice to lawyers to "discourage litigation."[5]

Treatment of Lincoln's law practice has been anecdotal. Although Lincoln handled thousands of cases, most biographers settled on discussing the same four or five. These cases became canonical: the Duff Armstrong murder case (the "Almanac Trial"); the *Effie Afton* case; the *Matson* case (sometimes paired with *Bailey v. Campbell*); the McLean County taxation

45

case; and the *Manny Reaper* case.[6] All five were discussed by Albert J. Beveridge in 1928.[7] They remained the only law cases mentioned by Benjamin Thomas in his 1952 biography and by Stephen Oates in his 1977 biography.[8] William E. Gienapp in a 2002 biography mentioned four of the five cases.[9] The canonical cases were the only law cases mentioned by Gienapp, Oates, and Thomas.

The best known of this handful is the Duff Armstrong murder case, which is also known as the Almanac Trial.[10] There, a witness testified that he could see Armstrong strike the fatal blow because the moon was high overhead. Lincoln, who defended Armstrong, helped secure an acquittal for his client by producing an almanac for the year that showed the moon was near the horizon at that time of night. Duff Armstrong was the son of Jack and Hannah Armstrong, friends of Lincoln from his early days in New Salem. The typical account tells how the widow Armstrong begged Lincoln to represent her son, how Lincoln emotionally argued Armstrong's innocence, and how Lincoln refused to charge a fee.[11] The typical account of Lincoln's defense of Duff resonates with the positive cultural image of the heroic criminal defense lawyer winning (against the odds) the acquittal of an innocent person. The case was first mentioned in campaign biographies written in 1860 and continues to be featured in books about Lincoln.[12] This case is so well known that I was told by a dean at a Chinese law school that he decided to become a lawyer after reading about the Almanac Trial in elementary school.

Lincoln in early biographies emerges as a country attorney who was uninterested in fees, who protected the poor and defenseless, who would not defend unjust causes, and who would not take advantage of legal technicalities. This view of Lincoln's law practice first appeared in campaign biographies published in 1860 and 1864. They devoted little space to Lincoln's law practice, and they barely concealed the attempt to combat the negative cultural stereotype about lawyers. John Locke Scripps, for example, asserted that Lincoln often represented poor clients for free when justice and right were on their side.[13] While the *Duff Armstrong* case appeared in at least six biographies, Lincoln's association with the Illinois Central Railroad was not mentioned once.[14] These campaign biographies set the tone for later ones. J. G. Holland wrote in 1866 that lawyer Lincoln's "desire for the establishment of exact justice always overcame his own selfish love of victory."[15]

The negative cultural image of lawyers and the positive cultural image of Lincoln were the two primary reasons that biographers generally paid little attention to lawyer Lincoln. The image of lawyer Lincoln clashes with the images of Lincoln as frontier hero or Great Emancipator. Within these images, there is little room for a successful lawyer.

The lack of attention to Lincoln's law practice changed with the Lincoln Legal Papers project. The problem with lack of access to documents disappeared when *The Law Practice of Abraham Lincoln: Complete Documentary Edition* was published in 2000.[16] This state-of-the-art electronic collection of over 100,000 legal documents culminated a decade-long project by the Illinois Historic Preservation Agency.[17]

The impact of the Lincoln Legal Papers project on Lincoln studies was felt before the publication of the electronic edition.[18] In 1995, David Donald became the first Lincoln biographer to use the materials from the Lincoln Legal Papers project, which he hailed as "perhaps the most important archival investigation now under way in the United States."[19] Although Donald finished his biography several years before the Lincoln Legal Papers project was complete, the book shows the influence of the project. One chapter on Lincoln, "At the Head of His Profession in This State,"[20] was based on "the hundreds of [then] unpublished documents in the files of the Lincoln Legal Papers. . . ."[21] Giving a fuller sense of the breadth of Lincoln's practice, Donald included cases that previous biographers had overlooked and gave examples of cases in circuit courts "of no great interest or consequence to anyone except the parties involved in the litigation."[22]

Since the publication of Donald's book, the impact of the Lincoln Legal Papers project has been easy to see. Five books about aspects of Lincoln's legal career have been published since 2002.[23] Moreover, recent books on Lincoln's presidency show a greater awareness of the possible influence of the law practice. For example, Burrus M. Carnahan probed the legal context of the Emancipation Proclamation because Lincoln had "earned his living by practicing law" and Lincoln would have viewed the issues raised by the Proclamation by "his practical knowledge of American law."[24] Phillip S. Paludan began an essay on Lincoln and the limits of constitutional authority with the deceptively simple sentence: "Abraham Lincoln was a lawyer."[25] Ronald C. White Jr. recently considered how the law practice influenced how Lincoln structured arguments and established tone in his major speeches.[26]

A Portrait of Lawyer Lincoln

But what do we learn about lawyer Lincoln from these thousands of documents? And what does lawyer Lincoln tell us about President Lincoln? I am sympathetic to those Lincoln scholars who complain that legal documents yield information grudgingly.[27] It is practically impossible based on what is left in any particular file—declaration, defensive pleadings, docket entries—to answer the simplest questions about the case. We now know with remarkable precision the results in Lincoln's litigation.[28] It is harder to answer other questions. Was this a case that Lincoln should have won? Or a case he should have lost? We really do not know.

We do know that Lincoln was a very busy lawyer. Cullom Davis, who directed the Lincoln Legal Papers project, noted the major finding of the accession process was that "Lincoln had a much larger and more active law practice than anyone had previously estimated."[29] The portrait of a man who was fundamentally disengaged from the practice of law, a man who really was a politician first and a lawyer second, is hard to reconcile with the five thousand-plus cases Lincoln or his partners handled in his twenty-five-year career. Lincoln's prepresidential political career has received more attention than his law practice; however, Davis also has convincingly argued that Lincoln's twin careers of law and politics had a symbiotic relationship.[30]

Lincoln was not just a trial lawyer who swayed local juries.[31] Lincoln's law practice reveals him to have been a very sharp tactician. Leonard Swett, one of Lincoln's colleagues, once described Lincoln's method of trying cases:

> as he entered the trial, where most lawyers would object, he would say he "reckoned" it would be fair to let this in or that and sometimes when his adversary could not quite prove what Lincoln Knew to be the truth he would say he "reckoned" it would be fair to admit the truth to be so & so. . . . When the whole thing is unravelled, the adversary begins to see that what he was so blandly giving away was simply what he couldnt get & keep. By giving away 6 points and carrying the 7th he carried his case and the whole case hanging on the 7th he traded away every thing which would give him the least aid in carrying that. any man who took Lincoln for a simple minded man would very soon wake [up with] his back in a ditch.[32]

He was also an excellent appellate lawyer, and argued hundreds of cases to the Illinois Supreme Court, where he developed sophisticated (and technical) legal arguments. He, or his partners, handled over four hundred appeals to the Illinois Supreme Court, and in nearly two hundred Lincoln had not tried the case in the circuit court but was hired for the appeal.[33] Lincoln's being hired for appeals meant he was a "lawyer's lawyer."

William Herndon thought Lincoln was a better appellate lawyer than trial lawyer: "He was greatest in my opinion as a lawyer in the Supreme Court of Illinois. There the cases were never hurried. The attorneys generally prepared their cases in the form of briefs, and the movements of the court and counsel were so slow that no one need be caught by surprise."[34] Lincoln handled so many appeals that he often established the precedent that would later defeat him in a subsequent appeal; in several appeals his most formidable opponent was himself.[35] He took advantage of legal technicalities when he could, arguing that appellants had failed to follow the formal requirements of pleadings and appeal bonds in order to obtain dismissals.[36]

On Lincoln's oral advocacy, let's hear again from Herndon describing Lincoln arguing before the Illinois Supreme Court:

> I heard him once argue a case and it was argued extremely well, it was logical, eloquent. In making his argument he referred to the history of the law, a useless part as I then thought. I know better now. After the speech was through and Lincoln had come into the law library room where the lawyers tell stories and prepare their cases, I said: "Lincoln, why did you go so far back in the history of the law as applicable to this case?" and to which he instantly replied: "I dare not trust this case on the presumptions that this court knows all things. I argued the case on the presumption that the court did not know anything."[37]

Lincoln's argument in that appeal would have been several hours long. It was not until 1853 that the Illinois Supreme Court limited the argument of counsel to two hours (each lawyer had two hours), except that by special permission opening argument could be up to three hours.[38] In 1858, the time allotted for each argument was restricted to one hour and the court noted that "counsel may file in addition, such written arguments as they shall think proper."[39]

Briefs in Lincoln's Illinois were not like modern briefs, but were "points and authorities," which meant a sentence or two of black letter law and then some citations.[40] The appellant or plaintiff in error had to file its brief of points and authorities the day before oral argument and the appellee's duty was to furnish its brief to the judges and opposing counsel "at the commencement of argument."[41]

Lincoln and Whig Lawyering

As a lawyer, Abraham Lincoln developed a distinctive Whiggish attitude toward law and the role of law in American society.[42] Lincoln had begun his political career as a Whig. Politically, Whigs like Lincoln were modernizing conservatives who favored internal improvements such as railroads to foster economic growth.[43] Whigs also believed that the rule of law provided a neutral means to resolve disputes. Lincoln was a Whig lawyer who embodied the Whig reverence for law and order.[44]

Lincoln, in his 1838 address on "The Perpetuation of Our Political Institutions," discussed recent incidents of civil disorder.[45] He was worried by the example of lawlessness that mobs set. To prevent disorder, reverence for the law needed to become the "political religion of the nation."[46] Lincoln, after saying there was "something of ill-omen amongst us," said he meant, "the increasing disregard for law which pervades the country; the growing disposition to substitute the wild and furious passions, in lieu of the sober judgements of Courts; and the worse than savage mobs, for the executive ministers of justice."[47]

Lincoln scholar Phillip Paludan concluded that Lincoln "spoke to perhaps the most compelling of the American traditions—that a country should be ruled by laws, and that legal-constitutional institutions should demand respect and devotion."[48] The question before Lincoln was, "What was to keep society from flying apart?"[49] Paludan said that Lincoln had the answer—"respect for legal institutions, for all laws, for the due legal process of doing things and for fellow citizens as lawmakers and law respecters."[50] Paludan elsewhere noted: "Lincoln's commitment to the rule of law had deep foundations. It arose from personal experience, gained strength from his faith that reason must triumph over passion as the source of democratic government and personal growth, found nurturance in his vocation as a lawyer, and was cemented in an environment where political rhetoric found its roots in constitutional debate."[51]

Lincoln's essentially political conception of a lawyer's role defined what a lawyer would do in his practice: represent clients faithfully. Lincoln possessed a service mentality; he was ready to represent any client. Part of this service mentality was the result of the economics of the law office in frontier Illinois. His partner Herndon remembered that there were not many retainers and that "the greatest as well as the least had to join the general scramble for practice."[52]

Whig politicians wanted to develop a commercial republic, but Whig lawyers were not the "shock troops of capitalism," as has been suggested by one historian.[53] Lincoln, like many other Whig lawyers, was not an instrumentalist; he did not see law as an instrument for him to implement pro-development or pro-capitalist legal rules.

The legal ideology of the Whigs forestalled the adoption of a litigation strategy dedicated to commercial interests. Lincoln's practice is often portrayed as becoming increasingly one-sided as he aligned with business corporations and railroads; but he also was regularly fighting *against* corporations and railroads throughout his career. For example, Lincoln is sometimes identified as a railroad lawyer, but he regularly represented six railroads (including the Illinois Central) and he regularly sued seven.[54] Lincoln took business as it came.[55]

Law and Community

As a Whig lawyer, Lincoln saw his role initially as representing one side—it did not matter which side—so long as the dispute was settled peacefully. In his 1838 address Lincoln mentioned the "executive ministers of justice."[56] But judges and juries would not always be necessary. Lincoln, like most antebellum lawyers, believed that lawyers should serve as peacemakers.[57] Lincoln famously wrote, "Discourage litigation. Persuade your neighbors to compromise whenever you can. . . . As a peace-maker the lawyer has a superior opportunity of being a good man."[58]

Antebellum lawyers like Lincoln celebrated the "sober judgements of Courts" as a means to maintain social order.[59] At the same time, however, they also believed that they should serve as peacemakers, preventing disputes from going to court. This peacemaking role is best shown in his slander cases, where Lincoln often took advantage of opportunities for mediation and compromise. He was able to resolve many cases by repairing the damage to the plaintiffs' reputation. In several instances, the defendant attested to the good reputation of the slandered plaintiff, which settled the case. In some cases, the defendant consented to a large judgment, which the plaintiff then agreed to reduce to a much smaller sum. In others, the plaintiff, after a jury had awarded damages, agreed to remit most or all of the award.

Slander cases in frontier Illinois were community oriented, regulating acceptable forms of behavior in small communities. Standing in a small community was based on reputation, and reputations were built or destroyed through gossip. Lincoln recognized the importance of reputation; he confessed in 1832 that his "peculiar ambition" was "being truly esteemed of my fellow men."[60]

Slander cases were different than other cases. One striking statistic is the relative lack of default judgments in slander cases. In all of Lincoln's slander cases, plaintiffs only obtained two default judgments, and one of the two was reversed on appeal to the Illinois Supreme Court. Thus, by my count, in all of Lincoln's slander cases, default judgments were obtained in roughly 2 percent of the cases.[61] About one-third of Lincoln's other cases ended with default judgments. Successful resolution of slander cases, however, apparently required some kind of formal appearance by the defendant. The goal of a plaintiff suing on a promissory note was to obtain a judgment that memorialized the debt; whether the defendant appeared in court was irrelevant.[62] The goal of a plaintiff in a slander suit was to vindicate honor and repair reputation. That goal required the defendant to participate by appearing in court.

Even in slander cases where litigants were emotionally invested in their lawsuits, Lincoln valued mediation and compromise. He did not try every slander claim; he often was able to settle them. In several instances, the parties settled before trial when the defendant agreed to a large adverse judgment, which the plaintiff then agreed to remit in part or in total. For example, in an 1840 Livingston County lawsuit, Stuart & Lincoln represented William Popejoy, who sued Isaac Wilson because he had said Popejoy had stolen meat. The case settled when Wilson in open court confessed judgment "for the sum of Two Thousand Dollars, the amount of Damages claimed in Plaintiff Declaration"; the judge then ordered Popejoy to recover the "Two Thousand dollars so confessed"; and "thereupon" Popejoy then agreed to remit the entire amount except court costs.[63] Popejoy only remitted the damages after Wilson in open court had confessed judgment for the entire claimed amount. The parties did not just announce a settlement where Wilson agreed to pay costs, but instead acted out a set piece that restored Popejoy's reputation.[64]

Other cases were settled before trial in the same fashion. Lincoln settled an 1853 Vermilion County case by having the defendant withdraw her plea and consent to a $5,000 judgment and having the plaintiff remit all but $50. The plaintiff, America Toney, had sued Emily Sconce for saying that after America had gone to her room with one Whitcomb late one evening the bed was "rattling and jiggling" and when America later came out of the room at three in the morning her clothes and hair were "rumpled," her face was "very red," and she was "very much excited."[65] In 1845, Lincoln and Herndon represented the plaintiff in a Sangamon County slander suit. The case was settled when the parties agreed to a $500 judgment, which the plaintiff agreed to remit except for costs. Lincoln pursued an identical strategy when he helped represent Dr. Julius Lehman in an 1859 McLean County lawsuit. Lehman sued another doctor, Herman Schroeder, for slander. The case was settled when Schroeder agreed in open court to a $5,000 judgment against him and Lehman agreed to remit all but $50 and to stay execution for three months.[66]

Henry Clay Whitney, an Urbana lawyer who was associated often with Lincoln on the circuit, recalled one slander case in which Lincoln, one of the defendant's lawyers, "made most strenuous and earnest efforts to compromise the case, which was accomplished by reason, solely, of his exertions."[67] The case arose in Kankakee County and involved a French Catholic priest named Chiniquy (from the French community of St. Anne's) and Peter Spink, a French Catholic from a nearby community. In a sermon, Chiniquy apparently accused Spink of perjury and refused to recant. Whitney noted that, after the suit was filed, "preparations were made for a 'fight to the finish,' by, not only the two principals, but the two respective neighborhoods, as well: for all became involved as principals or partisans."[68] When the case was transferred to Champaign County, "The principals, their lawyers and witnesses, and an immense retinue of followers, came to Urbana. The hotels were monopolized, and a large number camped out."[69] The case was tried twice and resulted in a mistrial twice. At the next term of court, "All came to our county, camp-outfits, musicians, parrots, pet dogs and all, and the outlook was, that all their scandal would have to be aired over again."[70] Lincoln then intervened; Whitney noted that Lincoln "abhorred that class of litigation, in which [there] was no utility, and he used his utmost influence with all parties, and finally effected a compromise."[71] After convincing the parties to settle, Lincoln prepared the agreement of dismissal. The parties agreed to divide court costs and to dismiss the case.[72]

The nature of these settlements suggest that slander suits were intended more to restore or repair reputation than to collect damages, and the lawyers involved in these cases were well aware of that.[73] Lincoln settled at least three slander cases by having his client affirm the good reputation of the plaintiff, thus repairing the plaintiff's reputation in the community.[74] As Lincoln later noted, "*Truth* is generally the best vindication against slander."[75]

Lincoln and the *Matson* Case

These slander cases showed Lincoln resolving disputes without the "sober judgements of Courts"—what was important for the lawyers and the parties was that the dispute was settled peacefully.[76] But let's look at another aspect of Whig lawyering. What was important for Whig lawyers was the rule of law, the "sober judgements of Courts"; the lawyer's role was to represent one side and leave the rest to the "executive ministers of justice."[77] This conception of Whig lawyering—taking business as it comes, not worrying about what side you take—has real limitations, which is shown by Lincoln's involvement in the *Matson* case.[78]

In the *Matson* case, Abraham Lincoln represented a Kentucky slaveowner named Robert Matson in an unsuccessful attempt to assert property rights to an African American woman named Jane Bryant and her four children.[79] This appears to be paradoxical for the man who would become the Great Emancipator. For those who doubt Lincoln's antislavery convictions or believe him to be a hypocrite, this case does not present any mysteries. But I agree with those who take Lincoln at his word, that he had "always hated slavery."[80]

Matson had bought land in Coles County in 1843, and he apparently had brought slaves from Kentucky every year to work on his farm. Matson would put on a little show, affirming that he had no intent to change the domicile of these slaves.[81] He did that because of how the law of freedom and slavery operated.[82]

In the 1840s, American courts, both North and South, generally accepted the proposition that slavery needed positive law to exist.[83] That principle had been established in a 1763 British case, *Somerset v. Stewart,* where Lord Mansfeld famously had stated that slavery was so odious it needed positive law to survive. If a slave was taken to England, where there wasn't a law of slavery, that slave became free.[84]

Massachusetts, probably the most influential state supreme court in this period, had accepted the *Somerset* principle in a case called *Commonwealth v. Aves.*[85] Other states also adopted this viewpoint, but made a sectional accommodation: Northern states allowed slaveowners brief transit or sojourns with slaves.[86] If a slave traveled through Illinois with his master, that did not operate to free the slave. Illinois accepted this principle in 1843.[87]

Robert Matson had left Jane and her children on his farm in Illinois for two years.[88] She was not part of his "annual migration." At the time, every court in the union would have ruled that she was free under those circumstances. The facts in the *Matson* case paralleled the facts in the *Dred Scott* case, where Dred Scott was taken to Illinois and the Wisconsin Territory by his master for a period of some years. It was clear under Missouri precedent that Dred Scott would have been free, except the Missouri Supreme Court, citing sectional tensions, changed the law in his very case.[89]

That would leave the question of why a Kentucky slaveowner would take five slaves to a free state and leave them there for two years. He may have counted on their ignorance. Lincoln in 1854 noted that it is good "book-law" that slaves became free when they entered a jurisdiction that did not have positive law that supported slavery. But, in actual practice, Lincoln questioned "who will inform the negro that he is free? . . . In ignorance of his legal emancipation, he is kept chopping, splitting and plowing."[90]

Robert Matson has been somewhat of a cipher in earlier accounts. I discovered lawsuits filed in Bourbon County, Kentucky, courts that presented a portrait of a real person, albeit a detestable one. There were lawsuits against his brother, including a slander suit, and there were family squabbles over land. There were many debt cases. And there were lawsuits that showed his slaves had tried to escape from him while in Kentucky.[91]

What precipitated the legal proceedings was Matson's apparently returning to Illinois intending to take Jane and her children back to Kentucky and sell them.[92] That is when she ran away. Lincoln ended up representing Matson, alongside Charleston lawyer Usher Linder.[93]

Some who have written about the case claim that Lincoln "threw the case away."[94] That's not true. He gave the best argument he could, stressing that Matson's intent was to keep his slaves temporarily in Illinois. Co-counsel Linder gave a more extreme argument that would have protected slave property in free states.[95] In 1858, when Lincoln warned of the next *Dred Scott* case that would make slavery national and make Illinois a slave state, the logic of that case would have been the same as Linder's logic in the *Matson* case—slavery was a property right that had to be protected in all jurisdictions.[96]

The case raises issues about the ethical roles of lawyers. Many who have written about the case seem to have assumed that the dominant legal ethic today—role morality—was dominant then. Lawyers today seem to have a particular problem with assuming that the legal culture of today is the same as Lincoln's.

It is not quite so simple. Different notions of legal ethics were being debated by antebellum lawyers. Treatise writer Timothy Hoffman argued in the 1820s that what was immoral for a person to do individually would be immoral still if that person acted as a lawyer. Hoffman said that a lawyer acted unethically if he pled the statute of limitations to a just debt. The statute of limitations did not change the character of the debt or the underlying obligation to pay it.[97] Other lawyers responded that it was not the lawyer's job to be judge and jury. Modern legal ethics arose from the conception of the lawyers' role advocated by Whig lawyers.[98]

Abolitionists severely criticized Northern lawyers who represented Southern slaveowners.[99] Lincoln's partner William Herndon only represented runaway slaves; Herndon never represented slaveowners. Lincoln and Herndon looked at the role of lawyers differently. Lincoln extolled the "sober judgement of Courts," while Herndon was more of an abolitionist who would not have considered helping a slaveowner.[100]

These developing notions of professional responsibility which minimized a lawyer's independence and moral autonomy, combined with Lincoln's notion of Whig lawyering, meant that it would not have been a quandary for him to represent Robert Matson. That is a problem for both Whig lawyering and for Abraham Lincoln.

At some level, the rule of law by itself is not enough. The rule of law becomes focused on procedure and process. Law professor Grant Gilmore once observed, "In Heaven there will be no law, and the lion will lie down with the lamb. . . . In Hell, there will be nothing but law, and due process will be meticulously observed."[101]

Lincoln as Lawyer and Lincoln as President

Lincoln in 1838 emphasized his commitment to the rule of law. This Whig reverence for law and order was strengthened by Lincoln's law practice. Phillip Paludan has noted that Lincoln's "law practice required that he know the rules and the procedures that settled disputes and distributed resources."[102] But in the 1850s Lincoln realized a commitment to the rule of law was not enough.[103] It was not until the Kansas-Nebraska Act of 1854, which drew Lincoln back to politics, that Lincoln began to connect the ideal of equality (the Declaration of Independence) with its processes (the Constitution).[104] Lincoln the Whig lawyer and Lincoln the Republican politician were quite different.

In his commitment to law and order, Lincoln did not seem to care much about the laws themselves—just that they were obeyed. This view appears to have changed in the wake of the Kansas-Nebraska Act in 1854 and the *Dred Scott* decision in 1857. Lincoln was now faced with the issue of slavery and its expansion into the territories. The Kansas-Nebraska Act had repealed the Missouri Compromise of 1820, which had allowed Missouri to enter the union as a slave state but for new states in the future had established a line at 36°30' whereby slavery was prohibited north of the line and permitted south of it. Illinois senator Stephen Douglas's bill made slavery north of the Missouri Compromise possible, as the question of slavery would be decided by the settlers in those territories.[105]

Lincoln began to think more about why slavery was wrong. He was incensed by Douglas's notion of popular sovereignty, where white settlers in a territory would vote on whether slavery would exist there, and he was incensed that Douglas did not care about the outcome. Lincoln complained in 1858 that Douglas was "blowing out the moral lights around us. When he says he 'cares not whether slavery is voted down or voted up'—that it is a sacred right of self government—he is in my judgment penetrating the human soul and eradicating the light of reason and the love of liberty in this American people."[106]

For a critique of popular sovereignty, Lincoln's devotion to law and order was useless by itself. Lincoln then went beyond a mere devotion to process, and began to look at the moral foundations of American democracy, particularly the Declaration of Independence. In an October 1854 speech that foreshadowed the Lincoln-Douglas debates, Lincoln grounded his attack on popular sovereignty on the "ancient faith" of the Declaration of Independence.[107]

Lincoln's critique of the Kansas-Nebraska Act was based on a Lockean theory of government that Jefferson had famously encapsulated in the Declaration of Independence. All men are created equal because all men have the natural rights of life, liberty, and the pursuit of happiness. Men enter the social compact to secure these rights. These rights were a priori: who has God-given rights was decided by God, not by voters.

Lincoln continued this critique four years later in his famous debates with Douglas. In the senate race of 1858, Lincoln held on to his moderate antislavery position: he opposed the extension of slavery into the territories because slavery was morally wrong, but he believed that the federal government did not have the authority to abolish slavery where it already existed.[108]

As Lincoln scholar Allen C. Guelzo writes in his recent book on the Lincoln-Douglas debates, Lincoln and Douglas represented competing visions of what a liberal democracy meant. Douglas believed that "liberal democracy existed only to provide a procedural framework for exercising rights," while Lincoln "insisted that liberal democracy had a higher purpose, which was the realization of a morally right political order."[109] Douglas in the debates said that he did not care whether "slavery was voted up or voted down" in the territories and that "whoever wants slavery has the right to have it."[110] Lincoln, on the other hand, said that blacks were "entitled to all the natural rights enumerated in the Declaration of Independence—the right to life, liberty, and the pursuit of happiness."[111] Slavery was a "moral, social and political evil."[112] Lincoln was now committed to more than a dedication to process; a liberal democracy needed more than the "sober judgements of Courts."

From his law practice, Lincoln developed certain habits of mind, ways for him to think about problems.[113] As his second law partner, Stephen T. Logan, noted, Lincoln learned how to "study out" his case.[114] This ability was shown by his mastery of military strategy during the Civil War.[115] As a lawyer, he learned to think strategically. He learned to express himself with clarity and precision. He thought about the importance of the rule of law.

From the constant interaction with clients, witnesses, juries, other lawyers, and judges, he sharpened his ability to read people. But what he gained from his law practice hardly predicts the end of slavery.

Notes

This essay was originally published in slightly different form in the *Northern Kentucky Law Review* 36, no. 2, and is reprinted here by permission.

1. Mark E. Steiner, *An Honest Calling: The Law Practice of Abraham Lincoln* 5 (2006). This section encapsulates the first chapter and freely incorporates material from that chapter. Material from the book is reprinted with permission of Northern Illinois University Press.

2. See, for example, *Young Mr. Lincoln* (Twentieth Century-Fox Film Corporation, 1939); Martha Brenner, *Abe Lincoln's Hat* (1994).

3. Steiner, *supra* note 1, at 5–6.

4. See, for example, John J. Duff, *A. Lincoln, Prairie Lawyer* (Rinehart, 1960); John P. Frank, *Lincoln as a Lawyer* (1961; reprint, Americana House, 1991); Frederick Trevor Hill, *Lincoln the Lawyer* (Century, 1906); Albert A. Woldman, *Lawyer Lincoln* (1936; reprint, Carroll and Graf, 1994).

5. Fragment: Notes for a Law Lecture (ca. 1850), in 2 *The Collected Works of Abraham Lincoln* 81–82 (Roy P. Basler, ed., Rutgers Univ. Press, 1953), available at http://quod.lib.umich.edu/l/lincoln/. A search (Lincoln /p "discourage litigation") in the JLR database in Westlaw resulted in 122 references to Lincoln's advice.

6. The canonical status of these cases is further indicated by their inclusion as the only law cases with entries in Mark E. Neely Jr., *The Abraham Lincoln Encyclopedia* 8, 96, 202–4, 207–8 (McGraw-Hill, 1982).

7. Albert Beveridge, *Abraham Lincoln: 1809–1858,* at 392–97, 561–71, 575–83, 584–96, 598–604 (Riverside, 1928).

8. Benjamin P. Thomas, *Abraham Lincoln: A Biography* 112, 157–60 (Knopf, 1976) (1952); Stephen B. Oates, *With Malice toward None: The Life of Abraham Lincoln* 101–2, 104, 136–37, 141–42, 266 (Harper Collins, 1994) (1977).

9. William E. Gienapp, *Abraham Lincoln and Civil War America: A Biography* 44–45 (Oxford Univ. Press, 2002).

10. See Daniel W. Stowell, "Moonlight Offers Little Light," 24 *J. Abraham Lincoln Ass'n* 66, 66–67 (2003), reviewing John Evangelist Walsh, *Moonlight: Abraham Lincoln and the Almanac Trial* (2000), available at http://www.historycooperative.org/view.php.

11. See Isaac Arnold, *The Life of Abraham Lincoln* 87–89 (Univ. of Nebraska Press, 1994) (1884).

12. Steiner, *supra* note 1, at 11.

13. John Locke Scripps, *The First Published Life of Abraham Lincoln* 44 (Cranbrook Press, 1900) (1860).

14. Steiner, *supra* note 1, at 11.

15. J. G. Holland, *Holland's Life of Abraham Lincoln* 130 (Univ. of Nebraska Press, 1998) (1866).

16. *The Law Practice of Abraham Lincoln: Complete Documentary Edition*, DVD-ROM (Martha L. Benner and Cullom Davis et al., eds., Univ. of Illinois Press, 2000), available at www.lawpracticeofabrahamlincoln.org

17. Paulette W. Campbell, "Reconstructing Lincoln's Law Practice," 22 *Humanities* 42 (January/February 2001), available at http://www.neh.gov/news/humanities/2001-01/lincolnslaw.html.

18. See, for example, William D. Beard, "'I have labored hard to find the law': Abraham Lincoln and the Alton and Sangamon Railroad," 85 *Ill. Hist. J.* 209 (1992), available at http://dig.lib.niu.edu/ISHS/ishs-1992winter/ishs-1992winter209.pdf.

19. David Herbert Donald, *Lincoln* 16 (Simon and Schuster, 1995).

20. Ibid. at 142–52.

21. Ibid. at 620.

22. Ibid. at 148.

23. See, for example, Allen D. Spiegel, *A. Lincoln, Esquire: A Shrewd, Sophisticated Lawyer in His Time* (Mercer Univ. Press, 2002); *In Tender Consideration: Women, Families, and the Law in Abraham Lincoln's Illinois* (Daniel W. Stowell, ed., Univ. of Illinois Press, 2002); Steiner, *supra* note 1; Brian Dirck, *Lincoln the Lawyer* (Univ. of Illinois Press, 2007); Julie M. Fenster, *The Case of Abraham Lincoln: A Story of Adultery, Murder, and the Making of a Great President* (Palgrave MacMillan, 2008).

24. Burrus M. Carnahan, *Act of Justice: Lincoln's Emancipation Proclamation and the Law of War* 2 (Univ. Press of Kentucky, 2007).

25. Phillip Shaw Paludan, "Lincoln and the Limits of Constitutional Authority," in *Lincoln and Freedom: Slavery, Emancipation, and the Thirteenth Amendment* 37 (Harold Holzer and Sara Vaughn Gabbard, eds., Southern Illinois Univ. Press, 2007).

26. Ronald C. White Jr., *The Eloquent President: A Portrait of Lincoln through His Words* 81–83, 272–73 (Random House, 2005).

27. See Mark E. Neely Jr., *The Last Best Hope of Earth: Abraham Lincoln and the Promise of America* 34 (Harvard Univ. Press, 1993).

28. See 1 *The Papers of Abraham Lincoln: Legal Documents and Cases* 61–62 (Daniel W. Stowell, ed., Univ. of Virginia Press, 2008) for a statistical breakdown of the 1,240 assumpsit cases in which Lincoln and his partners participated.

29. Herbert Mitgang, "Document Search Shows Lincoln the Railsplitter Was Polished Lawyer," *N. Y. Times,* February 15, 1993, at A12.

30. Cullom Davis, "Law and Politics: The Two Careers of Abraham Lincoln," 17 *Quarterly Journal of Ideology* 61 (1994).

31. For a good overview of Lincoln's practice, see John A. Lupton, "A. Lincoln, Esquire: The Evolution of a Lawyer," in Spiegel, *supra* note 23, at 18–49.

32. 1 *The Papers of Abraham Lincoln: Legal Documents and Cases, supra* note 28, at 21.

33. Ibid., at xxxvi.

34. William H. Herndon and Jesse W. Weik, *Herndon's Lincoln* 210–11 (Douglas L. Wilson and Rodney O. Davis, eds., Univ. of Illinois Press, 2006) (1888).

35. Compare *Grable v. Margrave,* 4 Ill. 372, 373 (1842) with *McNamara v. King,* 7 Ill. 432, 435–37 (1845); compare *Sprague v. Illinois River R.R.,* 19 Ill. 174 (1857) with *Banet v. Alton & Sangamon R.R.,* 13 Ill. 504 (1851).

36. See, for example, *Maus v. Worthing,* 4 Ill. 26, 26 (1841).

37. *The Hidden Lincoln: From the Letters and Papers of William H. Herndon* 428 (Emanuel Hertz, ed., Blue Ribbon Books, 1940).

38. Rule of the Illinois Supreme Court Adopted December Term, 1853, reprinted in 15 Ill. vi.

39. Rule of the Illinois Supreme Court Adopted at Springfield, January Term, 1858, reprinted in 18 Ill. vi.

40. For an early example of "Points and Authorities" written by Lincoln, see Report of Attorney's Argument (July 8, 1841), in 1 *The Papers of Abraham Lincoln: Legal Documents and Cases, supra* note 28, at 36–37.

41. Rules XX–XXII, Rules, Supreme Court of the State of Illinois, December Term, 1839, reprinted in 2 Ill. xv. In 1858, the court began requiring printed briefs. Rule XIII, Rules of Practice in the Supreme Court of the State of Illinois, Adopted at November Term, 1858, at Mount Vernon, reprinted in 19 Ill. xiv.

42. See generally Steiner, *supra* note 1.

43. Daniel Walker Howe, "Why Abraham Lincoln Was a Whig," 16 *J. Abraham Lincoln Ass'n* 26, 27–28 (1995), available at http://www.historycooperative. org/journals/jala/16.1/howe.html.

44. Ibid.

45. "Address before the Young Men's Lyceum of Springfield, Illinois" (January 27, 1838), in 1 *Collected Works of Abraham Lincoln, supra* note 5, at 108.

46. Ibid. at 112.

47. Ibid. at 109.

48. Phillip S. Paludan, "Lincoln, the Rule of Law, and the American Revolution," 70 *J. Ill. St. Hist. Soc'y* 10, 14 (1977).

49. Ibid.

50. Ibid.

51. Phillip S. Paludan, "Greeley, Colonization, and a 'Deputation of Negroes,'" in *Lincoln Emancipated: The President and the Politics of Race* 35 (Brian R. Dirck, ed., Northern Illinois Univ. Press, 2007).

52. Herndon and Weik, *supra* note 34, at 124.

53. Charles Sellers, *The Market Revolution: Jacksonian America 1815–1846,* at 47 (Oxford Univ. Press, 1991).

54. Steiner, *supra* note 1, at 64.

55. Thomas, *supra* note 8, at 158.

56. Address before the Young Men's Lyceum of Springfield, Illinois (January 27, 1838), in 1 *Collected Works of Abraham Lincoln, supra* note 5, at 109.

57. Fragment: Notes for a Law Lecture (ca. 1850), in 2 *Collected Works of Abraham Lincoln, supra* note 5, at 81.

58. Ibid.

59. Address before the Young Men's Lyceum of Springfield, Illinois (January 27, 1838), in 1 *Collected Works of Abraham Lincoln, supra* note 5, at 109.

60. "Communication to the People of Sangamo County" (March 9, 1832), in 1 *Collected Works of Abraham Lincoln, supra* note 5, at 5, 8.

61. Steiner, *supra* note 1, at 92.

62. Spiegel, *supra* note 23, at 53–54.

63. *The Law Practice of Abraham Lincoln, supra* note 16, Judgment, dated October 13, 1840 [61097], *Popejoy v. Wilson* [L02070] case file.

64. Ibid.

65. *The Law Practice of Abraham Lincoln, supra* note 16, Agreement [filed October Term 1853][5890], Judgment, dated October 29, 1853 [61811], Narratio, filed May 11, 1853 [61803], *Toney v. Sconce* [L02050] case file.

66. Ibid., Judgment, dated January 8, 1859 [53253], *Lehman v. Schroeder* [L01659], case file.

67. Henry C. Whitney, *Life on the Circuit with Lincoln* 136–37 (Estes and Lauriat, 1892).

68. Ibid. at 54.

69. Ibid.

70. Ibid. at 55.

71. Ibid.

72. *The Law Practice of Abraham Lincoln, supra* note 16, Judgment, dated October Term, 1856, *Spink v. Chiniquy* [L01448] case file.

73. Steiner, *supra* note 1, at 97.

74. Ibid.

75. Abraham Lincoln to Edwin M. Stanton (July 14, 1864), in 7 *Collected Works of Abraham Lincoln, supra* note 5, at 440.

76. Woldman, *supra* note 4, at 30.

77. Ibid.

78. This section draws extensively from the fifth chapter of Steiner, *supra* note 1, at 103–36.

79. Ibid. at 103.

80. Speech at Chicago, Illinois (July 10, 1858), in 2 *Collected Works of Abraham Lincoln, supra* note 5, at 484, 492. On Lincoln's hatred of slavery, see generally George M. Fredrickson, *Big Enough to Be Inconsistent: Abraham Lincoln Confronts Slavery and Race* 81 (Harvard Univ. Press, 2008); James Oakes, *The Radical and the Republican: Frederick Douglass, Abraham Lincoln, and the Triumph of Antislavery Politics* 132 (Norton, 2007); Phillip Shaw Paludan, "Lincoln and Negro Slavery: I Haven't Got Time for the Pain," 27 *J. Abraham Lincoln Ass'n* 1 (2006), available at http://www.historycooperative.org/journals/jala/27.2/paludan.html.

81. Steiner, *supra* note 1, at 119.

82. See generally Paul Finkelman, *An Imperfect Union: Slavery, Federalism and Comity* (Univ. of North Carolina Press, 1981).

83. Don E. Fehrenbacher, *The Dred Scott Case: Its Significance in American Law and Politics* 54–56 (Oxford Univ. Press, 1978).

84. *Somerset v. Stewart,* 98 Eng. Rep. 499 (K. B. 1772).

85. *Commonwealth v. Aves,* 35 Mass. 193 (1836).

86. Fehrenbacher, *supra* note 83, at 54–56.

87. *Willard v. People,* 5 Ill. 461, 472–73 (1843).

88. Steiner, *supra* note 1, at 119.

89. *Scott, a Man of Color v. Emerson,* 15 Mo. 576, 592 (1852).

90. Speech at Peoria, Illinois (October 16, 1854), in 2 *Collected Works of Abraham Lincoln, supra* note 5, at 247, 262.

91. Steiner, *supra* note 1, at 105–6.

92. Ibid. at 107–8.

93. Ibid. at 108–9.

94. This myth dies hard. See Paul Finkelman, "Abraham Lincoln: Prairie Lawyer," in *America's Lawyer-Presidents: From Law Office to Oval Office* 129, 134 (Norman Gross, ed., Northwestern Univ. Press, 2004).

95. Steiner, *supra* note 1, at 119–23.

96. Speech at Springfield, Illinois (June 16, 1858), in 2 *Collected Works of Abraham Lincoln, supra* note 5, at 461, 464–65.

97. Steiner, *supra* note 1, at 133–34.

98. Ibid. at 131–34.

99. Ibid. at 131.

100. Ibid. at 127–28.

101. Grant Gilmore, *The Ages of American Law* 111 (Yale Univ. Press, 1977).

102. Phillip S. Paludan, "Lincoln's Prewar Constitutional Vision," 15 *J. Abraham Lincoln Ass'n* 1, 8 (1994) available at http://www.historycooperative.org/journals/jala/15.2/paludan.html. This paragraph depends heavily on Paludan's article.

103. Ibid. at 14.

104. Ibid. at 13–14.

105. David Herbert Donald, *Liberty and Union* 59–63 (D. C. Heath, 1978).

106. First Debate with Stephen A. Douglas at Ottawa, Illinois (August 21, 1858), in 3 *The Collected Works of Abraham Lincoln, supra* note 5, at 30.

107. Speech at Peoria, Illinois (October 16, 1854), in 2 *The Collected Works of Abraham Lincoln, supra* note 5, at 267.

108. William C. Harris, *Lincoln's Rise to the Presidency* 121–22 (Univ. Press of Kansas, 2007).

109. Allen C. Guelzo, *Lincoln and Douglas: The Debates that Changed America* 313–14 (Simon and Schuster, 2008).

110. Speech at Indianapolis, Indiana (September 19, 1859), in 3 *The Collected Works of Abraham Lincoln, supra* note 5, at 469.

111. First Debate with Stephen A. Douglas at Ottawa, Illinois (August 21, 1858), in 3 *The Collected Works of Abraham Lincoln, supra* note 5, at 16.

112. Fifth Debate with Stephen A. Douglas, at Galesburg, Illinois (October 7, 1858), in 3 *The Collected Works of Abraham Lincoln, supra* note 5, at 226.

113. Phillip Shaw Paludan, "'Dictator Lincoln': Surveying Lincoln and the Constitution," 21 *OAH Mag. of Hist.* 8, 10 (January 2007) ("Thinking like a lawyer was a profound part of his makeup.").

114. "Stephen T. Logan Talks about Lincoln," *Bull. Lincoln Centennial Ass'n* 3 (September 1, 1928).

115. James M. McPherson, *Tried by War: Abraham Lincoln as Commander in Chief* 3 (Penguin, 2008). Michael Burlingame reached a similar conclusion: "Lincoln acquired a better understanding of strategy than most of his generals" (2 Michael Burlingame, *Abraham Lincoln: A Life* 248 [Johns Hopkins Univ. Press, 2008]).

A. Lincoln, Respectable
"Prairie Lawyer"
Brian Dirck

In 1860, Americans did not have bumpers or stickers, but they had that same mentality. Candidate Lincoln had a lot of "bumper sticker" moments—more so than most, perhaps, because voters knew so little about him. People looked hard for a catchphrase or an easy concept that would neatly summarize him in their minds. "Railsplitter" was a big one, with its connotations of a hardworking frontier farmer (even though Lincoln hated farming). "Humble" and "Honest" were also useful handles, as was the fact that he hailed from the frontier.

One of the more popular bumper stickers attached to Lincoln was "prairie lawyer." The *New York Evening Express,* for example, described Lincoln as a "very respectable lawyer in Illinois," while the *New York Times,* with a bit more haughtiness, called him "a lawyer of some local Illinois reputation." Others were much less charitable. A London journalist sniffed that Lincoln was nothing more than a "village attorney." Abolitionist Wendell Phillips called him a "little country advocate," and in early 1861 Secretary of State William Seward sneered that his new boss was "a little Illinois lawyer." Even during the 1864 election Lincoln was dismissed by some in the press as a "third rate backwoods" attorney.

These were not compliments. Calling the president a mere "village" lawyer was a way of cutting him down to size, of implying that he was no statesman but rather a small-minded toiler of the type who hung out on the courthouse steps, drumming up nickel and dime cases and eking out a dubious living.[1]

In the decades following Lincoln's death, things changed drastically.

Americans discovered just how much they loved that "third-rate attorney," and they transformed him into the Great Emancipator and Great American with which we are all so familiar. In the process, some Lincoln mythmakers further deified their man by making him out to be a lawyer superhero, a combination of Atticus Finch, John Marshall, and William Blackstone all rolled into one. Or conversely, they turned "country lawyer" into a compliment. Lincoln "practiced law like a pioneer," wrote Emanuel Hertz in his 1931 biography, "with the pioneer ideas of fairness, of justice, of right dealing."[2]

But more often Americans downplay or even ignore entirely Lincoln's legal career. It is hard to say why, exactly. Boredom is one explanation. Early Lincoln scholar Ida Tarbell bluntly asserted that "most of his cases were utterly uninteresting."[3] Intimidation is another possible explanation, with people frightened away from Lincoln's law practice because of a felt need to master esoteric legal concepts in order to do the subject justice. Or maybe we have such an extremely ambivalent attitude toward the legal profession that we are unwilling to sully the name of the Great Emancipator by focusing too much on what was an extensive but mostly pedestrian practice.

Or maybe we just do not know what we can learn about Lincoln from his days spent in the courtroom. After all, we are talking about thousands of cases spanning a quarter-century. They are now available in the DVD-ROM format of the Lincoln Legal Papers project, truly a wondrous collection of material. Given the sheer number of cases unearthed by the LLP, one thing is very clear: Lincoln took his law practice seriously, and I think the law practice is worth our attention if we are to understand this very complex man. I would like to offer a brief sketch concerning what I discovered about the Lincoln law practice in the course of writing *Lincoln the Lawyer*. And second, I would like to offer some speculation concerning what we might be able to learn about Lincoln from his practice. What did the law practice do for him and to him, in terms of his overall personality, intellect, and worldview?

To begin with: why exactly did he want to become a lawyer? Lincoln never said, but we can hazard a few guesses. Unlike business, it required relatively little in the way of financial resources or start-up costs, it offered a higher ceiling of reward for hard work than farming, and, unlike the military, it did not possess an ossified pay and rank structure that hindered upward progress.

Lincoln took advantage of the law's informality to gain a fair amount of legal experience before he ever was licensed. He was asked by neighbors to draw up the deeds for various real estate transactions; one picturesque account has Lincoln drafting a deed while tilling a cornfield, using the plow handle and a piece of wood for a makeshift desk. He also wrote the summons for a debt collection case and various other pieces of boilerplate legal paperwork.[4]

In 1837 his name was entered into the Sangamon County, Illinois, court record book of Judge Stephen T. Logan as "a person of good moral character." Five months later he was formally licensed to practice law in the state, after passing some sort of bar exam: probably a few pertinent questions were put to him by an older member of the Illinois bar, who then pronounced his answers satisfactory.

After brief partnerships with John Todd Stuart—Mary's cousin, by the way—and Stephen Logan (who returned to the bar because he thought he could earn more money there than on the bench), Lincoln partnered with Billy Herndon, a younger man who had actually been studying for the bar while clerking in Lincoln and Logan's office. Billy was a good choice, overall. He knew how to do research, he was bright, and he was diligent. Still, he had his faults. He was given to existential meanderings about the meaning of life that at times drove Lincoln nuts. He was also a drinking man and became more so as the years went by. He had no sense of humor and did not get many of Lincoln's stories and jokes—a real problem for anyone who hung around with Abraham Lincoln for very long.[5]

Lincoln certainly was not the perfect law partner, either. He was supremely disorganized (as was Herndon—their law office was by all accounts an epic mess), he tended to read newspapers out loud while stretched out on a beat-up couch in the office corner ("a habit which used to annoy me beyond endurance," Billy grumbled), and he would allow Tad, Willie, and Robert to wreak havoc on their office, pulling down books, papers, and inkstands, and piling it all on the floor with no rebuke at all.[6]

Still, in a peculiar way the odd couple of Lincoln and Herndon worked, and prospered. By the mid-1850s their practice was earning both men a comfortable living. While Billy managed the books and did most of the paperwork, Lincoln plied the courtrooms up and down the Eighth Judicial Circuit, a wide swath of central Illinois that encompassed hundreds of square miles of territory. The firm of Lincoln & Herndon created a thriving practice that reached into over a dozen counties and litigated cases from local justice of the peace courts to the Illinois Supreme Court and the federal circuit. Lincoln and Herndon were even involved in four cases that eventually reached the U.S. Supreme Court.

So what sort of business did all of this activity create? The numbers indicate a very large, diverse practice. Lincoln was an attorney of record in a little over five thousand extant cases. "Attorney of record" could mean a lot of things: an active litigator, of course, but also an informal advisor of sorts. Lincoln's name appears on documents related to quite a few cases in which his exact role is unknown and probably unknowable. At times, Lincoln entered into formal partnerships with other attorneys on the circuit and advertised as such in local newspapers. Unthinkable today, this was actually a fairly common practice at the time.[7]

The circuit, and the practice of law in general, was a highly informal, fluid thing. Lincoln was even sworn in as a circuit judge on occasion, filling in for his friend (and later Supreme Court justice) David Davis and disposing of an astonishingly large number of cases—over three hundred—in this manner. Judge Lincoln's cases ran the gamut: probate settlements, contract disputes, property sales, debt collection, divorce, and a few criminal cases (thirty-two). Most were rather perfunctory proceedings. To cite but one example, in October 1859 the DeWitt County prosecutor indicted Choice Bland, John Book, William Catterlin, and Robert Phares for gambling. The men pled guilty, and Lincoln from the bench duly recorded their plea.[8]

Lincoln's legal career in general was characterized by many such straightforward, uncomplicated proceedings. This is not to say that he did not face some extraordinarily complex and convoluted litigation. He did, and some of it must have been truly mind-numbing. To give just one example, in 1859 a man named James Barrett hired the firm of P.A. Dorwin and Company to construct a distillery for him, at a cost of $2,836.19. To pay for this, Barrett mortgaged the ground upon which the distillery stood to a variety of other individuals and companies. Mr. Barrett overextended himself financially, however, and only paid the Dorwin firm about $1,800. Dorwin sued Barrett and the people to whom Barrett had mortgaged the land, and won a judgment for the balance owed the firm (the other defendants defaulted). But Barrett could not pay the balance, so the Sangamon County court sold the land to three of the mortgagers to pay the money. But a fourth defendant, the Columbus Machine Manufacturing Company, hired Lincoln, who discovered that the original contract for the distillery had a minor technical error (it failed to specify the exact date upon which the job was to be completed). Lincoln pounced on the paperwork mistake and got the judgment reversed (thus at least temporarily getting his client off the hook for paying its part of the original debt). The whole affair was appealed up to the state supreme court, which eventually reversed the original court's ruling for the Columbus Machine Manufacturing Company, and sometime in 1860 Lincoln's client had to pay up.[9]

Such was life at Lincoln & Herndon. But the truth is that most of the cases that came their way were more clear-cut and less demanding. For example, in 1841 Congress passed a nationwide bankruptcy bill, and soon thereafter Lincoln (probably along with many other members of the American bar) was swamped with clients looking for a fresh start. During 1842 he therefore found himself in what was (for him) an unusual place: the U.S. district court's dark wood-paneled room on the first floor of Springfield's capitol building, petitioning federal justices for discharges of debt under the new law. He litigated seventy-three such cases in seventeen months, nineteen alone during the month of October 1842. The proceedings were highly routinized; in one of those October cases, for example, he petitioned the court for bankruptcy relief on behalf of Henry A. Craw, who owned only a thirty-nine-acre plot of land and $60 worth of assets, but who owed a whopping $14,000 worth of debts. The court granted Craw's bankruptcy petition.

Lincoln's bankruptcy litigation bonanza was short-lived because Congress, for a variety of political reasons, quickly repealed the act. Lincoln brought his last known bankruptcy petition before the federal court in June 1843. It likely was not much of a moneymaker for him, anyway, since a bankrupt client was by definition unable to afford much in the way of lawyer's fees. Bankruptcy was so unusual that Lincoln did not quite know what the going rate for a discharge petition should be, confessing to a colleague that "I can not say there is any custom on the subject." One bankruptcy client, James Gambrell, could only pay Lincoln with a $20 promissory note for some firewood, a dubious reward at best.[10]

The truncated bankruptcy branch of Lincoln's litigation reveals a larger fact about Lincoln's practice: its foundation was debt collection. Of the five thousand cases, 2,600 involved some form of debtor-creditor litigation. In 1837—his first full year as a lawyer—he was involved in ninety-one cases, sixty-five of which entailed some form of debt collection. That is close to 75 percent. Five years later Lincoln was involved in 219 cases, 175 of which likewise involved debt collection—nearly 80 percent.[11]

Debt was something of a specialty for Lincoln during his early career. In 1842 many of the nondebt cases were handled by Logan only, whereas there were few debt cases that did not involve Lincoln in some way. There were relatively few cases during 1842 in which Lincoln was the lone representative of Logan & Lincoln that did not involve debt collection issues. In fact, Logan himself retained Lincoln twice in 1842 as his attorney to recover debts, from John Wilbourn for a $239 note, and then from a man named Littleton Gardner for another debt of about the same amount. Lincoln won the Wilbourn case for his partner; Logan later dismissed the case against Gardner.[12]

As the senior member of Logan & Lincoln, Logan seemed disposed to leave debt collection to his junior partner, unless the case was inordinately complex or involved an appeal to the Illinois Supreme Court. When Lincoln went solo that year, it usually involved relatively simple debt litigation. In November 1842, for example, Lincoln appeared in the Christian County courthouse to represent the interests of Alexander Ralston. Three years previously, Ralston had given a $100 promissory note to a man named John Gilbert, and Gilbert in turn gave the note to Henry Hardin. When Hardin tried to collect on the note with Ralston, the latter refused to pay, claiming that the note had expired and, moreover, that he had already made good on the debt by giving various dry goods to Gilbert as part of their new business partnership. The court apparently did not accept this explanation—perhaps Gilbert disputed it, or maybe Ralston did not properly document his little business labyrinth—and awarded Hardin $143 to cover the note and (presumably) court costs.[13]

Most of Lincoln's debt cases were such straightforward, bread-and-butter lawsuits. It was good, steady work. Debt cases that only involved collection on a promissory note earned Lincoln anywhere from $5 to $50, depending on the circumstances—the number and amount of the notes, perhaps the distance Lincoln had to travel (Sangamon County court cases usually cost his client about $10), and possibly whether the case involved a jury trial or an appeal. Not a lot of cash, to be sure, but the volume made up for the low return.

I am not suggesting that Lincoln specialized in debt collection matters, in the modern sense of, say, a lawyer advertising as a family law practitioner and handling only custody disputes. Lawyers in Lincoln's day did not really think that way, and, while there were attorneys who tended to favor one or the other type of case, few could afford a tunnel vision–style specialization. Rather, in Lincoln's case I think debt collection acted as something of a foundation. It was steady, guaranteed work that he knew would always be there to pay the bills and help him get by while he simultaneously took cases involving contracts, probate, negligence, and so on.

Lincoln had an awful lot of "and so on." Packed around the debt collection cases, year in and year out, were just about every conceivable form of litigation. There were 121 divorce cases. Lincoln and Herndon helped settle thirty-four wills and resolved various contract disputes a whopping two thousand times. The firm handled eighty-three larceny cases, involving the theft of (among other things) cash, horses, cows, sheep, sheepskin, chickens, eggs (stands to reason if you stole one you would probably take the other, I suppose), bacon, ham, fruit trees, a saddle, clothes, a plough, a clevis pin (which is part of a plough), and hogs. At least one such case involved slander as well, by the way: farmer David Adkins apparently resented Lincoln's client Robert Hines's calling him a "hog thief."[14]

Lincoln and Herndon litigated eighty-eight slander cases, whereby their neighbors accused one another of lying, perjury, thievery (the most common such insult), forgery, prostitution, bestiality, general sexual misconduct, and general bad character, as in 1842 when John Bradford called William Dormody "a damned rogue." Dormody hired Lincoln and sued Bradford but lost (the reasons are not clear). In one rather curious case, Lincoln in 1850 represented Daniel Gollogher, who accused a Shelby County schoolteacher named Emily Fancher of inflating her roll to get more money from the local school fund, and told someone that Fancher's father should take her "back to Wisconsin to the bad house where he found her & then the sores on her neck would vanish away." Oddly enough, the jury found Gollogher guilty of slander where the falsifying of school rolls was concerned, but not guilty concerning the aspersions cast on her sexual conduct.[15]

Race could get mixed up in this, too. In 1855, Lincoln represented a DeWitt County man named Charles Dungey whose brother-in-law habitually called him "Black Bill" and claimed that Dungey had African American ancestry. This was a very serious matter, for under the state's notorious 1853 "black laws" Dungey could have had his marriage voided (the laws forbade the marriage of whites to people with more than a quarter of African American blood) and been subjected to all sorts of humiliating restrictions. Lincoln won the case for his client.[16]

Interestingly enough, however, these were mostly civil matters; Lincoln was not much of a criminal lawyer. He appeared as an attorney of record in only 194 extant criminal law cases during the entire course of his career—not a lot, in the context of a practice that spanned a quarter-century and five thousand cases.[17] This may reflect the possibility that there just was not a lot of criminal law business out there; there were, after all, surely a lot more debtors than murderers or thieves in Illinois. Or maybe Lincoln was not comfortable doing criminal law, preferring instead cases that involved economics and business matters: as Lincoln scholar Gabor Boritt pointed out, economics was Lincoln's primary interest, at least before 1854.[18]

Aside from these two things—his debt collection and his relative lack of criminal law experience—not too many generalizations are possible concerning the type of law he practiced. As the years went by he does seem to have been earning larger retainers, and toward the end of the 1850s he found himself representing more well-heeled clients and earning subsequently larger rewards. In 1857 he tried a case involving a steamboat named the *Effie Afton,* which sank after crashing into a bridge spanning the Mississippi River at Rock Island, Illinois. Lincoln represented the bridge owners, who were sued by the owners of the vessel and its cargo; the case resulted in a hung jury. Five years earlier he was involved in what was according to Herndon "the most important lawsuit Lincoln and I conducted," involving tax exemption issues for the powerful Illinois Central Railroad. Lincoln represented the railroad and won, netting Lincoln and Herndon thousands of dollars in fees (after they sued the railroad to collect), and getting them considerable attention in Illinois' legal and business circles.[19]

But he did not evolve into an exclusively big business lawyer, or what we would now call a "corporate lawyer." Even at the very end of his practice, as he stood on the cusp of the presidency, Lincoln continued to collect debts—although the records indicate that he and Billy were less likely to take the really small debt cases, lawsuits over a few dollars, preferring instead cases that involved debts that were at least in the $100-plus range. In April 1860 he represented a man named Charles Duff, who sued John S. Dennis to collect on a $163.15 promissory note. Dennis did not show up, and Lincoln's client won his case. Aside from the comparatively larger amount of money involved, this case was not substantively different from the debt cases Lincoln had litigated as a young attorney in 1837.[20]

In fact, what is most impressive about the law practice is how ill-suited it is for nearly all of the pat generalizations that have been made about Lincoln over the years. His law practice just does not lend itself well to bumper sticker generalities. There are at least three of these bearing special notice.

First, there is the idea that Lincoln was a backwoods John Marshall, a special sort of attorney whom everyone knew was destined for great things. But as a whole the Lincoln law practice was unremarkable. It existed largely within the circle of Illinois' Eighth Judicial Circuit, rarely rising much higher than the state supreme court and generating no truly notable legal precedents. Lincoln was, as we have seen, primarily involved in debt collection, but that was not terribly unique, either. Many other American lawyers of his day apparently earned their living in much the same way.

Second, many of Lincoln's admirers have wanted to make him out as some sort of legal giant who only handled cases touching on the great moral issues of the day. You see this a lot in the early biographies of Lincoln, and it still resonates with the popular reading audience today: the notion that Lincoln cherry-picked his clients because of their moral worth, avoiding overtly guilty people and immoral lawsuits. "His conscience would not permit him to support a cause which he believed to be unjust, or to defend a person whom he knew to be guilty," reads James Baldwin's "true life" of Lincoln, published in 1904. Ida Tarbell believed Lincoln actively sought cases involving miscarriages of justice, and "where he saw injustice he was quick to offer his services to the wronged party." If Lincoln discovered in the course of a trial that his client was in the wrong, he suddenly became listless and ineffective. "No possible fee would induce him to become the instrument of injustice under cover of legal form and merely technical right," according to an 1885 account.[21]

There is no pattern in the Lincoln law practice indicating anything of the kind. He represented plaintiffs and defendants, the guilty and the innocent, the rich and the poor, and nearly all of the various possible sides in divorce cases, contract disputes, property disputes, and so forth. It is possible, I suppose, that Lincoln tried to screen from his practice people he thought were sleazy in some fashion—but then, if he did, how would we know? We have no way of reliably documenting the cases he *did not* take, and in the absence of such data, we can only address the cases he did take. And those cases strongly suggest that Lincoln represented all sorts of people from all walks of life.

Even where there is a detectable pattern, we must be very careful in our conclusions. In his debt-related litigation, for example, he seems to have represented creditors more often than debtors. Some might take from this the notion that Lincoln sympathized more with businessmen and bankers than he did with those in society who were under financial strain. It might tempt some to go one step further and place Lincoln in an ongoing debate among legal historians concerning the extent to which antebellum American lawyers were complicit in the creation of a capitalist system that tolerated tremendous inequities between rich and poor. Tempting, yes, but reckless, for there are too many variables involved. Lincoln may well have taken on more creditor clients because many debtors fled the state when their finances came crashing down upon them—in other words, creditors simply may have been more inclined to be physically present in Illinois and therefore more likely to hire Lincoln.

Third, there has also grown up around Lincoln the reputation that he was an unskilled technical lawyer who got by on backwoods moxy and folksy charm. He did not bother with technicalities, he did not know or much care about the intricate structure of the common law, and he rarely needed to open a law book. Instead, it has been argued, he used his innate abilities, his fundamental common sense, and his force of logic to win cases, without having to know all those little tricks about how to draft interrogatories, writs, and other trifles that bedeviled the lesser lights of the Illinois bar. He did not even have to sue for his fees, presumably because he was such a nice guy and because grubbing for cash like a common lawyer was beneath him, somehow.

This is nonsense. As we saw in the distillery dispute, Lincoln most assuredly did win cases because of his knowledge of the law's structure and his sharp eye for technical detail. The law practice abounds with examples of Lincoln's ability to properly draft, say, a writ of replevin, or understand the crucial difference between a writ of trespass and a writ of trespass on the case.

Was he a good jury lawyer who could give a good speech and charm the jury box and the gallery with folksy stories? Sure. But such skills went hand in hand with the technical expertise Lincoln had to possess in order to be a competent attorney. Lincoln drew no distinction between them: all were necessary for him to be what he was, a good attorney. And he did, incidentally, sometimes have to sue clients to get paid: nineteen times, to be exact.[22]

I think Lincoln's law practice taught him the value of what I call "grease." He worked constantly in the interstices of the economy and the social structure, he slipped among the wheels of his community and quietly eased their operation. Think about it this way: as a lawyer, Lincoln was always between things. He stood between creditors and debtors, between embattled husbands and wives, between parents and children (I am thinking about custody disputes here: Lincoln and Herndon litigated thirty-two such cases), between business partners and neighbors.[23] And the things he stood between were nearly always in a state of flux, or tension. Creditors dunned debtors, husbands and wives divorced, business partners sued one another over company assets, family members battled over estate settlements. Read any of the court documents of the period, and you quickly find how nasty and even brutal these affairs could be.

Day in and day out, Lincoln stared at the heat and friction created by the failings of human beings at war with one another. In a sense, he witnessed over five thousand little civil wars before he got the big one in 1861. Lincoln was for all these people a lubricant: he allowed business relationships, families, friendships, and so forth to function without overheating, without seizing and locking up. Note, for instance, what he did as a debt collection lawyer: in an age before there were collection agencies, his existence gave creditors at least some peace of mind, knowing that, if worse came to worse, they could always bring a lawsuit to collect what was owed them. Would a person with money have been as ready to loan it out if there had been no lawyer like Lincoln around? Surely not. Would a person who needed money have been as likely to go borrow it if he had not known that he could hire a guy like Lincoln to mitigate the damage somewhat should his particular business venture fail? Again, I rather doubt it.

If Lincoln and other lawyers like him had not been there to provide this ease of mind—this grease—then the wheels of the frontier economy in Illinois would most certainly have slowed tremendously: the machine of progress would have locked up, because in the Illinois of Lincoln's age there was little cash to fund entrepreneurial ventures. Indeed, those little promissory notes and IOUs that dominated Lincoln's practice *were* cash, in a very real sense. Some of them changed hands four or five times before finally landing on Lincoln's desk as exhibit A in this or that debt collection case. I would bet he probably got heartily sick of all those little scraps of paper, and that he spent more time than he liked untangling the relationships they represented. But if he had not been there to do this, one wonders where the economy of Illinois might ultimately have ended up.

The same goes for the various social relationships. By litigating slander proceedings, neighborhood quarrels of all shapes and sizes, even the relatively few criminal cases he saw, Lincoln kept the machine of society rumbling along instead of exploding in paroxysms of rage and violence. Everyone knows of course how violent the antebellum American frontier could be: but how much more would this have been the case had there been no legal recourse to satisfy the multitude of tensions and conflicts that arose naturally from the collision of disparate human beings in an unsettled place?

Heaven knows this probably was not a pleasant way to earn a living, though to his credit there is no record of Lincoln's ever grumbling about his lot in life as "grease." But pleasant or not, it was a great education into the ways people interacted with one another. And surely this education spilled over into other areas of Lincoln's life. People who knew Lincoln often noted his affability, both in his personal relationships and especially in politics. He seemed to instinctively know how to get warring factions of politicians to work together, or with him, and this was an absolutely invaluable leadership trait during a civil war that was filled with George McClellans, Benjamin "Beast" Butlers, Charles Sumners, and the like. Lincoln's friends (and later on, historians) usually marked this down as a personality trait, a function of what has been termed his essentially passive nature. Perhaps. But could we not also suggest that, during the course of a law practice whose primary function was to grease the creaky wheels of society, Lincoln learned the value of negotiation, accommodation, and compromise? And perhaps he came also to understand the value of institutions that facilitated such things.

So that is my bumper sticker for Lincoln the "prairie lawyer." He was a form of legal, economic, and social grease. Not very romantic, to be sure, and probably not very exciting, but wholly necessary to the development not only of the man himself but also of his times.

Notes

1. Brian Dirck, *Lincoln the Lawyer* (Urbana: Univ. of Illinois Press, 2007), 143–44.

2. Emanuel Hertz, *Abraham Lincoln: A New Portrait*, 2 vols. (New York: Liveright, 1931), 1:99; for other examples of lawyerly Lincoln hagiography, see, for example, William E. Curtis, *True Life of Abraham Lincoln* (Philadelphia: J. B. Lippincott, 1903), 83; Isaac Arnold, *The Life of Abraham Lincoln* (Chicago:

Jansen, McClury, 1885), 59; John T. Richards, *Abraham Lincoln: The Lawyer-Statesman* (Boston: Houghton-Mifflin, 1916), 21; Henry B. Kranz, *Abraham Lincoln: A New Portrait* (New York: Putnam, 1959).

3. Ida M. Tarbell, *The Life of Abraham Lincoln*, 2 vols. (New York: Lincoln Historical Society, 1924), 2:155.

4. Deed for Cox et al., June 1834, in *The Law Practice of Abraham Lincoln: Complete Documentary Edition,* ed. Martha L. Benner and Cullom Davis (Urbana: Univ. of Illinois Press, 2000), DVD-ROM, hereafter cited as LPAL); deed for Colson et al., July 1834, LPAL; also, Mentor Graham, interview with William H. Herndon, in *Herndon's Informants: Letters, Interviews, and Statements about Abraham Lincoln,* ed. Douglas L. Wilson and Rodney O. Davis (Urbana: Univ. of Illinois Press, 1997), 8–11.

5. See generally David Donald, *Lincoln's Herndon: A Biography*, 2nd ed. (New York: Da Capo, 1989); and Dirck, *Lincoln the Lawyer*, 29–31.

6. The Herndon quote is in William H. Herndon, *Herndon's Life of Lincoln: The History and Personal Recollections of Abraham Lincoln* (1888; reprint, New York: Da Capo Press, 1983), 256; on Lincoln's law offices generally, see ibid., 254–57; Paul M. Angle, "Where Lincoln Practiced Law," *Lincoln Centennial Association Papers* (1927), 22–28; Francis Fisher Browne, *The Everyday Life of Abraham Lincoln* (1887; reprint, Lincoln: Univ. of Nebraska Press, 1994), 223; and Gibson W. Harris, "My Recollections of Abraham Lincoln," *Farm and Fireside*, December 1, 1904.

7. Numbers based on search string "Abraham Lincoln" as an attorney of record, LPAL.

8. The *Law Practice of Abraham Lincoln* database lists 321 cases in which he served as a judge; see also Henry C. Whitney, *Life on the Circuit with Lincoln* (Boston: Estes and Lauriat, 1892), 78.

9. Abraham Lincoln to Peter Ambos, June 21, 1859, in *The Collected Works of Abraham Lincoln*, ed. Roy P. Basler, 9 vols. (New Brunswick: Rutgers Univ. Press, 1953) (hereafter cited as *CW*), 3:386–387; Abraham Lincoln to Samuel Galloway, July 27, 1859, *CW*, 3:393; *Ambos v. James A. Barrett & Co.*, 1851, LPAL.

10. Data search for "bankruptcy," LPAL; *in re Craw*, 1842; Abraham Lincoln to Frederick A. Thomas, July 11, 1842, *CW*, 1:290.

11. Numbers based on search string "Abraham Lincoln" as an attorney of record for the years 1837 and 1842, LPAL.

12. Search string for "Abraham Lincoln," as an attorney of record, 1842, LPAL; *Logan v. Gardner*, 1842, LPAL; and *Logan v. Wilbourn*, 1842, LPAL.

13. *Ralston v. Gilbert*, 1842, ibid.

14. Numbers based on search strings for divorce, probate, contract, and larceny, with cases listing Lincoln as an attorney of record, LPAL.

15. Search string for slander cases listing Lincoln as an attorney of record, LPAL; *People v. Adkins*, 1839, LPAL; *Dormondy v. Bradford*, 1842, LPAL; *Fancher v. Gollogher*, 1850, LPAL; see also Mark Steiner, "The Lawyer as Peacemaker: Law and Community in Abraham Lincoln's Slander Cases," *Journal of the Abraham Lincoln Association* 16 (1995): 5–9, and passim.

16. *Dungey v. Spencer*, 1853, LPAL.

17. Search string for criminal law cases in which Lincoln appeared as an attorney of record, LPAL; see also my discussion of these matters in Dirck, *Lincoln the Lawyer*, 106–19.

18. Gabor Boritt, *Lincoln and the Economics of the American Dream*, 2nd ed. (Urbana: Univ. of Illinois Press, 1994).

19. See Lincoln's speech to the jury in the Rock Island Bridge Case, September 22, 1857, *CW,* 2:415–422; Herndon, *Herndon's Lincoln*, 284; *Illinois Central Railroad v. McClean County, Illinois*, 1853–1855, LPAL; Dirck, *Lincoln the Lawyer*, 97–99.

20. *Duff v. Dennis*, 1860, LPAL.

21. James Baldwin, *Abraham Lincoln: A True Life* (New York: American Books, 1904), 129; Tarbell, *The Life of Abraham Lincoln*, 2:42, 44–45; William O. Stoddard, *Abraham Lincoln: The True Story of a Great Life* (New York: Fords, Howard, and Hulbert, 1885), 127–28.

22. Numbers based on search string of cases involving lawyer's fees of which Lincoln was an attorney of record, LPAL.

23. Search string of cases involving custody disputes in which Lincoln was an attorney of record, LPAL.

Part Two

The Illinois Years

A. Lincoln, Debtor-Creditor Lawyer

Roger Billings

Introduction

Biographers of Abraham Lincoln's legal career tend to focus on his most famous cases. The Rock Island Bridge, Illinois Central Railroad, McCormick Reaper, Duff Armstrong, and Matson slave cases are well known. Little attention is paid, however, to the routine debtor-creditor cases that were the bread and butter of Lincoln's practice. One can imagine Lincoln's arrival at a county courthouse in the Illinois Eighth Judicial Circuit where potential clients were waiting to hire him to defend a debtor or collect on a note. The Lincoln Legal Papers bring to light the importance of debtor-creditor cases in Lincoln's law practice, cases he needed to make a living, but which were often routine and boring.[1] Debtor-creditor work required a minimum of the trial work Lincoln loved and a maximum of document drafting. When Lincoln did sue on a note, the chances of the debtor showing up in court were slim, and Lincoln's court appearance often resulted in a default judgment.

Putting the spotlight on Lincoln's debtor-creditor cases leads to a more balanced portrait of Lincoln's career while revealing the everyday problems caused by the shortage of money on the frontier. Lincoln's work in the debtor-creditor field occurred during tumultuous developments in the U.S. economy, when banks were not capable of supporting business growth, and trade was carried on with personal notes rather than bank loans or the sale of stocks and bonds. Thanks to the Lincoln Legal Papers, we can study an Illinois circuit lawyer as he practiced during the panic-stricken 1830s and the railroad-building and corporation-forming 1840s and 1850s. We find in Lincoln a leading lawyer who excelled in litigation but was relegated mostly to debtor-creditor work.

Was Lincoln a Specialist?

Lawyers in the small county seats on the Eighth Judicial Circuit had too little business to practice law full time, let alone specialize. They were forced to supplement their legal work with other work, such as farming.[2] Lincoln, on the other hand, practiced in the state capital, where he could make a living as a full-time lawyer, provided he was willing to take any kind of case. Restriction of a law practice to one kind of case would have been impossible, although the Lincoln Legal Papers show that Lincoln had more debtor-creditor cases than any other kind. Specialization as a debtor-creditor lawyer was not unknown. Lincoln's great patron, Judge David Davis, had a so-called collection practice in Bloomington, Illinois, before he became a judge on the Eighth Circuit.[3]

The Lincoln Legal Papers reveal the breadth of Lincoln's debtor-creditor practice. If one clicks on the term "Business" in the index, a table titled "A Statistical Portrait: Common Subjects" appears. The editors developed the table as a general guide to a variety of topics within his legal practice. It shows in descending order of frequency those topics that describe a hundred or more Lincoln cases. The most common topic assigned to Lincoln's cases is "Debtor and Creditor," with 3,145 cases, followed by "Contracts" (subentry: "Breach of Contract.") with 2,322, and "Negotiable Instruments" (subentry: "Promissory Notes.") with 1,892. Skipping the fourth-largest topic, "Real Property," the fifth-largest is "Default Judgment" with 1,351 cases. A default judgment is most often a judgment on an overdue mortgage or promissory note, in other words, a debtor-creditor case. Contracts, too, frequently involve the creation of debt. Thus, four out of the five largest topics reflect Lincoln's huge debtor-creditor practice. In contrast, there are only 821 cases dealing with "estates," 318 dealing with "criminal offenses," and 110 dealing with "divorce." Under another index heading, "A Statistical Portrait: Legal Actions," the editors make the point even clearer. In a pie chart called "Debt-related Actions Compared to Other Actions by Division," Lincoln's practice is broken down into "Debt-related actions (62%)," "Other common law actions (21%)," "Other chancery actions (17%)," and "Other probate actions (1%)." For the first time, the Lincoln Legal Papers clearly document that Lincoln, like his contemporaries, concentrated on debtor-creditor law.

Lincoln himself became a plaintiff when his clients neglected to pay his fee. In most of Lincoln's debtor-creditor cases the fee was about $10, a relatively small fee in his day.[4] Even so, his second partner, Stephen T. Logan, advised him to be diligent in collecting fees, and there are a number of fee collection cases where Lincoln appears in the record as plaintiff.[5] The best-known example is his suit against the Illinois Central Railroad to collect a $5,000 fee, the largest he ever charged.[6] He would sue to collect even a $20 fee, however, and sometimes would be forced to take a fee note payable in goods because of the shortage of currency, as the following note illustrates:

Springfield, Feb. 24, 1842

On or before the first day of November next I promise to pay A. Lincoln twenty dollars in good fire wood about four feet in length, at the selling price when delivered, to be delivered at any place designated by said Lincoln, in the city of Springfield—for value received.

James Gambrell[7]

The First Promissory Notes

Promissory notes were widely used in nineteenth-century Illinois in lieu of scarce currency, and they figured prominently in Lincoln's private and professional life. While he was experimenting with ways to earn a living in New Salem he found it easy to borrow by drafting and signing notes, and sometimes he obliged friends by cosigning theirs. He undoubtedly copied notes he saw in New Salem and probably had access to a printed form book, such as *Story's Notes*. One of the first things he did in New Salem was to hang around the justice of the peace court, presided over by Bowling Green, where he saw many kinds of legal documents and even wrote documents for the justice.[8] He was acutely aware of the significance of notes. In Lincoln's "Communication to the People of Sangamo County," dated March 9, 1832, he noted the local practice of lending money at exorbitant interest rates and bemoaned that it seemed "we are never to have an end to this baneful and corroding system . . . unless there be a law made setting a limit to the rates of usury."[9] Even so, the people of New Salem pressed young Lincoln into service to draft their legal documents. Among the documents he drafted was the following:

March 8, 1832

Mr. James Rutledge please to pay the bearer David P. Nelson thirty
dollars and this shall be your receipt for the same.
March 8th, 1832.

A. Lincoln
for D. Offutt[10]

This document is similar to a bank check and is called a draft. Lincoln signs
for Offutt, who is the drawer, Nelson is the payee, and Rutledge is the banker.
Offutt was simply paying his debt to Nelson with money Rutledge already owed
Offutt. Instead of Offutt paying Nelson directly, he just ordered Rutledge to
pay. Unfortunately, we do not know the collection history of the Offutt draft.
We do know, however, that with the words "pay the bearer David P. Nelson"
Lincoln probably was trying to make the draft negotiable. The importance
of negotiability was, and still is, that Nelson could easily transfer the draft to
another person, who then would acquire the right to collect the draft against
Rutledge. In case Rutledge did not admit his obligation to pay, the transferee
could still collect from Offutt. The transferee would be called a "holder in due
course" and could ignore almost every argument of Offutt that he should be
excused from paying. It was important in Lincoln's time for documents such as
drafts and promissory notes to be negotiable, for they were substitutes for cash.

About ten months after drafting the Offutt note, Lincoln signed another
document, this time as a cosigner. Vincent A. Bogue chartered a small river
steamer called the *Talisman* to carry goods to market and paid Lincoln the
handsome sum of $40 to act as assistant pilot for passage up the Sangamon
River.[11] When the steamer arrived at New Salem, Bogue sold goods off the
Talisman to Nelson Ally, a local tavern proprietor, who paid Bogue with a
printed note which reads as follows:

$104.87½   No. 13   October 30, 1832
SIX MONTHS after date we or either of us, promise to pay to J.D.
HENRY Sheriff of Sangamon County, or order, (for the benefit of
the creditors of V.A. Bogue) the sum of one hundred & four dollars
Eighty Seven ½ cents, value received this 30th Oct., 1832.

Nelson Ally
A. Lincoln[12]

This second note contained an explicit promise by the signers to pay, and it, too, was negotiable because it contained the words "or order." The words "or order," like the word "bearer" in the Offutt note, made this note easily transferable. It was made payable to the sheriff, who would use the proceeds to pay some of Bogue's creditors. For some reason Lincoln signed it himself, perhaps as a favor to Ally, for apparently Lincoln himself did not owe anything to Bogue. As cosigner he became a gratuitous "accommodation maker," equally liable with Ally to pay Sheriff Henry.[13] Ally defaulted on the note and the sheriff sued on behalf of the creditors, Henry Emmerson and James McCandless. Judgment was entered against both Ally and Lincoln in the Sangamon Circuit Court on September 13, 1833.[14] The court's files reflect that the note was paid off in installments by several persons, but Lincoln paid none of the installments.[15] Perhaps Lincoln, at twenty-four years of age, was judgment proof.[16] In any event, he escaped liability on the note.

In the 1830s, when credit was easy,[17] Lincoln and William F. Berry teamed up to buy one of the three stores operating in tiny New Salem. Lincoln paid for his half by drafting and signing a note payable to J. Rowan Herndon.[18] Lincoln's credit was dubious, but Herndon believed him to be thoroughly honest and accepted the note.[19] Lincoln proceeded to sign notes to other creditors and accumulated what he called a "national debt" of around $1,100.[20] Although he defaulted on all of them, he eventually paid them off and was debt free when he purchased his first home in 1844 for $1,200.[21]

Another note related to the Lincoln and Berry store recently came to light, and it clearly indicates the use of notes in lieu of currency. The note, although in Berry's handwriting, was signed "Lincoln & Berry" and given as payment for merchandise for the Lincoln and Berry store from the merchants Augustus Knapp and Thomas Pogue. Knapp and Pogue operated a flour mill, distillery, pork packing, and general merchandise store in Beardstown, with a branch in the settlement of Pappsville where Lincoln and Berry bought supplies.[22] The note is another example of "order paper" and reads as follows:

$52 36/100   New Salem   14 May, 1833
One day after date I promise to pay to the order of Knapp & Pogue
the sum of fifty two Dollars 36/100 for value Recd of them at the rate
of twelve percent interest from Date until final paymt.
                    Lincoln & Berry[23]

The note is payable at sight because it states that the holder can demand payment the very next day, like the Offutt "bearer" note. It was so negotiable that it could substitute for currency, and Knapp and Pogue did use the note as currency because they endorsed the back:

> Beardstown 3rd December 1833 pay to Wm. Watkins or order the within amount.
>
> Knapp & Pogue

Endorsing and delivering the note transferred the right to payment to William Watkins, a livestock breeder, who probably sold hogs to Knapp & Pogue in exchange for Lincoln & Berry's note. When Watkins took the note he was gambling that it would be easily collectible. Watkins was mistaken. When he asked Lincoln or Berry for payment he was refused, for documents show that Watkins sued Lincoln and Berry on the note in Bowling Green's justice of the peace court.[24] Berry "confessed judgment," by which he admitted liability, and the court awarded Watkins a judgment for $53.[25] He was not to collect until later, however, for Lincoln and Berry posted bond and appealed to the Circuit Court of Sangamon County.[26] The court ruled for Watkins and awarded $57.86 in damages.[27] The clerk, C. R. Matheny, then issued a writ of execution to the sheriff of Sangamon County that said, "We [the court] command you [the sheriff] that of the goods and chattels, lands and tenements of Abram Lincoln & Wm. F. Berry late of your county you cause to be made the sum of Fifty Seven Dollars and 86 cents. . . ."[28] The final act for this note transaction is recorded on the reverse of the writ. Berry is given credit for payments of $24.50 on August 5 and $17.40 on August 25.[29] Perhaps Watkins accepted this as final payment, because there is no further record of collection on the note nor any indication Lincoln was involved personally in the process.

By that time Lincoln had learned the hard way about the creation and collection of debt. For example, in 1834 a judgment was entered against him on behalf of Peter Van Bergen for $154 and an execution was issued under this judgment, which caused the sheriff to seize everything of value Lincoln owned: his horse, saddle, bridle, compass, chain, and other surveying instruments. This gave rise to the well-known incident whereby "Uncle Jimmie Short" bid all of the property in and gave it back to Lincoln.[30]

By 1849 Lincoln's situation had improved dramatically, and he had money to lend. In those days individuals with extra cash were the source of capital, not banks, and so Lincoln carefully made loans to persons he trusted in return for their promissory notes at the legal rate of 10 percent interest. We know about these notes because of the pioneering research of Harry E. Pratt, who devoted a whole chapter to Lincoln, "The Money Lender," in his classic book, *The Personal Finances of Abraham Lincoln.*[31] Pratt discovered Lincoln's 1861 memorandum to Robert Irwin, cashier of the Springfield Marine and Fire Insurance Company, where Lincoln had his checking account. The memorandum directed Irwin to collect ten interest-bearing notes and mortgages worth a face value of $9,337.90 while Lincoln was away in Washington.[32] The memorandum revealed investments worth about three times the value of Lincoln's substantial house on Eighth and Jackson streets, which was insured in 1861 for $3,200.[33]

A Newly Minted Debtor-Creditor Lawyer

When Lincoln started practicing law in 1837 with his first partner, John Todd Stuart, he had read Blackstone and other authorities but had little practical experience except for handling notes. His personal experience in New Salem had familiarized him with much of what he needed to know in the practice of debtor-creditor law.

After he got a judgment his client would need to get a writ of execution authorizing the sheriff to levy on the debtor's property using roughly the same procedure that is still in use.[34] The negotiable notes he drafted in New Salem have changed little in form, and the checks he drew on the Springfield Marine and Fire Insurance Company are nearly identical to modern checks. The rules governing checks and notes in today's version of the Illinois Uniform Commercial Code would be familiar to Lincoln.

Lincoln needed tutoring in the general practice of law, but he would not receive it from his partner. Stuart simply turned the bulk of his law practice over to Lincoln in order to free himself to run for political office. Fortunately for Lincoln, most of the practice was on the familiar ground of debtor-creditor law.[35] The easy credit everyone had experienced in New Salem had gone bad. The people of Sangamon County faced a crisis of too little currency with which to repay debts after the demise of the Second Bank of the United States in 1832, and President Andrew Jackson's "Specie Circular" in 1836.[36] As a result, demand for debtor-creditor work was brisk.

After three years with Stuart, the ambitious Lincoln saw a chance to improve his skills by accepting Stephen Trigg Logan's offer to join him in practice. The exact reasons Lincoln left Stuart are not documented, but Lincoln and Stuart did part amicably and remained lifelong friends. A lot was going on in Lincoln's private life at the time of their parting. The "fatal first of January"[37] 1841, when he was scheduled to marry Mary Todd, came and went without a wedding. He wrote Stuart, "I am now the most miserable man living.... If I could be myself I would rather remain at home with *Judge Logan*" (emphasis added).[38] The reference to Logan was prophetic, coming just before Logan became his partner. Logan was happy to have Lincoln as the replacement for his former partner, Edward D. Baker, whom he found reckless in money matters.[39] He knew Lincoln from previous encounters in the courts and their association in the Truett murder case.[40]

On April 15, 1841, Lincoln was sufficiently recovered from the "fatal first of January" to be at work for Logan, winning a huge judgment of $16,000 for the plaintiff in *Kellogg v. Crane* in an action on a debt in Tazewell County.[41] Logan was everything Lincoln was not: methodical, industrious, particular, painstaking, and precise. In appearance he was small, gnome-like, stern faced, and craggy.[42] Although Lincoln was disorderly, Logan admired his ability and set about changing his habits.[43] He tutored Lincoln in all aspects of the practice and sent him off to the courthouses on the Eighth Judicial Circuit while he himself stayed in Springfield. Lincoln also spent time in Springfield, as evidenced by his work on bankruptcy cases tried in the federal court there. Logan and Lincoln remained partners until 1844, when Logan's son joined his father and Lincoln went on to form a new partnership with William Herndon.

The New Partner's Bankruptcy Practice

When Lincoln began to practice law the panic of 1837 had already begun. Many citizens of Springfield, as elsewhere in the United States, could not repay their debts because there was not enough currency in circulation and their assets were tied up in real estate. In response to the panic the second U.S. bankruptcy law was enacted in 1841,[44] and it further nudged Lincoln's practice toward debtor-creditor law. He already had some of the skills needed to practice bankruptcy law since he knew firsthand about foreclosure and the taking of property under a levy of execution.

By February 1842, Logan and Lincoln were handling numerous Sangamon County bankruptcy cases as well as referral cases from lawyers outside the county. The referral lawyers found it too expensive to come to the federal court at Springfield to handle uncontested bankruptcies at a mere $10 per case. On the other hand, it was profitable for Lincoln to handle them in bulk, and he did so, requiring the out-of-town lawyers to pay $10 in advance and up to $20 more from time to time for court costs and newspaper ads.[45] Those newspaper ads, required by the court as a notification to creditors about debtors who were filing bankruptcy, are practically the only records we have of Lincoln's bankruptcy practice. The Chicago fire of 1871 destroyed most of the case files of the federal courts in Illinois.[46]

The bankruptcy law was repealed March 31, 1843, but it lasted long enough to make Lincoln an experienced debtor-creditor lawyer right at the beginning of his career. Persons who filed bankruptcy had to disclose their entire credit record, just as they do today, by filling out detailed schedules of all known debts and all the assets that are available to pay those debts. Falsifying the schedules is grounds for denial of a discharge in bankruptcy.[47] Even an innocent omission of a single debt will cause that debt not to be discharged.[48] Lincoln wrote to one of his referral attorneys: "Be sure that [the schedules] contain the creditors *names,* their *residences,* the *amounts* due each, the debtors *names,* their *residences,* and the *amounts* they owe, also all property and where located."[49]

Another consequence of Lincoln's bankruptcy practice was the need to take promissory notes instead of cash for fees. Lincoln could require payments up front from out-of-town referral lawyers, but it was not as easy to require cash of his own Sangamon County clients. They were often destitute when they filed bankruptcy, and Lincoln had to accept their notes for fees and expenses. One such note called for payment to be made in firewood, because Lincoln must have doubted that the client would be able to pay in cash.[50] He reluctantly took notes in payment for fees throughout his career and was diligent in collecting them.[51]

By the time Congress repealed the second U.S. bankruptcy law, Lincoln and Logan had handled seventy-seven bankruptcy cases, the most of any Springfield lawyers.[52] The repeal, however, did not mean that Lincoln ceased practicing a common law form of bankruptcy, for Illinois insolvency law, including the law of assignment for the benefit of creditors and compositions, remained an alternative to federal bankruptcy law.

Banknotes, Specie, and Money

"Money" is a flexible concept that denotes generally anything of value that a creditor will accept in payment of debt. Governments, however, pass laws designating the types of money which *must* be accepted by creditors. Such money is called "legal tender," and it usually consists of government-minted coins and government-printed paper money. In the Legal Tender Cases of 1867 and 1868, the Supreme Court ruled that the paper "greenbacks" Salmon P. Chase issued under the Legal Tender Act to finance the Civil War had to be accepted at face value as legal tender.[53] But when Lincoln practiced law in the Eighth Judicial Circuit there was not yet any paper designated as legal tender. Rather, there was only hard currency in the form of gold and silver coins and bars of gold and silver called "bullion" or "specie."[54] Payment of debt in specie was highly desirable, but there was a shortage of specie, and so promissory notes of state-chartered banks (banknotes) had to be used as a substitute. The problem was that banknotes were not legal tender and creditors could refuse to take them. They would demand specie unless they had agreed in advance to accept banknotes. Promissory notes of unincorporated agencies, insurance companies, and railroads were in circulation, but they, too, were not legal tender.

Banknotes were payable in specie, but frequently the banks did not have enough. The State Bank of Illinois, established at Springfield in 1835, and the State Bank of Shawneetown had ceased redeeming their banknotes in specie by 1842.[55] An individual who could not pay in banknotes or specie could expect the creditor to seize his land. One thing the individual might do was hire a lawyer like Lincoln to forestall that result.

Many a bank that could not pay its notes in specie would close its doors, and all of the notes would become worthless. The State Bank of Illinois, for example, was ordered in 1843 to liquidate in five years.[56] The reason banks failed is a complicated subject, but a few basic reasons are readily discernable. Banks in Illinois were chartered by the state, and there was no national bank to force them to discipline themselves. As agents of the state they were expected to lend money by issuing their notes to finance the railroads and the other public works which Lincoln favored during his years in the legislature. By the time Lincoln retired from the legislature in 1841, however, the banks had issued too many notes to redeem them for specie, and creditors would devalue their banknotes. For example, creditors might require $100 in face value of a bank's notes to pay off a debt of $10.

One of Lincoln's cases from this period, *Todd v. Ware,* involved a disagreement over whether the creditor had agreed that payment could be made in devalued banknotes.[57] In 1841 Lincoln's future father-in-law, Robert S. Todd, gave three notes to Nathaniel Ware for about $400 apiece and secured them by a mortgage. Failure of Todd to pay off the notes would result in foreclosure on his real estate. In 1842 Todd tendered some notes of the State Bank of Illinois as payment, but Ware refused to accept them at face value. Todd then engaged Lincoln to file suit against Ware, seeking a decree that Ware must accept the notes. Lincoln argued that under the loan agreement Todd could pay Ware "in current bankable paper, received on deposit at the State Bank of Illinois," and that "current bankable paper" meant the banknotes Todd tendered must be accepted at face value. But Lincoln lost the case. The court decided that the bank's notes were not "current bankable paper" because the bank was in bad repute and its paper was circulating at a discount of 40 to 50 percent. It found that Todd and Ware could not have had in mind that the debt could be repaid at 50 cents on the dollar. *Todd v. Ware* illustrates that Lincoln practiced debtor-creditor law during the Dark Ages of monetary policy.[58]

The Routine Practice of Debtor-Creditor Law

Lincoln is described by most biographers as a trial lawyer who left the office work to his third partner, Billy Herndon. The result was that Lincoln drafted relatively few promissory notes but regularly went to court to collect them. When he had to file a complaint, however, he followed a precise format, because, if the wording deviated in any way from the common law requirement, the complaint could be dismissed. Therefore, Lincoln was careful to use the correct forms. It is said that in his saddlebags he carried only the Illinois Statutes and perhaps one other lawbook, *Story's Notes.* A long complaint for a complicated case could extend over several handwritten pages. For example, the complaint Lincoln wrote for *Todd v. Ware* was three pages long and contained over seven hundred words. A short printed form was often all that was necessary, however, and might read, "the plaintiff states that he holds a note on the defendants [inserting their names] in substance as followeth: [and the substance of the note follows]. Yet the debt remains unpaid wherefore he prays judgment for his debt and damage, for the detention of the same, together with his costs."[59]

Over the years complaints to collect notes have changed little. A modern Illinois complaint to collect on a note requires no formal language and might be as brief as a Lincoln complaint.

> 1. On_____[date], at _____[city], _____ County, Illinois, defendant was indebted to plaintiff for $_____, and made and delivered to plaintiff_____[his or her] written promissory, dated the above date, in which _____[he or she] promised to pay plaintiff $_____, principal, _____ days after date with interest at the rate of _____per cent per annum. A copy of the note, marked "Exhibit A," is attached and incorporated by reference.
> 2. Defendants have not paid the principal of $_____ in whole or in part or the interest.
> 3. Plaintiff requests Defendant be ordered to pay to plaintiff whatever amount due.

Once a collection case was started with a properly filed complaint, a default judgment was usually the result, because then, as now, few defendants took the trouble to contest their debts. Sometimes there was a default judgment even if the note being sued upon was lost. In a letter to Joshua Speed, Lincoln wrote: "Herndon showed me a couple of letters of yours concerning your note against Judge Browne. . . . We do not remember ever having had the note. . . . You mention in your letter that you have our receipt for the note. I wish you would, at once, send a copy of the receipt to Logan. . . . I wish Logan to see by the receipt, whether he or I, by reference to it sufficiently describe the note, on oath, to recover on it as a lost instrument. . . ."[60] Lincoln knew that he could do what commercial lawyers still can do: prove the existence of a lost instrument and sue upon it. Thus, Lincoln and Herndon could sue Judge Brown without producing it in court.[61]

While getting a default judgment was relatively easy, debtors still had to be pursued and their property seized. Lincoln would file writs of execution to request the sheriff (or constable) to seize property of the debtor. That property could consist of personal property, such as a horse and wagon, but more often it consisted of real property. After seizing property, the sheriff would conduct a sale and the proceeds would be turned over to Lincoln on behalf of his client. Lincoln spent a lot of his time collecting from debtors in the same manner as creditors collected from him in New Salem.

Lincoln for the Defense

As a plaintiff's lawyer Lincoln would sue on a note, obtain judgment, and draft an order to the clerk requesting that a writ of execution be directed to the sheriff. The writ usually concluded Lincoln's work for plaintiffs, but sometimes his clients were defendants who would wind up on the wrong end of the writ. An example of this is the 1847 case of *Hill v. Masters & Goodpasture*.[62] The case is exceptional in that unlike the majority of their cases, Lincoln and his partner, Silas W. Robbins, tried to offer a defense. The presumption in those days was that debtors summoned to court were "guilty" and most of them did not even appear in court. If they did appear it was to have their lawyers "confess judgment," that is, admit of liability on the note.

This case illustrates once again that notes were the currency of Lincoln's time. Four notes were involved, and they seemed to flow back and forth among the parties like cash. Squire D. Masters and William B. Goodpasture gave their note to Thomas Anno as payment for land. The note was payable in a combination of goods and dollars as follows:

> On or before the first day of December 1846 I promise to pay to Thos. Anno a good span of horses and good wagon in payment in part for lands bought of him the amount of indebtedness to said Anno yet remaining being $257. The amount above the horses and wagon due to said Anno to draw inters from date.
>
> S. D. Masters
>
> June 2. 1846
>
> Wm. B. Goodpasture
>
> A.H. Goodpasture witness[63]

Anno, the payee of the note, assigned it to Thomas Hill as follows:

I assign the within note to Samuel Hill as collateral security on two
notes of hand that Hill holds against Anno, one dated January 29
1846 for one hundred thirteen dollars and fourteen cents. The other
one hundred and thirty dollars dated Jany th 24.1843—

This 16th day Nov. 1846
Thos. Anno[64]

The writing reveals that Anno assigned the note "as collateral security" for
two prior notes he had given Hill (notes 1 and 2 below). This assignment
gave Hill the right to collect from Masters and Goodpasture, but only if
Anno failed to pay the first two notes. In other words, Hill's right to collect
from Masters and Goodpasture would only arise if Anno defaulted to Hill
on the first two notes. That is exactly what must have happened, because
Hill sued Masters and Goodpasture. This is how the case looks in diagram:

<u>promises to pay Hill</u>
Notes 1 & 2   <u>$113 note dated Jan. 29, 1846</u>
<u>and $130 note dated Jan. 24, 1843</u>
Thomas Anno>>>>>>>>>>>>>>>>> Samuel Hill
maker (two notes)   payee (two notes)

<u>promise to pay Anno</u>   <u>Anno assigns note</u>
Note 3   horses & wagon or $257, note   to Hill as security
dated June 2, 1846   for notes 1 & 2

S.D. Masters & Wm. B.   >>>>>>>>>>Thomas Anno
>>>>>>>> Samuel Hill
Goodpasture, makers   payee   assignee

<u>promise to pay Masters</u>
Note 4   corn or $198, note dated
June 2, 1846
Thomas Anno   >>>>>>>>>   Squire D. Masters
maker   payee

After Hill filed suit, Masters and Goodpasture hired Silas W. Robbins as their attorney. Lincoln was not immediately involved in the case because only Robbins's name appears on the first pleading for the defense, in which Robbins argues that the note "is not for the direct payment of money or property, but indirectly for both, without saying how much either and therefore the law does not authorize this proceeding."[65] Robbins was arguing that the case should be dismissed. This initial and murky plea was followed by two more pleas in Robbins's hand but signed "Lincoln & Robbins," indicating Lincoln had now entered the case. Lincoln was doing what he did almost everywhere he went on the Eighth Judicial Circuit, forming an ad hoc partnership with a local lawyer. Robbins must have approached Lincoln when he arrived for the May term of the Circuit Court for Menard County in 1847.

The case well illustrates the difficulty frontiersmen had in finding cash and the role lawyers played in collecting notes as substitutes for cash. It appears that Masters and Goodpasture could not come up with the cash to pay the note sued upon by Hill, and so Lincoln and Robbins devised a tactic called "set-off" as a substitute.[66] Masters was holding a note payable to him and signed by Thomas Anno (note 4 above.) In the note Anno promised to pay Masters "twelve bushels of corn per acre for a hundred and ten acres or its equivalent in cash."[67] Why not offer to assign this note to Hill as a set-off for the $257 owed Hill? In other words, why not swap one note for another? In their plea offering the set-off, Lincoln and Robbins assured Hill that the Anno note remained "fully undischarged"[68] and that the equivalent in cash of the corn amounted to $198. They were assuring Hill that the Anno note was good. If Hill accepted the Anno note, Masters and Goodpasture would settle most of their $257 debt. But success depended on Hill having a high opinion of Anno's note.

The tactic did not work, and the court entered judgment against Lincoln's clients for $257, plus $6.42 in damages and $9.76 in costs.[69] Armed with a judgment in his favor, Hill wrote an order to the clerk for a writ of execution. The clerk then issued the writ of execution to be carried out by the sheriff. The writ stated "of the goods and chattels, lands and tenements of Squire D. Masters and William B. Goodpaster . . . you cause to be made two hundred and fifty seven dollars debt . . . and have that money ready at the Clerk's office of our said Circuit Court within ninety days from the date hereof. . . ."[70] This ancient language for writs of execution continues in use today.

No record is available to explain what the sheriff did to collect the debt, but after a few years one of the codefendants was released. The last document in the case reads:

> The Clerk of the Menard Circuit Court will enter the judgment in
> the case of Saml Hill vs. S.D. Masters satisfied—
> Petersburg Jany—29—1850
> Samuel Hill[71]

Robbins and Lincoln lost this case, but at least they offered a defense. The case illustrates the note-based payment system in Illinois and the hazards of collection. Just getting a judgment in court did not bring satisfaction to a plaintiff like Hill. After judgment he had to wait for the sheriff to seize whatever property of the debtor he could find. Frequently the sheriff reported back to the court that nothing of value was found and the note would prove to be worthless. Hill was lucky, for it appears he collected something from Masters.

Most of the wealth in antebellum Illinois was in possessions, not bank accounts or currency. Land, the produce of land, horses and wagons, and even surveying instruments were the currency of the day, and lawyers used notes to transfer ownership rights to others. The lawyers on the Eighth Judicial Circuit were the necessary agents to make trade possible, and they were a close-knit group. The two plaintiff lawyers who opposed Lincoln in the Hill case were John Todd Stuart, Lincoln's former partner, and Benjamin S. Edwards, Stuart's present partner, and also the son of Lincoln's brother-in-law, Ninian Edwards. A final irony was that the case took place in Petersburg, near the abandoned village of New Salem, where Lincoln first read law.

An Unusual Collection Case

Many of Lincoln's collection cases were routine, but a few remained open for years. One such difficult case came to Lincoln as a referral from out of state, the case of *Kelly v. Blackledge,* which had been filed in Columbiana County, Ohio.[72] The case illustrates what Lincoln did as a referral attorney, how difficult it was to find property of the debtor, and how diligent Lincoln had to be to close the case.

In 1838 James Kelly, a building contractor in Columbiana County, sold his share in a mill to his partner, Nathan Harris, for $2,687.50. Harris paid Kelly by signing a series of promissory notes, and Jesse D. Blackledge, a wealthy resident of Pickaway County, also signed the notes as security. Today, we would call Blackledge a guarantor or an "accommodation party."[73]

In 1845, when the notes were overdue, Kelly sued both Harris and Blackledge. After considerable litigation, judgment was entered against the two men in 1847 for $632.59, $0.01 in damages, and costs of $7.36. Kelly's attorney then caused levy to be made against Harris's property, but the sheriff's return said, "No goods, chattels, etc." This "nulla bona"[74] return cleared the way for a writ to the sheriff in Pickaway County for levy against Blackledge's property, and this time the return said, "Not found in my bailiwick." It seems Blackledge had left the county. Kelly was stymied, but he kept trying to levy on Harris, and the sheriff eventually seized Harris's bay mare and two-horse wagon, which sold for $26.87. The balance of over $600 remained to be collected.

Three years later Kelly's new attorney, A. L. Brewer, learned that Blackledge was living in Logan County, Illinois, and the race was on to collect from him.[75] An Illinois attorney was needed, and so in 1851 Brewer paid the clerk of court for a transcript of the judgment and sent it to Abraham Lincoln. Lincoln decided to sue Blackledge, but there was more delay because the sheriff for some reason failed to serve process notifying Blackledge that he was being sued, and, furthermore, Lincoln had to send the transcript back to Ohio to get the authentication of record corrected. Brewer was getting nervous about the delay and wrote Lincoln in November 1852 that he would very much like to hear how Lincoln was getting along with the claim. Lincoln said, "I ordered an alias[76] for the next April term. It was all I could do."[77]

In early 1853 Blackledge died before anything came of the "alias," and any satisfaction of the claim would now have to come from filing a new case against Blackledge's estate. In September of that year Lincoln's partner, William Herndon, filed Kelly's claim in Blackledge's estate, but even more delay ensued, as explained by Lincoln himself in a letter to Brewer:

Mar. 16, 1855

A. L. Brewer, Esq.
Dear Sir:
Your letter of the 8th is just received. It has all the while been understood that the estate of Blackledge is solvent & that the Kelly

claim is good. After I sent back to you & got the authentication of record corrected, I commenced a suit in the circuit court; and about that time Blackledge died. The case is not in the county of my residence; so that I am only there at the terms of the circuit court. At the first term after B's death, my partner, who was attending court in that county that term dismissed the suit and filed the record in the Probate Court as a claim against the estate. This we both thought was the best way of doing. Last fall I turned out of my way to come by that county to see after the claim; and was surprized to be told that the claim had not been allowed or acted on.

On the 2nd. of April court takes me there again, when I shall give special attention to the matter.

Yours &c.

A. Lincoln[78]

It got worse. On July 27 Lincoln reported to Brewer that the judge in probate court inexplicably decided not to allow the claim. Lincoln appealed, and finally was able to report to Brewer on November 5 that "the [circuit] court decided for us and we got judgment for the amount of the old judgment and interest."[79] An affidavit on file in the Logan County courthouse stated that all claims against the estate were paid, presumably including Kelly's.[80] It took ten long years for Harris to collect on his notes, and Lincoln worked for him half of the time.

Perhaps it was the tedium of the *Kelly v. Blackledge* case that led to Lincoln's outburst in a letter to another important client. The client was S.C. Davis & Co., St. Louis, Missouri, wholesale merchants who had retained Lincoln & Herndon to collect bad accounts in Illinois. Lincoln wrote them a letter dated November 17, 1858, right after his debates with Douglas, saying, "I will try to 'explain how our' (your) 'interests have been so much neglected,' as you choose to express it."[81] He went on to say sarcastically that judgments had been obtained but that selling land on execution was a delicate matter requiring careful examination of titles and a canvas of half the state. He explained that because he had received no instructions on how to proceed he hired a young man who spent three or four weeks visiting all of the localities to make an accurate report on titles and values. He said he had written S.C. Davis & Co. asking whether Lincoln & Herndon should sell the real estate and bid in for S.C. Davis & Co. but there was no reply.

Lincoln continued: "My mind is made up. I will have no more to do with this class of business. I can do business in court, but I cannot, and will not, follow executions all over the world."[82]

Conclusion

Lincoln not too subtly suggested that one of his best clients, S.C. Davis & Co., take its business elsewhere. He was then handling major railroad cases and collection work was a bother. In the end, however, he stayed with the client.[83] Perhaps the moral of the story is that debtor-creditor law was indeed his bread and butter, and even as his political career was taking off he could not abandon it. Right up to his election, debtor-creditor cases continued to put food on his table and help finance his political career.

Notes

This essay was originally published in slightly different form in the *Journal of Illinois History* 8, no. 2 (summer 2005), and is reprinted here by permission.

1. Benner, Martha L., and Cullom Davis, eds., *The Law Practice of Abraham Lincoln: Complete Documentary Edition,* DVD-ROM (Urbana: Univ. of Illinois Press, 2000), hereafter cited as LPAL. A project of the Illinois Historic Preservation Agency begun in 1984, the Lincoln Legal Papers includes over 1.5 million discrete facts about Lincoln's legal career and over 200,000 documentary images.

2. John J. Duff, *A. Lincoln, Prairie Lawyer* (New York: Rinehart, 1960), 177–78.

3. Ibid., 183.

4. Ibid., 123–28; John P. Frank, *Lincoln as a Lawyer* (Urbana: Univ. of Illinois Press, 1961), 40; Albert A. Woldman, *Lawyer Lincoln* (Boston: Houghton Mifflin, 1936), 42–44.

5. William H. Townsend, *Lincoln the Litigant* (Boston: Houghton Mifflin, 1925), 4–8.

6. Frank, *Lincoln as a Lawyer,* 40.

7. Promissory note, February 24, 1842, *In re Gambrel,* LPAL.

8. John A. Lupton, "The Law Practice of Abraham Lincoln: A Narrative Overview," www.papersofabrahamlincoln.org/narrative_overview.htm, accessed March 15, 2005.

9. Roy P. Basler, Marion Delores Pratt, and Lloyd A. Dunlap, eds., *The Col-*

lected Works of Abraham Lincoln, 9 vols. (New Brunswick, N.J.: Rutgers Univ. Press, 1953–1955), 1:5–9, hereafter cited as *CW.* "Communication to the People of Sangamo County" was published in the *Sangamo Journal,* March 15, 1832.

10. *CW,* 1:4.

11. Harry E. Pratt, *The Personal Finances of Abraham Lincoln* (Springfield, Ill.: Abraham Lincoln Association, 1942), 9; Benjamin P. Thomas, *Abraham Lincoln* (New York: Knopf, 1952), 52–53.

12. Promissory note, October 30, 1832, *Henry for use of McCandless & Emmerson v. Ally & Lincoln,* LPAL.

13. The rule on accommodation makers is found today in the Uniform Commercial Code § 3-419(b). The more common name for "accommodation maker" is "guarantor." This law is found in Illinois at 810 ILCS 5/3-419(b).

14. Pratt, 10; Thomas, 52–53.

15. Ibid.

16. "Judgment proof" is the term debt collectors use when a debtor is known to have no money to pay.

17. Thomas, 70.

18. David Herbert Donald, *Lincoln* (New York: Simon and Schuster, 1995), 47.

19. Wm. H. Herndon and Jesse W. Weik, *Herndon's Lincoln: The True Story of a Great Life,* 3 vols. (Chicago: Belford, Clarke, 1889), 1:107.

20. Thomas P. Reep, *Lincoln at New Salem* (Petersburg: Old New Salem League, 1927), 65; Pratt, 14.

21. Donald, 96; Pratt, 15.

22. Thomas F. Schwartz, "Finding the Missing Link: A Promissory Note and the Lost Town of Pappsville," *Bulletin of the 55th Annual Meeting of the Lincoln Fellowship of Wisconsin Held at Milwaukee, Wisconsin, April 22, 1995,* Historical Bulletin Number 51 (1996).

23. Promissory note, December 3, 1833, *Watkins v. Lincoln & Berry,* LPAL. The note is not in Lincoln's handwriting but in Berry's. Lincoln's name is signed by Berry. It was perfectly legal then, as now, for one partner to sign a document on behalf of the partnership.

24. Judgment, December 24, 1833, *Watkins v. Lincoln & Berry,* LPAL.

25. JP transcript, March 1, 1834, *Watkins v. Lincoln & Berry* appeal, LPAL.

26. Appeal bond and writ of supersedeas, December 25, 1833, *Watkins v. Lincoln & Berry* appeal to the Sangamon County Circuit Court, LPAL.

27. Order and judgment docket, April 26, 1834, *Watkins v. Lincoln & Berry* appeal to the Sangamon County Circuit Court, LPAL.

28. Writ of execution, August 25, 1834, *Watkins v. Lincoln & Berry* appeal to

the Sangamon County Circuit Court, LPAL. The language of this writ is similar to language still in use for writs of execution.

29. Writ of execution, August 25, 1834, *Watkins v. Lincoln & Berry* appeal to the Sangamon County Circuit Court, LPAL.

30. Townsend, 68–70; *Vanbergen v. Lincoln et al.,* LPAL.

31. Pratt, 71–82.

32. Pratt, 82.

33. Pratt, Hartford Fire Insurance Company policy.

34. Lincoln probably learned about writs by reading William Blackstone, *Commentaries on the Laws of England, Book the Third* (Oxford: Clarendon Press, 1768), 412–21.

35. John A. Lupton, "The Law Practice of Abraham Lincoln: A Narrative Overview," www.papersofabrahamlincoln.org/narrative_overview.htm, accessed March 15, 2005.

36. *Dictionary of American Biography* (New York: Charles Scribner's Sons, 1932), 5:532–533.

37. Abraham Lincoln to Joshua F. Speed, March 27, 1842, *CW,* 1:282.

38. Abraham Lincoln to John T. Stuart, January 23, 1841, *CW,* 1:229.

39. Mark E. Neely Jr., *The Abraham Lincoln Encyclopedia* (New York: Mc-Graw Hill, 1982), 194.

40. Duff, 54, 80.

41. *Kellogg v. Crane,* LPAL; Duff, 81.

42. Woldman, 38.

43. Duff, 80.

44. "An Act to Establish a Uniform System of Bankruptcy throughout the United States," U.S. Statutes at Large, vol. 5, 27th Cong., Sec. 1, ch. 9, 1841, 440–49. See generally, Edward J. Balleisen, *Navigating Failure, Bankruptcy and Commercial Society in Antebellum America* (Chapel Hill: Univ. of North Carolina Press, 2001).

45. Duff, 232.

46. Duff, 230.

47. Bankruptcy Code, 11 U.S.C. § 727(a)(4).

48. 11 U.S.C. § 523(a)(3).

49. *CW,* 1:270.

50. Duff, 233.

51. Townsend, 4–8.

52. Duff, 231.

53. Legal Tender Cases, 79 U.S. (12 Wall.) 457 (1871). Ironically, Chase himself opposed making his greenbacks legal tender.

54. For a discussion of money as it existed in pre–Civil War Illinois, see, Paul M. Angle, *Here I Have Lived* (New Brunswick, N.J.: Rutgers Univ. Press, 1935). See, generally, John F. Chown, *A History of Money* (London: Routledge and the Institute of Economic Affairs, 1994); and Jason Goodwin, *Greenback* (New York: Holt, 2003).

55. Angle, 120–21, 170.

56. Angle, 170.

57. *Todd v. Ware,* LPAL. See generally Frank, 31–36, 71–76.

58. A. W. Coats and Ross M. Robertson, *Essays in American Economic History* (New York: Barnes and Noble, 1970), 113.

59. Frank, 37.

60. Washington, Dec. 25, 1848. *CW,* 2:17. See Friend, "Abraham Lincoln and a Missing Promissory Note," *Commercial Law Journal,* November, 1968, 349.

61. Uniform Commercial Code § 3-109. This law is found in Illinois at 810 ILCS 5/3-109.

62. *Hill v. Masters & Goodpasture,* LPAL.

63. Petition, promissory note, June 2, 1846, *Hill v. Masters & Goodpasture,* LPAL.

64. Petition, promissory note, June 2, 1846, *Hill v. Masters & Goodpasture,* LPAL.

65. Undated demurrer, joinder, filed May 4, 1847, *Hill v. Masters & Goodpasture,* LPAL.

66. Plea, May 5, 1847, *Hill v. Masters & Goodpasture,* LPAL.

67. Undated plea, filed May 5, 1847, *Hill v. Masters & Goodpasture,* LPAL.

68. That is, no one had yet collected it.

69. Execution docket, April 4, 1848, *Hill v. Masters & Goodpasture,* LPAL.

70. Order for writ of execution, April 28, 1848, writ of execution, May 4, 1848, *Hill v. Masters & Goodpasture,* LPAL.

71. Order, January 29, 1850, *Hill v. Masters & Goodpasture,* LPAL.

72. *Kelly v. Blackledge,* LPAL. Henry C. Friend, "Abraham Lincoln as a Receiving Attorney: Kelly vs. Blackledge," *Commercial Law Journal* (February 1949): 27. Friend was able to put together the facts of this case because Lincoln was obliged to report by mail to his client attorney, or forwarder, what he did, what the judges did, and what his partner, William H. Herndon, did. The fire that burned the courthouse of Logan County in 1857 destroyed documents pertaining to the case, but Lincoln's correspondence survives.

73. Uniform Commercial Code § 3-419. This law is found in Illinois at 810 ILCS 5/3-419.

74. Latin for "no goods."

75. The process of locating an absent debtor today is called "skip-tracing."

76. An "Alias" is issued after the first instrument has not been effective (Bryan A. Garner, *Blacks Law Dictionary,* 8th ed. [Eagan, Minn.: West Group, 2004]). In this case it probably referred to an "alias process," or second summons notifying Blackledge that he was being sued. The alias version of the summons would begin, "as we have before commanded you." Index, Glossary, LPAL.

77. *CW,* 2:161.

78. *CW,* 2:315.

79. *CW,* 2:327.

80. Friend at n. 30.

81. *CW,* 3:338.

82. *CW,* 3:338.

83. Duff, 229–30; Frank, 41; Friend, 46, citing Angle, *New Letters and Papers of Lincoln,* 200–201.

Lincoln and Illinois Real Estate

The Making of a Mortgage Lawyer

Roger Billings

When Kentucky was part of Virginia the holders of land warrants had to provide a survey and description of their claims at their own expense. The surveys were unprofessional, using marks on trees, movable stones, and dry creeks to show division lines. By the time Lincoln's father began to buy land in Kentucky, the titles were almost bound to be disputed, and those who could afford lawyers were the most likely to succeed. Thomas Lincoln bought his first 238 acres in 1803 near Mill Creek, another 348½ acres near Hodgensville in 1808 (called the Sinking Springs farm), and another 230 acres near Knob Creek in 1811. He lost thirty-eight acres of the Mill Creek purchase because of an erroneous recording of the survey, and he lost the Sinking Springs farm in litigation over the title; he similarly lost the Knob Creek farm over a claim to prior title in an "ejection suit" against Thomas and nine neighbors by the Middleton heirs of Philadelphia.[1] Louis A. Warren reports, and most historians agree, that Thomas Lincoln left Kentucky for Indiana to settle in a state "where land once purchased could be retained."[2] It is also true that he much preferred a free state, for he was an antislavery man.[3]

There is no evidence of just how much the young Lincoln understood his father's troubles with titles. It seems, however, that he must have learned something about them and they must have been on his mind as an element of his family history when he left his father and settled in the frontier town of New Salem, Illinois. In any event, he soon learned about real estate matters in his capacity as assistant to the county surveyor, John Calhoun. To get that job he taught himself the principles of trigonometry, read books to learn the surveyor's trade, and eventually conducted complicated surveys.

According to historian David Donald, "all his work was careful and meticulously accurate."[4] Thus, in his mid-twenties and not yet a student of the law, Lincoln was skilled in determining the metes and bounds of a parcel of land, ironically a skill that would have been invaluable to his father. And surveying was not the only thing he did in New Salem that supported a possible future as a lawyer. New Salem residents called upon Lincoln to draft basic legal documents for them. And so, when John T. Stuart of Springfield suggested that Lincoln should study law the idea sounded good. As Benjamin Thomas wrote, "Lincoln had always liked the law," having read the Revised Statutes of Indiana and listened to the trials in the Spencer County, Indiana, courthouse.[5]

Lincoln probably first learned about mortgages after he acquired four volumes of Blackstone's *Commentaries* and set about reading them from cover to cover. William Blackstone was an English lawyer who saw that there was a need to organize the common law. The common law is law that is made by judges, not by legislatures. If there is no legislative act on a particular legal issue, a judge is supposed to find the leading judicial decision and follow it. Blackstone simply collected the decisions and explained them.

Sir William Blackstone wrote an analytical treatise on the common law entitled *Commentaries on the Law of England.* They were originally a course of lectures on the laws of England that he read in the University of Oxford. The *Commentaries* were published in four volumes over 1765–1769. An American edition was published in Philadelphia in 1771–1772 and sold out on its first printing of 1,400 copies.[6] A number of other editions followed. Lawyers in antebellum Illinois relied on Blackstone as the primary source of law. The reason this treatise on English law was so important in America is that when the United States began its existence as a new country in 1789 the states adopted the common law of England as the law of the United States. Courts in the United States as well as state legislatures could make their own laws, so that the English law, which was frozen as of 1789, would be replaced eventually. But when Lincoln practiced law most of the English common law was still valid.

The precise edition of Blackstone that Lincoln studied is not known, but it might have been the one suggested in *The Law Practice of Abraham Lincoln*: William Blackstone, *Commentaries on the Laws of England,* 4 vols. (New York: Collins and Hannay, 1832).[7] Some of Blackstone's words on mortgages which Lincoln read were as follows:

Analysis
Book II—Of the Rights of Things
Chapter X. Of Estates Upon Condition

6. Estates in gage, *in vadio,* or in pledge, are estates granted as a security for money lent; being, I. *In vivo vadio,* or living gage; where the profits of land are granted till a debt be paid, upon which payment the grantor's estate will revive. II. *In mortuo vadio,* in dead, or mort gage; where an estate is granted, on condition to be void at a day certain, if the grantor then repays the money borrowed; on failure of which, the estate becomes absolutely dead to the grantor.

Mortgages gave lenders some assurance that their loans would be repaid. Yet not all borrowers had land to mortgage, and there was always a flourishing business for the lawyers suing on defaulted notes which were not backed by a mortgage at all.

Lincoln had over three thousand cases dealing with debtor and creditor issues.[8] Over half of these cases related to negotiable instruments—specifically promissory notes.[9] Some were guaranteed by someone other than the debtor (cosigned), but overwhelmingly the transactions were not secured with collateral. Instead creditors seized a debtor's personal and real property with a variety of writs similar to those in use today. *The Papers of Abraham Lincoln* describes them as follows:

Writ of Scire Facias—a writ requesting judicial enforcement of a previous court order. It was commonly used to seek enforcement of a judgment that was more than one year old, after which normal writs of execution were not longer available. If the defendant appeared to defend against the writ of scire facias, the case proceeded like other actions. The defendant had to demonstrate why the plaintiff should not receive the benefit of the earlier decree. Litigants occasionally used this writ as a method of foreclosing a mortgage.

Writ of Attachment—an order for a sheriff to seize a debtor's real or personal property to secure a creditor's claim before the court; a writ authorizing a sheriff to arrest and bring before the court an individual whom that court held in contempt of court.

Writ of Execution—an order for a sheriff to seize and sell real or personal property in satisfaction of a judgment. This writ and a writ of fieri facias were functionally interchangeable.

Writ of Fieri Facias—a writ of execution that directed a sheriff to seize the losing party's personal goods or real property and sell them to raise funds to pay the winning party the amount of money owed from a judgment by the court. This writ and a writ of execution were functionally interchangeable.

Writ of Possession—a writ of execution, usually in an action of ejectment, that ordered a sheriff to seize specific real property that the losing party had failed to turn over to the winning party as ordered by the court.

Writ of Venditioni Exponas—a writ of execution that directed a sheriff to sell property that he had seized under a writ of fieri facias but that remained unsold.[10]

Real Estate Mortgages

When a note was secured, it was typically secured with real property and only in rare instances with chattel mortgages. In many cases, the debtor could redeem the property by paying the debt, but a strict foreclosure or completed sale barred the right to redeem the land forever.[11] The promissory note looked similar to a check today, stating the name of the parties, date of the transaction, amount promised, date due, and interest amount due. The mortgage or deed was a lengthier document, typically describing the land to be transferred, the reason for the mortgage, a statement voiding the mortgage if the note was paid, and the names of the parties. The mortgage deed was typically recorded by the clerk in the county court. The terminology of mortgage practice in Lincoln's day is quite similar to Blackstone's terminology, and most of it is still in use today. They include the terms "conveyance," "dower," "ejectment," "foreclosure," "mechanics lien," "partition," "quiet title," "redemption," "quit claim deed," "right of way," "specific performance," and "usury."[12]

Many mortgage loan cases were routine and required little or no litigation. For instance, on November 18, 1844, Charles Dunn gave a promissory note to Charles Hurst for $180.75, with a combination of real and personal property as collateral. The collateral consisted of a forty-acre tract of real estate in Sangamon County and "three head of horses, one buggy and harness, one wagon and four sets of harnesses."[13] A man named John Williams paid off the note on January 16, 1852, and so foreclosure on the collateral was unnecessary. The loan was like a delinquent automobile installment loan that is paid up so as to avoid repossession. We may reasonably assume that Lincoln negotiated the settlement of many bad loans without litigation.

Similarly, in *Ambos v. Barret et ux,* James Barret gave four promissory notes to Ambos that totaled $8,700.[14] Barret secured the notes with a mortgage, and eventually sold part of the property to fulfill the payment of the debt.[15]

Approximately two hundred of Lincoln's cases dealing with promissory notes involved mortgage foreclosures.[16] In *Blair v. Babb et al.,* Blair gave three promissory notes to Babb totaling $3,450[17] and secured the notes with a mortgage on 240 acres.[18] Blair passed away before satisfying his obligation, so Babb sued to foreclose on the mortgage. The court ruled for Babb in the amount of $2,233. When Blair's heirs did not pay the judgment, the court foreclosed on the mortgage.[19] On June 14, 1857, Henry Dresser signed a promissory note to Condell, Jones & Co. for $595.79 which read, "on or before the first day of January 1848, I promise to pay to Condell, Jones & Co. or order six hundred and ninety six dollars 79 cents for value received with interest hereon from the date hereof at the rate of twelve percent per annum."[20] The note was secured with a mortgage on several lots in Springfield.[21] Dresser failed to pay the note, so Condell, Jones & Co. sued to foreclose the mortgage.[22] The court ruled for Condell and sold the property at a public auction to satisfy the judgment.

Chattel Mortgages

CHATTEL MORTGAGES IN THE ANCIENT WORLD

There is evidence that in the ancient world lending among individuals was common. Rules of conduct in Exodus and Deuteronomy indicate that not only was there lending but personal property collateral was used to assure repayment of loans. Use of personal property collateral today is a routine incidence of lending, but the collateral in ancient days was pledged, something not often done in Lincoln's day, or even today. Pledges are made when the debtor gives the creditor something to hold until loan repayment. The pledge can be any kind of valuable personal property. The key is that the lender takes possession of something of value owned by the debtor. When the loan is repaid the pledge is returned. When the loan is not repaid the creditor can sell the pledge. This is one version of what we now call chattel mortgage lending.

The ancient Israelites were sensitive to the injustice that can occur in the pledge process. They recognized that in taking a pledge the creditor could deprive a debtor of what he needs to make a living. Israelites were so sensitive to the possibility of abuse by creditors that the Bible did not allow any interest to be charged for loans to fellow Israelites. Below are some references to chattel mortgages in Exodus and Deuteronomy.[23] Note that in the last Old Testament reference to lending in Proverbs, lending is discouraged altogether:

Exodus 22:25–27
If you lend money to one of my people among you who is needy do not be like a moneylender; charge him no interest. If you take your neighbor's cloak as a pledge, return it to him by sunset, because his cloak is the only covering he has for his body. What else will he sleep in?

Deuteronomy 15:1–3
At the end of every seven years you must cancel debts. This is how it is to be done: Every creditor shall cancel the loan he has made to his fellow Israelite. He shall not require payment from his fellow Israelite or brother, because the Lord's time for canceling debts has been proclaimed. You may require payment from a foreigner, but you must cancel any debt your brother owes you.

Deuteronomy 24:6
Do not take a pair of millstones—not even the upper one—as security for a debt, because that would be taking a man's livelihood as security.

Deuteronomy 24:10–13
When you make a loan of any kind to your neighbor, do not go into his house to get what he is offering as a pledge. Stay outside

and let the man to whom you are making the loan bring the pledge out to you. If the man is poor, do not go to sleep with his pledge in your possession. Return his cloak to him by sunset so that he may sleep in it.

Proverbs 11:15
He who puts up security for another will surely suffer, but whoever refuses to strike hands in pledge is safe.

Proverbs 22:26
Do not be a man who strikes hands in pledge or puts up security for debts.

Lending historically has had an unsavory reputation. The Muslim religion prohibits loans with interest altogether. And Shakespeare puts lenders like Shylock in *The Merchant of Venice* in a bad light. We can be sure that Lincoln read these Bible passages as well as Shakespeare. What he thought of them we will never know, but we do know that his law practice included chattel mortgage financing and that if he was to make a living as a lawyer he could not be bothered by the morality of lending. In fact, notes (whether or not secured with a mortgage) were a necessary substitute for money, which was in short supply.

When Lincoln read those Bible passages as a youth he might have pondered what they meant. The Old Testament told him that lenders should be fair to borrowers and that Israelites should not make loans to one another for interest.[24] In those passages he first encountered the word "pledge," which is what results when the borrower gives something valuable to the lender to hold until the loan is repaid. The Bible mentions two kinds of pledged property: a pair of millstones and outer garments or cloaks. It cautions that if the lender takes a neighbor's cloak as a pledge it must be returned by sunset, because it is needed to sleep in. Cloaks must have been poor collateral if the lender had to collect them each morning and return them each night! "A pair of millstones" is a more interesting kind of collateral. Millstones were equipment used to grind wheat into flour. They were undoubtedly valuable possessions, but they were a means for the owner to make a livelihood and taking them as a pledge would deprive the debtor of their use. That is why Deuteronomy says in verse 24:6, "Do not take a pair of millstones—not even

the upper—as security for a debt, because that would be taking a man's livelihood as security." A later reference to pledges in the Old Testament further
discourages borrowers from taking pledges. It says, "Do not be a man who
strikes hands in pledge or puts up security for debts; if you lack the means
to pay, your very bed will be snatched from under you."[25]

Chattel Mortgages in Lincoln's Day

Today, of course, we have strayed away from these biblical injunctions and
now see collateralized debt as a necessary evil. Indeed, banks rarely make a
loan on the signature of the borrower alone. The system of taking collateral
for loans has become quite sophisticated and includes conditional sales
contracts, inventory financing, and equipment financing, all of which are
represented among Lincoln's cases. Instead of pledges, where the lender
takes and holds property of the borrower, the borrower is allowed to keep
this collateral and use it to earn money to pay back the loan. To warn others
that the lender claims certain property of the debtor as collateral, banks file
a notice called a financing statement at a central office, such as the secretary
of state's office. The financing statement is the rough equivalent of the real
estate mortgage filed in the courthouse.

If anyone buys or uses this collateral while the financing statement is in
force, the lender who filed the financing statement can seize the collateral
in an action for replevin, an action well-known to Lincoln. There is an exception: the buyer of inventory does not have to worry about the financing
statement. For example, if you buy a washing machine from Sears, you do
not have to worry about the fact that a bank claims a security interest in all
of Sears's inventory. With that exception debtors are not allowed to sell the
collateral while it is subject to a chattel mortgage. But some do it anyway, and
that precipitates a fight over who has priority in the collateral. In Lincoln's
times there was no system similar to the filing of financing statements until
1856, and this made litigation over priority in collateral more likely.

Lincoln was involved in collateralized loans as early as 1842. The case
of *Stapleford v. Lewis*[26] involved inventory financing, one of the most complex kinds of chattel financing. And so, the earliest case in Lincoln's career
as a chattel mortgage lawyer was quite challenging, and Lincoln had been
in practice less than five years. The case involved a store in Springfield

owned by a man named Thomas Lewis who had arrived in Springfield in 1837, about the same time as Lincoln. He was a shoemaker by trade and also tried his hand at practicing law, banking, and publishing.[27] Sometime before 1842 Lewis sold his store to a man named Torrey. Torrey paid Lewis, not in cash, but with three promissory notes for a total of $1,500 secured by a chattel mortgage on the store's inventory. In other words, Torrey agreed that if he did not repay the notes Lewis could seize the store's inventory and sell it to liquidate the loan. The store was a general store and might have served customers much like those of Sears, Walmart, Target, or JCPenney. The merchandise in its inventory included staples for Springfield of the 1840s: "twenty sides of Sole Leather, three half boxes of Tobacco, one Box of Candles, three Reams of Wrapping Paper, one-half Barrel of Rice, one-half Barrel of Sugar, fifty pounds of Coffee, five kegs of Nails, forty-four Boxes of Blacking, twelve Gallons of Lamp Oil, three tin Pans, three Coffee Pots, and eighteen pairs of Boots."[28]

Torrey failed to pay Lewis on the first note, and so Lewis sued Torrey to gain possession of the store inventory. This is called a foreclosure suit, similar to foreclosure suits to sell mortgaged real estate, except the collateral involved here was store merchandise, not real estate. The judge ruled for Lewis and gave him the right to order the constable to levy execution on all the merchandise in the store's inventory. "Levy execution" is what the constable or sheriff does when he seizes collateral pursuant to a court judgment. And in *Lewis v. Stapleford,* that is exactly what the constable did. He seized the inventory and impounded it. Here is where the real trouble in the case began. If the constable had done what Lewis expected, he would simply have turned over the collateral or at least sold it and given the proceeds to Lewis. But for unknown reasons he did neither. He simply impounded the collateral and did not turn it over to the lender. Lewis then hired the firm of Logan & Lincoln to bring an action of replevin to recover the merchandise from the constable, Stapleford.

There is a strong hint of why the constable did not turn over the merchandise to Lewis. In the affidavit to the court claiming the right to seize the inventory, Logan and Lincoln stated that there were no other persons who claimed priority in Lewis's property. The affidavit said that the goods in inventory "have not been taken for any tax, assessment, or fine levied by virtue of any law of this state, nor seized under any execution or attachment against the goods and chattels."[29] But perhaps the constable who impounded the goods thought otherwise, for he knew that without any system for financing statements the claimants to a debtor's property were on a first-come, first-served basis. Maybe the constable wanted to wait awhile to see if there were any claimants other than Lewis to Torrey's store inventory. What is certain is that, because the constable would not release the inventory to Lewis, Lincoln and Logan had to file an action against the constable to force him to release it. The jury ruled for Lewis and awarded $1 in damages. Of course, the damages were unimportant. What Lewis wanted, and what Logan and Lincoln got for him, was the right to seize and sell the inventory.

A long period of about fifteen years intervened before Lincoln was again involved in complex chattel mortgage litigation. By this time Illinois had passed a statute that created the forerunner of the financing statement. The Illinois Statues of 1856 specified that "No mortgage on personal property shall be valid as against the rights and interests of any third person or persons, unless . . . the said mortgage be acknowledged and recorded" by the recorder of the county in which the debtor resides.[30] The statute would be an obstacle that Lincoln and his third partner, Herndon, could not overcome for their client in the case of *Gregg et al. v. Sanford*.[31] The case was argued in the Illinois Supreme Court at its January term, 1860, at Springfield. This time the inventory was hogs, not store merchandise. Hiram Sanford had loaned $1,758 to Moses and David Edmiston to purchase hogs and corn so that they could fatten them for market. The hogs were to be sold in Madison, Indiana, and the proceeds used to pay back Sanford's loan. The Edmistons gave Sanford a chattel mortgage on all the hogs they bought with his money, but Sanford did not record the mortgage under the 1856 statute. The mortgage provided that if the Edmistons defaulted Sanford could take possession of the hogs and sell them to pay the indebtedness.

The Edmistons defaulted, but before Sanford could seize any hogs another creditor named Gregg got a judgment and had the sheriff levy on 150 hogs. Sanford hired Lincoln and Herndon to get an injunction to prohibit the sheriff from selling the hogs for the benefit of Gregg. And so it came down to a classic priority case: two creditors both going after the assets of the same debtor. Lincoln and Herndon were awarded an injunction in the Edgar County Circuit Court, but they lost in the Supreme Court. The Supreme Court ruled that since Sanford's chattel mortgage was not filed, the hogs belonged to whichever of the two creditors seized them first. Gregg seized them first and so Sanford's chattel mortgage was second in priority.

Had Sanford filed the mortgage in the Edgar County courthouse he would have had priority. The rule is remarkably like the rule in the present-day Illinois Uniform Commercial Code (UCC).

A second case further illustrates the risk lenders assumed when they did not take advantage of the 1856 statute. In *Cass v. Perkins*,[32] Cass was the holder of a $600 note secured by a chattel mortgage on three horses, one two-horse wagon, and a leather harness. The note was due to be paid by the borrower, Ford, on July 1, 1859. But Ford defaulted and so four days after the note was due, on July 4, the lender Cass seized the horses and wagon of Ford. Complicating matters, there was a second lender who also claimed the horses and wagon. This was a lender who had a note, but unlike Cass he did not have a chattel mortgage to secure the note.

Ford had now defaulted to both Cass and the second lender. On June 25, before Cass seized the horses and wagon of Ford, the second lender got a writ of execution which authorized the sheriff to seize goods belonging to Ford. The sheriff, however, did not seize the horses and wagon from Cass until July 6. Cass protested that he had previously seized the horses and wagon on July 4, two days before the sheriff, and that he should have priority. He said his chattel mortgage was superior to the other lender's mere writ of execution. But the Illinois Supreme Court disagreed. It said the one who delivered a writ of execution to the sheriff should have priority. If Cass wanted to seize the horses and wagon under the authority of the chattel mortgage, he should have acted within twenty-four hours after Ford defaulted on July 1. Instead, he waited until July 4. The delay was inexcusable and misleading to other lenders. Lincoln and Herndon represented Cass and lost the case. The 1856 law calling for filing chattel mortgages in the courthouse was designed to avoid this kind of dispute. If Cass had filed, he would have had priority over the other lender's writ of execution. Without the filing the court decided the lenders were on almost equal footing in a race to seize the collateral.

Another chattel mortgage case which is a forerunner of today's "purchase money security interest" law is the St. Nicholas Hotel case, *Miller & Scott v. Wickersham*.[33] Miller and Scott were St. Louis merchants that sold furniture to Wickersham for his hotel in Springfield. Wickersham signed a note for $1,851.46 and also got some friends named Constant and Matteson to sign the note as "sureties" (cosigners). As sureties, they were liable to pay off the lenders, Miller and Scott, if Wickersham defaulted. Concerned that Miller and Scott might call upon them to pay, they took the precaution of getting a chattel mortgage on the hotel's furnishings from Wickersham, which would allow them to reimburse themselves after paying Miller and Scott.

Wickersham defaulted on the loan to Miller and Scott. Then he sold the hotel furnishings and kept the proceeds for himself and the sureties, Constant and Matteson, instead of paying off the lenders, Miller and Scott. Lincoln and Herndon argued in the Illinois Supreme Court that Miller and Scott had priority to the money. Again, Lincoln and Herndon lost. The court said that the sureties, Constant and Matteson, had taken possession of the chattels and this gave them priority in them over Miller and Scott. One wonders why Miller and Scott did not themselves take a chattel mortgage on Wickersham's hotel furnishings. We cannot blame Lincoln and Herndon for the oversight because they were only called in as litigators.

Conclusion

Lincoln's real estate mortgage practice would be familiar to any present-day mortgage lawyer. The chattel mortgage practice was more primitive compared with today's practice in the field of law called secured transactions. But the handful of cases involving chattel mortgages are remarkable for their reflection of the basic principles of present-day law.

Notes

This essay was originally prepared for the Conference on Illinois History, October 18, 2007. It is printed here in slightly different form.

1. Louis A. Warren, *Lincoln's Youth* (New York: Appleton, 1959), 12–13; David Herbert Donald, *Lincoln* (New York: Simon and Schuster, 1995), 24.

2. Warren, *Lincoln's Youth*, 13.

3. Ibid.

4. Donald, *Lincoln*, 52.

5. Benjamin Thomas, *Abraham Lincoln* (New York: Random House, 1952), 42.

6. Greg Bailey, "Blackstone in America," *Early American Review* (spring 1997), www.earlyamerica.com/review/Spring97/blackstone.

7. "Legal History: Contemporary Legal Resources," in *The Law Practice of Abraham Lincoln: Complete Documentary Edition,* ed. Martha L. Benner and

Cullom Davis (Urbana: Univ. of Illinois Press, 2000), DVD-ROM (hereafter cited as LPAL).

8. "Common Subjects of Cases," in "A Statistical Portrait," LPAL. The author acknowledges the able assistance of his research assistant, Jodi Henry, in compiling materials to illustrate real estate and chattel mortgages.

9. Ibid.

10. Glossary, LPAL.

11. "Common Subjects of Cases," in "A Statistical Portrait," LPAL.

12. Glossary, LPAL. Daniel W. Stowell et al., eds., *The Papers of Abraham Lincoln: Legal Documents and Cases,* 4 vols. (Charlottesville: Univ. of Virginia Press, 2008), 4: 389–404.

13. Deed Record, January 16, 1852, promissory note for Dunn & Hurst, LPAL.

14. Promissory Note, October 9, 1857, *Ambos v. Barret,* LPAL.

15. See *Ambos v. Barret,* LPAL. (Note that Barret had secured another note to Von Phul using one thousand acres of the same property.)

16. A mortgage foreclosure is an action to recover real property claimed under a mortgage. See Glossary, LPAL.

17. Promissory Note, November 5, 1836, *Babb v. Blair et al.,* LPAL.

18. Real Estate Mortgage, November 5, 1836, *Babb v. Blair et al.,* LPAL.

19. See generally *Babb v. Blair et al.,* LPAL.

20. Promissory Note, June 15, 1847, *Condell, Jones & Co. v. Dresser et ux,* LPAL.

21. Bill to Foreclose Mortgage, August 13, 1849, *Condell, Jones & Co. v. Dresser et ux,* LPAL.

22. Ibid.

23. Bible quotes are from the New International Version, Archeological Study Bible (Grand Rapids, Mich.: Zondervan, 2005), 696.

24. Exodus 22:25 (NIV).

25. Proverbs 22:26–27 (NIV).

26. LPAL, File ID L03838.

27. LPAL, biographical sketch of Thomas Lewis.

28. LPAL, affidavit in *Stapleford v. Lewis.*

29. LPAL, affidavit in *Lewis v. Stapleford.*

30. Norman H. Purple, *A Compilation of the Statutes of the State of Illinois* (Chicago: Keen and Lee, 1856), chapter 20, "Chattel Mortgages: Statutes," LPAL.

31. 24 *Illinois Reports* 17 (1860).

32. *Cass v. Perkins,* LPAL.

33. *Miller & Scott v. Wickersham,* LPAL.

The Power of Lincoln's Legal Words

John A. Lupton

Samuel Moulton was a contemporary of Abraham Lincoln's on the Eighth Judicial Circuit. He was notorious for his poor penmanship. One day, his colleagues decided to play a trick on him. They found a bug, dipped its legs in ink, and let the bug run across a piece of paper. They took this paper to Moulton, who was also well known for being quite near-sighted, for him to read. Moulton looked at it and said, "I wrote it, but I'll be damned if I can read it now."[1] Moulton was certainly not the only lawyer in Lincoln's antebellum America writing his own documents. During the nearly twenty-five years that Lincoln practiced law in the courts of Illinois, lawyers almost always wrote their own documents. Attorneys needed to write well in a handwriting sense, but more importantly they needed to write well in a cohesive sense.

Lincoln was a successful member of the bar, earning a decent income to provide a respectable middle-class life for his family. His life as a lawyer has recently drawn considerable attention, mainly due to the publication of his legal documents.[2] A number of scholars have focused their attention on Lincoln's law practice generally or on specific cases. A separate genre of Lincoln scholarship has examined Lincoln's writing, most notably in specific speeches.[3] Largely absent in this voluminous scholarship is a discussion of Lincoln's legal writing ability. Was Lincoln a good legal writer? Did the way Lincoln wrote legal documents affect the outcome of his cases? Did Lincoln, the legal writer, influence Lincoln, the political and presidential writer?

Before a discussion of the content of Lincoln's legal writing can take place, an examination of his actual handwriting is necessary. Lincoln's handwriting was excellent compared to that of his contemporaries.[4] He had a clear and bold handwriting that distinguished him from many of his peers. With well-formed and consistent letters, Lincoln was probably a slow and deliber-

119

ate writer. He clearly took time to form letters and words, which mirrored the way he thought. In describing Lincoln, Daniel Kilham Dodge suggested that "clear thinking is the basis of all clear writing."[5] James C. Conkling, one of Lincoln's contemporaries, described him as a slow and deliberate thinker, pondering heavily on issues and considering all arguments before making a firm decision.[6] William Herndon, Lincoln's third law partner, noted that Lincoln "was truly a great lawyer" in the Illinois Supreme Court because it gave attorneys "time, ample time, to read the record and gather up the facts of the case . . . stating the facts in a condensed form . . . [and] time to hunt up the law and to argue the case."[7] Lincoln's thought process was manifested through his penmanship.

Understanding how Lincoln wrote helps to inform how we understand what he wrote. Lincoln himself wrote for his Discoveries and Inventions lecture that "*writing*—the act of communicating thoughts to the mind, through the eye—is the greatest invention of the world."[8] While a clerk and postmaster in New Salem, Illinois, Lincoln began to learn the tools of legal writing. As early as 1834, he began to read law books, giving him his first true exposure to the formality of legal documents. Lincoln's experience in drafting legislation in the Illinois General Assembly in the 1830s should not be underestimated in its role in helping him learn to draft legal documents. Fred Kaplan noted that Lincoln's "ability to think and write coherently that marked his success as a legislator began to characterize his performance in the law."[9] Receiving his license to practice law in 1836, he earnestly began a career that would last for a quarter-century. In his partnership with John T. Stuart, Lincoln was largely untutored, learning the law himself as he handled cases in the Illinois court system. His second law partner, Stephen T. Logan, was more of a taskmaster, teaching Lincoln the proper practices of a legal career. After Lincoln began his third and final partnership with William H. Herndon, he took this knowledge, along with his innate gift of words, and became one of the top attorneys in Illinois.[10]

Lincoln's notes for a law lecture best portray his thoughts on how to practice law, and several letters he wrote to prospective lawyers illustrate his legal advice and suggested path for attaining a legal education. Lincoln frequently used legal analogies in speeches and debates. Other attorneys sought his advice or opinions on specific legal questions, and Lincoln would respond with well-thought-out replies. Lincoln was not a legal theorist, however, nor did he seek any judicial office from which he could express legal doctrine. As a result, there are no opinions or treatises written by Lincoln that might offer some insight into Lincoln the legal writer.[11]

Generally, it is very difficult to determine how well an attorney wrote from most case documents because of their formulaic nature. Form books of the antebellum period contained the specific words to use in declarations in replevin, or pleas in debt, or replications in assumpsit, as examples. Hence, the content of one declaration to recover a promissory note was pretty similar to another declaration to recover a promissory note.[12] However, even these formulaic documents reveal some information about Lincoln's legal writings—that Lincoln followed the standard legal practices of the day, that he believed in a legal system of form and structure, and that he understood that deviance from that form could present problems for clients and a lawyer's reputation.

One example of deviance from form occurred with Stephen A. Douglas, Lincoln's chief political rival for twenty-five years. Douglas did not practice much law and only ventured into the law to further his political ambitions. One of the first rungs in his rise up the legal and political ladder was serving as a state's attorney for the First Judicial Circuit in 1835. In McLean County, one of the first counties in which he practiced as a state's attorney, Douglas wrote all of the indictments with the court name of M'Lean. John T. Stuart, who would later become Lincoln's first law partner, saw the error and motioned the court to quash all of the indictments because there was no such county in Illinois named M'Lean. The judge asked Douglas to respond, but he threw the burden of proof back to Stuart. Stuart requested a recess to examine the statute books, and to his surprise the statute that created McLean County actually spelled it as M'Lean. The court denied Stuart's motion to quash, and the cases continued. Douglas later compared the written engrossed legislation to the printed statutes and found that there was a misprint in the printed version.[13]

While Lincoln occasionally misspelled words, he probably would not have made this kind of error. The most cited mistake in Lincoln's law practice comes from a letter, not a legal document. In 1859, Lincoln helped his friend Ward Hill Lamon, the state's attorney for the Eighth Judicial Circuit, write indictments for the upcoming spring 1860 term. Lincoln wrote an indictment against Henry Musick and three others for sending a threatening letter. Lincoln and Lamon disagreed as to the wording: Lamon thought the threat needed to be spelled out specifically, but Lincoln thought the statute said that it could be general. When the case came before the court, the defense attorney motioned to quash the indictment because it was not specific. In March 1860, Lamon wrote to Lincoln, who was in Chicago arguing a different case, wanting the specific statute to which Lincoln referred. Lamon noted that "quashing an indictment written by a prominent candidate for the presidency of the U.S. by a little court like [David] Davis's will not sound well in history." Lincoln defended his original assumption that "there is no necessity for setting out the letter *haec verba*. Our Statute, as I think, relaxes the high degree of technical certainty formerly required." Lincoln continued, "If, after all, the indictment shall be quashed, it will only prove that my *forte* is as a Statesman, rather than as a Prossecutor." The court quashed the indictment.[14] Indictments, of course, follow the example of formulaic legal documents. The verbiage Lincoln used was not based on his writing skill but on how he interpreted the specific statute that guided threatening-letter actions in court.

In most cases, Lincoln was acutely aware of the finer details of the law. Eli Blankenship and Jesse Trailor, the executors of an estate, sued John Williams, executor of another estate, to collect a debt. The case was originally tried before Thomas Moffett, a probate justice of the peace who was acting in the capacity of a regular justice of the peace. Moffett found for the plaintiffs Blankenship and Trailor and awarded $43, well below the jurisdictional limit of $100 for probate justices of the peace, but over the jurisdictional limit of $20 for regular justices of the peace. Williams retained Lincoln and appealed the case to the circuit court. Lincoln argued that the justice of the peace signed his documents as the probate justice of the peace but entered them in his regular justice's docket, and that that position had the $20 limit in debt cases. The circuit court agreed with the lower court and affirmed the judgment. Lincoln wrote a bill of exceptions in which he restated the complicated jurisdictional issue by simply referring to the seal Moffett used as a regular seal, not a probate seal. Williams continued to employ Lincoln in the appeal to the Illinois Supreme Court, which agreed with Lincoln and reversed the judgment because regular justices of the peace only had jurisdiction where the statute granted it, and Moffett was operating under the jurisdiction of a regular justice of the peace, not a probate justice of the peace.[15]

Lincoln crafted prose in writing his bill of exceptions, rather than simply following the guidelines of crafting documents from a form book. Bills of exception and jury instructions were two types of legal documents that lent themselves to more creative and less formulaic writing. Jury instructions were written instructions given to the jury by the court to assist them in determining the law, not the facts, of the case. Typically, attorneys who wanted instructions in a case prepared them and submitted them to the court. The judge considered them and would mark "given" or "refused," depending on his assessment of the propriety of a particular instruction. In a number of opinions, the Illinois Supreme Court commented on jury instructions that they should be few and simple, concise, not argumentative, and not misleading. Bills of exceptions were typically written by an attorney and signed by the presiding judge. During the course of a trial, either party could allege an exception to a decision by the court—if the judge mistook the law or the attorneys on either side presumed the judge mistook the law. The bill of exceptions itself should have copies of all pertinent documents to support getting the decision reversed.[16] While much of the content of a bill of exceptions could simply be copies of documents, attorneys still needed to explain the finer details of the case.[17]

Jury instructions and bills of exceptions tell us much about Lincoln the legal writer. The content of these instructions and exceptions and the variety of cases to which they belong offer a wonderful representative lens into Lincoln's law practice, and more particularly, Lincoln the legal writer. In comparison to other attorneys, Lincoln's jury instructions and bills of exceptions were not too different in terms of length. The presiding judges corrected or changed Lincoln's documents as frequently as they changed other attorneys' documents. Lincoln sometimes corrected his own documents, but not as frequently as other attorneys corrected their own. Most striking about Lincoln's instructions and bills was not the length or the editing, but the content.

In a number of instructions, as expected, Lincoln was clearly being a strong advocate for his client. In many cases, Lincoln understood the crux of the case, and it was reflected in his jury instructions. In *Alton & Sangamon Railroad v. Carpenter*, the railroad condemned forty acres of Carpenter's property, but the parties could not agree on adequate compensation. Commissioners appointed by a justice of the peace awarded Carpenter $100, but he appealed the decision to the circuit court. As the attorney for the railroad, Lincoln instructed the jury to consider the economic advantages and deduct them from "the damages done to the land by the construction of the railroad." The court refused the instruction, and the jury awarded Carpenter

$326. Lincoln appealed the judgment to the Illinois Supreme Court, arguing that the circuit court erred by not allowing the instruction to the jury. The supreme court agreed with Lincoln, reasoning that the statutes never contemplated paying damages to a landowner for the privilege of having a railroad constructed through his lands when the value added to the land was equal to the injury.[18]

In another case, *Fairchild v. Capps & St. Clair,* Chauncey Fairchild made a contract with John Capps and Cicero St. Clair to sell them wheat from his property. When Capps and St. Clair refused to purchase five hundred bushels for a total of $500, Fairchild sued them for a breach of contract. Lincoln wrote the jury instruction for Capps and St. Clair, arguing that if "both parties understood a crop of *fall* wheat to be growing and for which they both intended to contract, and that the wheat tendered by the plaintiff to the defendants was *Spring* wheat, and not fall wheat, they the jury, are to find for the *defendants.*" The jury found Lincoln's clients not guilty, recognizing, as did Lincoln, that fall wheat was more desirable, and thus more expensive, than the cheaper spring wheat.[19]

One final example is *Mallory v. Elkin,* in which Garret Elkin lost money playing cards to John Haynes. With no money in hand, Elkin gave Haynes a promissory note for $125 to cover the gambling debt. Haynes assigned the note to Egbert Mallory, and when Elkin failed to pay when the note became due, Mallory sued him to recover the debt. Lincoln instructed "the jury that if they are satisfied from the evidence the note in question was given for money won by gaming at cards, they are to find for the defendant." Lincoln understood that notes were given for the payment of money or property, not for gambling, and conveyed that to the jury, who agreed, and decided for the defendant.[20]

Of course, Lincoln did not win every case in which he was a lawyer. In fact, he lost quite a few. The great majority of his cases involved the collection of debt, and in a creditor-friendly legal environment, Lincoln won the great majority of his cases when he was representing the creditor-plaintiff and lost the great majority of his cases when he was representing the debtor-defendant. Whether he won or lost his case, he made himself clear. Douglas Wilson argued that "achieving clarity, it seemed, was a large part of his obsession." Fred Kaplan concurred that "as a lawyer and politician, he had struggled with the precise use of language to communicate ideas."[21]

In *Richardson & Hopkins v. Johnson,* William Richardson and Horace

Hopkins owned a winery and employed Henry Brush and Bob Thompson to transport and sell the alcohol. Brush and Thompson spent the night at Johnson's City Hotel in Springfield, Illinois, carrying nearly $3,500 in cash with them. Johnson locked $3,000 of it in his safe, but Brush decided to keep $370 in the pocket of his pants, which he left on a chair at the foot of the bed. The next morning, Brush found the door to their room wide open, his pants in the hallway, and the money in them gone. Richardson and Hopkins sued Johnson to recover the money since Johnson, as the owner of the hotel, failed to provide a secure environment for his guests, more specifically, the agents of Richardson and Hopkins. Lincoln represented Johnson and argued—as reflected in his jury instruction—that since Brush chose not to leave his money in the safe, even though he was aware of the safe's existence, then the jury should find for the defendant. The court refused the instruction, and the jury found for Richardson and Hopkins for $290. Lincoln wrote the bill of exceptions concisely summarizing all of the testimony in the case and recording the refused instruction. He appealed the case to the Illinois Supreme Court, but lost when the court affirmed the judgment by noting that the innkeeper was responsible for the theft unless he could prove otherwise. The court reasoned that the laws were particularly hard on innkeepers but founded on considerations of public utility and deemed essential to ensure a high degree of security to travelers.[22]

Another business owner who had a criminal action against him also had a difficult legal battle because the laws, as they were written, heavily favored the prosecution in manslaughter cases, in which the burden of proof was not as strict as in murder cases. A man by the name of Samuel Dehaven entered Thomas Patterson's store to buy some goods on credit, but Patterson refused to give him any more credit. Dehaven allegedly picked up a shovel in a menacing manner, and Patterson responded by throwing a two-pound weight at Dehaven, hitting him in the temple. Dehaven died a few days later, and Patterson was indicted for manslaughter. Lincoln defended him and in his jury instructions argued that, first, if Patterson threw the weight because of a reasonable fear that he was in danger, then the jury should find Patterson not guilty; second, if the jury had any reasonable doubt that Patterson was fearful of being in danger, they should find him not guilty; and third, if the jury had any reasonable doubt of Patterson's guilt, they should acquit him. Lincoln was clearly attempting to put reasonable doubt in the jury's minds, and that might have worked had Patterson been charged with murder. The jury found Patterson guilty of manslaughter and sentenced him to three years in the penitentiary. One year later, Lincoln joined in a petition to the governor for his pardon, and the governor granted it.[23]

In the previous two cases, Lincoln fought hard for his client with strong and emphatic jury instructions and bills of exceptions. In a number of other cases, Lincoln appeared to expect an adverse decision for his client, and his instructions to the jury highlighted mitigating factors. In *Selby v. Dunlap,* James Dunlap had beaten Paul Selby with a cane because Selby had written editorials in his newspaper about Dunlap's financial misdeeds. Selby sued Dunlap in a civil action of assault and battery, requesting $10,000 in damages. Lincoln represented the defendant Dunlap, and in his instruction to the jury he wrote that "in case they find the issue for the plaintiff, they are to consider all the circumstances . . . and give such an amount of damages, and such an amount only, as, in their common judgment, they think right, between the parties." Lincoln knew the law and facts were against him in this case, and his primary purpose as Dunlap's attorney was to mitigate the damages. In this capacity, Lincoln was successful. He technically lost the case, but won with respect to the amount of damages his client had to pay. While the jury found for the plaintiff, they awarded damages of only $30, not even near 1 percent of what was requested.[24]

Lincoln also wrote jury instructions in such a manner as to mitigate the damages that the juries would assess against his clients in several slander cases. In one he wrote, "if [the jury] believe he spoke the words, with intent to impute false swearing, but so much in the heat of passion as to be free from all deliberate malice, this is to go in mitigation of damages." In another slander case, Lincoln wrote, "if they find for the plaintiff, they are to assess such an amount of damages, as will be a reasonable compensation to the plaintiff for the injury done him in his feelings . . . and as will also be a proper example to the community, and a due punishment of the defendant for the wrong done." Lincoln understood, as Mark Steiner has pointed out, that the purpose of slander cases was not so much to gain monetary awards, but to restore the good name of the aggrieved party.[25]

These slander examples show that Lincoln was presenting a balanced argument to the jury. In a surprisingly large number of cases, Lincoln wrote very balanced instructions, almost giving the other side of the case as much weight as his own. Douglas Wilson recognized this trait in Lincoln's politics, particularly in his 1854 Peoria speech, which had a "balancing restraint."[26]

Daniel Kilham Dodge extended his argument to the legal arena in noting that in Lincoln's speeches, "as in his arguments before the bar, he is always strictly logical and fair."[27] This ability to explain in writing the opposition's argument supports what a number of contemporaries said about Lincoln's oral arguments in court. Leonard Swett noted that Lincoln would give away six of seven points in a case, but the seventh Lincoln fought for the hardest, knowing the final decision would rest on that seventh point. Schuyler Colfax commented that Lincoln could state the opposition's argument better than the opposition's attorneys.[28]

One final example of Lincoln's writing a surprisingly balanced jury instruction comes from one of his most famous cases, *People v. Armstrong,* popularly known as the "Almanac case." William "Duff" Armstrong, James Norris, and Preston Metzker were drinking at a camp meeting and got into a scuffle. Norris allegedly hit Metzker with a piece of wood on the back of his head, and Armstrong allegedly hit Metzker with a slung shot (a handheld weapon consisting of a small, heavy weight attached to a strap with which to hold the weapon) on the front of the head. Metzker died a few days later. The state's attorney indicted Norris and Armstrong for murder. The court separated the cases, and a jury found Norris guilty of manslaughter. Lincoln then became involved in the defense of Duff Armstrong because he was the son of Lincoln's very good friends from his New Salem days Jack and Hannah Armstrong. Jack Armstrong and Lincoln famously wrestled at the beginning of Lincoln's time there, earning Lincoln the respect of the community.[29]

In the legendary version of this case, the star witness for the prosecution saw Armstrong strike Metzker with the slung shot. This witness knew it was Armstrong because he could see him by the light of the moon high in the sky. Lincoln summoned an almanac, which showed that the moon was actually low in the sky, so there would have been no light with which to see. Lincoln's rebuttal shattered the prosecution's main argument, and the jury acquitted Armstrong.

Much of that legend was true, but there was much more involved in the prosecution and the defense than the light of the moon and the almanac. In fact, the almanac was only a minor aspect to the case, but it certainly received much more attention because of its drama.[30] Lincoln's main defense was explained very well in his jury instructions: "The Court instructs the jury, That if they have any reasonable doubt as to whether Metzker came to his death by the blow on the eye, or by the blow on the back of the head, they are to find the defendant 'Not guilty' unless they also believe from the evidence, beyond reasonable doubt, that *Armstrong* and *Norris acted by concert*, against Metzker, and that Norris struck the blow on the back of the head. That if they believe from the evidence that Norris killed Metzker, they are to acquit Armstrong, unless they also believe beyond a reasonable doubt that Armstrong acted in concert with Norris in the killing, or purpose to kill or hurt Metzker."[31]

Lincoln argued that Norris had already been tried and convicted of Metzker's death, so unless the jury believed that Armstrong and Norris acted in unison, Armstrong should be acquitted. Also, a doctor testified that the blow Norris dealt to the back of Metzker's head could have caused the damage in the front of the skull. More importantly, though, it was never quite clear from the testimony which blow to the head resulted in Metzker's death: was it Norris's blow, Armstrong's blow, or was it when Metzker fell off his horse and hit his head? Since that was unresolved, and Norris was already found guilty, then Armstrong should be acquitted.

These were the principal reasons—not the almanac—that the jury acquitted Armstrong. The jury instructions pointed to Norris's being the guilty party, but offered a balanced view that if Armstrong and Norris worked in unison, then Armstrong *should* be found guilty. William Walker, Lincoln's co-counsel in the case, remarked that the jury instructions are "in Lincolns own hand writing Carefully prepaired while the prosecution Closed the argument."[32] Noticeably absent from the instructions was anything about an almanac. If the jury instructions captured Lincoln's primary argument, then the almanac was not as important as the doctor's testimony.

Largely dismissed as formulaic, standard legal documents such as declarations and pleas do not illuminate Lincoln the legal writer. Jury instructions and bills of exceptions, however, manifest Lincoln's thought process and writing ability. Lincoln wrote well-thought-out jury instructions and bills of exceptions. He had far fewer strike-outs and interlineations than his contemporaries, suggesting that he already knew in his head exactly—or nearly exactly—what he planned to write. The content was largely legal and not folksy language, as might be expected from oral arguments to juries and judges. Daniel Kilham Dodge agreed that Lincoln frequently used anecdotes and humor to emphasize his meaning orally, but his writings "show a comparatively slight use of them."[33] While strong and clear, Lincoln's legal writing probably did not affect the outcome of most of his cases. Lincoln won cases in which the law was on his side, and when the law was not on his side, he could not convince a jury—in writing—that he should win.

As president, Lincoln penned some of the most perceptive and thought-provoking words in our nation's history. Not all lawyers who became president, of course, have had successful presidential administrations. However, what separates Lincoln from the twenty-five other lawyers who became president is the length and intensity of his legal career. Many lawyer-presidents fit the mold of an Andrew Jackson, who used the law as a stepping stone to political office.[34] Lincoln actually worked hard and made a living from the practice of law, which "was the best possible preparation for the . . . state papers of the early 'sixties."[35] This sustained legal experience allowed him to become a better lawyer and a better writer as time progressed and to "apply the fire of his own genius as a writer-speaker to the desperate issues of his world" in 1861.[36]

Exclusive of the law, Lincoln was extremely intelligent and had an innate ability to deal with many different types of personalities. Those attributes suited him well in his vocation of the law. His continued experience as a lawyer honed those abilities, refined them, and gave him real-world training in personal conflict and dispute resolution. His innate ability and legal training combined to make him uniquely suited to deal with the Civil War—the greatest legal question in our country's existence. The power of Lincoln's written words as a lawyer helped to explain the law to juries and to summarize the facts in bills of exceptions. The power of Lincoln's words as president helped to explain the Civil War to the masses and to guide the country through its most difficult legal crisis.

Notes

1. John M. Palmer, ed., *The Bench and Bar of Illinois: Historical and Reminiscent*, 2 vols. (Chicago: Lewis Publishing Co., 1899), 1:468.

2. Martha L. Benner and Cullom Davis et al., eds., *The Law Practice of Abraham Lincoln: Complete Documentary Edition*, DVD-ROM (Urbana: Univ. of Illinois Press, 2000); Martha L. Benner and Cullom Davis et al., eds., *The Law Practice of Abraham Lincoln: Complete Documentary Edition*, 2nd edition (Springfield: Illinois Historic Preservation Agency, 2009), http://www.lawpracticeofabrahamlincoln.org, hereafter cited as LPAL; and Daniel W. Stowell et al., eds., *The Papers of Abraham Lincoln: Legal Documents and Cases*, 4 vols. (Charlottesville: Univ. of Virginia Press, 2008).

3. For the former, see Mark E. Steiner, *An Honest Calling: The Law Practice of Abraham Lincoln* (DeKalb: Northern Illinois Univ. Press, 2006); Brian Dirck, *Lincoln the Lawyer* (Urbana: Univ. of Illinois Press, 2007); John Evangelist Walsh, *Moonlight: Abraham Lincoln and the Almanac Trial* (New York: St. Martin's, 2000); Julie M. Fenster, *The Case of Abraham Lincoln: A Story of Adultery, Murder, and the Making of a Great President* (New York: Palgrave, Macmillan, 2007). For the latter, see Garry Wills, *Lincoln at Gettysburg: The Words That Remade America* (New York: Simon and Schuster, 1992); Ronald C. White Jr., *Lincoln's Greatest Speech: The Second Inaugural* (New York: Simon and Schuster, 2002); Harold Holzer, *Lincoln at Cooper Union: The Speech That Made Abraham Lincoln President* (New York: Simon and Schuster, 2004); Douglas L. Wilson, *Lincoln's Sword: The Presidency and the Power of Words* (New York: Knopf, 2007); Lewis E. Lehrman, *Lincoln at Peoria: The Turning Point* (Mechanicsburg, Pa.: Stackpole Books, 2008); Fred Kaplan, *Lincoln: The Biography of a Writer* (New York: Harper, 2008).

4. Roy P. Basler, ed., *Abraham Lincoln: His Speeches and Writings* (Norwalk, Conn.: East Press, 2003), xxv–vi.

5. Daniel Kilham Dodge, *Abraham Lincoln: Master of Words* (New York: D. Appleton and Co., 1924), 8.

6. Rufus Rockwell Wilson, *Lincoln among his Friends: A Sheaf of Intimate Memories* (Caldwell, Idaho: Caxton Printers, 1942), 107.

7. William H. Herndon and Jessie W. Weik, *Herndon's Life of Lincoln,* with an introduction by Paul M. Angle (1889; reprint, New York: Da Capo, 1983), 272.

8. Wilson, *Lincoln's Sword,* 41.

9. Kaplan, *Lincoln: The Biography of a Writer,* 102.

10. John A. Lupton, "A. Lincoln, Esquire: The Evolution of a Lawyer," in Allen D. Spiegel, *A. Lincoln, Esquire: A Shrewd, Sophisticated Lawyer in His Time* (Macon, Ga.: Mercer Univ. Press, 2002), 24, 25, 28.

11. Stowell et al., eds., *The Papers of Abraham Lincoln,* 1:3, 10, 12–13, 14, 20; 4:230, 234, 238, 241, 248–50.

12. Alexander Hamilton, *The Illinois Form Book and Practical Guide* (St. Louis: B. L. Turnbull, 1835), 85–159; Sabin D. Puterbaugh, *Illinois Pleading and Practice: A Practical Treatise on the Forms of Common Law Actions, Pleading and Practice Now in Use in the State of Illinois* (Chicago: Callaghan and Cutler, 1867), 70–86.

13. Robert W. Johannsen, *Stephen A. Douglas* (New York: Oxford Univ. Press, 1973), 33–34.

14. *People v. Musick et al.,* LPAL.

15. *Williams et al. v. Blankenship and Trailor,* LPAL.

16. Puterbaugh, *Illinois Pleading and Practice,* 591, 633–38.

17. *The Law Practice of Abraham Lincoln: Complete Documentary Edition* contains more than one thousand cases in which a jury heard or decided a case. However, it contains only one hundred cases in which a jury instruction written by Lincoln is extant. It also contains only 160 cases with a bill of exceptions and only forty-four by Lincoln. Presumably, there were many more jury cases, jury instructions, and bills of exceptions than what has survived today, but due to fires, floods, and theft, many have disappeared.

18. *Alton and Sangamon Railroad v. Carpenter,* LPAL.

19. *Fairchild v. Capps and St. Clair,* LPAL.

20. *Mallory v. Elkin,* LPAL.

21. Wilson, *Lincoln's Sword,* 21; Kaplan, *Lincoln: The Biography of a Writer,* 292.

22. *Richardson & Hopkins v. Johnson,* LPAL.

23. *People v. Patterson,* LPAL.

24. *Selby v. Dunlap,* LPAL.

25. *Ramsey v. Marteny,* LPAL; *Campbell v. Smith,* LPAL; Steiner, *An Honest Calling,* 94.

26. Wilson, *Lincoln's Sword,* 39.

27. Daniel Kilham Dodge, *Abraham Lincoln: The Evolution of His Literary Style* (Urbana: Univ. of Illinois Press, 1900), 41.

28. "Reminiscence of Leonard Swett," August 29, 1887, Stowell et al., eds., *The Papers of Abraham Lincoln,* 1:21; Allen Thorndike Rice, ed., *Reminiscences of Abraham Lincoln by Distinguished Men of His Time* (New York: North American Review, 1888), 333–34.

29. Douglas L. Wilson, *Honor's Voice: The Transformation of Abraham Lincoln* (New York: Knopf, 1998), 19–51; Kenneth J. Winkle, *The Young Eagle: The Rise of Abraham Lincoln* (Dallas, Tex.: Taylor Publishing, 2001), 67–68; *People v. Armstrong,* LPAL.

30. Daniel W. Stowell, "Murder at a Methodist Camp Meeting: The Origins of Abraham Lincoln's Most Famous Trial," *Journal of the Illinois State Historical Society* 101 (fall/winter 2008): 229, 232.

31. *People v. Armstrong,* LPAL.

32. Douglas L. Wilson and Rodney O. Davis, *Herndon's Informants: Letters, Interviews, and Statements about Abraham Lincoln* (Urbana: Univ. of Illinois Press, 1998), 341.

33. Dodge, *Abraham Lincoln: The Evolution of His Literary Style,* 34.

34. Norman Gross, ed., *America's Lawyer-Presidents: From Law Office to Oval Office* (Evanston, Ill.: Northwestern Univ. Press, 2004).

35. Dodge, *Abraham Lincoln: Master of Words,* 6.

36. Kaplan, *Lincoln: The Biography of a Writer,* 292.

Competence, Diligence, and Getting Paid

Lincoln's Lessons for Today's Ethical Lawyer

William T. Ellis and Billie J. Ellis Jr.

Lincoln practiced law for twenty-four years. During this time, there was virtually no formal system in place to regulate the conduct of lawyers. Without the help of a code, creed, or manual, Lincoln navigated through an astonishingly eclectic, broad-reaching practice guided only by his own judgment, informed by his own ethical intuition. Today, lawyers have at their disposal a cornucopia of guidelines and creeds espousing the principles of proper, lawyerly behavior, not to mention the official, national guideline created by the ABA: the Model Rules of Professional Conduct. And yet, to many, lawyers are no more ethical now than they were in the nineteenth century. According to Aristotle, people ultimately do not learn to act ethically through codes and commandments, but through other people. Taking Aristotle's insight to heart, this chapter presents Lincoln as an ethical role model for today's lawyer.

To help review Lincoln's appraisal of ethical problems within his practice, and to link his solutions to these problems with contemporary practice, this chapter will juxtapose Lincoln's actions and decisions with three especially important model rules. Features of Lincoln's practice will be examined in light of Rules 1.1 and 1.3, dealing with competence and diligence, and Rule 1.5, dealing with fees. Lincoln not only complied with these rules before they existed, but aspired beyond them. Despite the obvious fact that Lincoln practiced law more than 150 years ago, his ethical aspiration provides a powerful model for twenty-first-century lawyers.

Expressions of the Aspirational Drive

Since the adoption of the Model Rules, which allegedly removed the aspirational tenor of earlier lawyer codes of conduct and replaced it with only minimum, mandatory requirements, efforts have been under way to increase the ethical standards of lawyers. We see today a proliferation of ethics courses in law schools and ethics articles in law journals. According to the Association of American Law Schools, there has been a six-fold increase in the number of law professors teaching courses in legal ethics in the past ten years.[1] Twenty years ago, the *Georgetown Journal of Legal Ethics* was created, the first legal periodical dedicated solely to the topic of ethics.[2] There are currently four other journals dedicated to ethics: *The Journal of the Legal Profession, The Journal for the Institute for the Study of Legal Ethics, The Notre Dame Journal of Law, Ethics, and Public Policy,* and *The Professional Lawyer.*[3] All of these journals were created within the last three decades. Other recent publications, while not focusing exclusively on ethics, highlight its importance, including the *Lawyers' Manual on Professional Conduct;*[4] the Hazard, Hodes, and Jarvis treatise;[5] Ronald Rotunda's recent one-volume book for the ABA;[6] and Tom Morgan's book comparing the Restatement of Law Governing Lawyers with the ABA Model Rules.[7] The number of law review articles dealing with legal ethics has also been on the rise. It is worth noting that these articles increasingly propose idealistic concepts, perhaps compensating for the lack of ethical drive observed in practice. One such article goes so far as to introduce an atonement theory to legal ethics, a self-sacrifice concept borrowed from medieval Christian theology.[8] Another argues that the modern lawyer should find guidance in Bushido, the warrior code of the samurai.[9]

In addition to the surge in ethically centered legal publications, the 1986 Stanley Commission Report, by an ABA-appointed commission to study the issue of professionalism, ushered in a new enthusiasm for ethics in law among legal practitioners. The report bemoaned the imminent consequences of the Model Rules: an increasing fear over breaking mandatory standards coupled with a decline in personal, higher standards.[10] The professional movement produced a series of purely aspirational codes, most notably the Lawyer's Creed of Professionalism.[11] The Lawyer's Creed maintains that the lawyer, in addition to providing zealous advocacy on behalf of the client, must adhere to the system of justice and the common good:

I will be a vigorous and zealous advocate on behalf of my client, while recognizing, as an officer of the court, that excessive zeal may be detrimental to my client's interests as well as to the proper functioning of our system of justice:

. . . I will remember that, in addition to commitment to my client's cause, my responsibilities as a lawyer include devotion to the public good.[12]

While the Model Rules are expected to be carried out as law, the Lawyer's Creed, with its aspirational undertones, is not. The Lawyer's Creed is meant to influence and persuade lawyers to elevate their personal ethical standards. If this is the intention, it begs the question as to whether or not the creeds are actually persuasive. Although a definitive answer is impossible, most would agree that the rise of these creeds has failed to create an ethical renaissance in the legal profession.

THE LIMITATIONS OF A "CODE/CREED" APPROACH

The Model Rules remain the official form of guidance for lawyer behavior. In light of this, other codes and creeds easily end up appearing superfluous. The obligatory Model Rules encourage those referring to them to think a certain way: in terms of what is allowed, and what is not. Aspirational documents like the Lawyer's Creed, however, are voluntary, and wish to encourage one to not only avoid discipline, but to strive for virtue, above the required minimum standard for conduct.[13] Yet the fact that these creeds are separate from the Model Rules frustrates this attempt. To a mind-set already conditioned by mandatory black letter statements, voluntary creeds often seem less than compelling. For lawyers to actually follow the guidelines of something like the Lawyer's Creed, they must be inspired, or personally motivated, to do so. Because the Creed is voluntary and not legally enforceable, the source of this inspiration must be old-fashioned conscience. In other words, the lawyer must be inspired to act ethically for the sake of acting ethically. Herein lies the difficulty. A lack of conscience and ethical drive are the very problems the aspirational creeds try to solve. These creeds, therefore, are not a remedy, but rather a symptom of the disease. Outside the classroom and Continuing Legal Education hypotheticals, with clients at stake, a lawyer is unlikely to be motivated by any document such as the Lawyer's Creed unless he already possesses a strong ethical conscience.

Aristotle's Theory

The argument proffered above—that voluntary, aspirational creeds are un-likely to affect any but the most ethical attorneys, and therefore will have a minimal impact on attorneys at large—is based on a rationale that can be traced back to ancient Greece. The word *ethics* derives from the Greek *ethos*, meaning habit.[14] Of course, a habit is an internalized, repeated, or innate principle that naturally springs from within a person, without reference to an outside rule or commandment.[15] Many of us tend to think of an ethical person as someone who has ethical habits, such as honesty and fairness. This belief finds expression in the common parlance "conscience." Ethical people have an ethical conscience, an innate moral reasoning capacity. We would not consider a person ethical who, lacking conscience, had to consult a manual on how to behave every time an ethical situation arose.

The idea that an ethical person must possess ethical habits is common sense today, but it was cutting-edge philosophical theory when originally es-poused by Aristotle. Aristotle, of course, was never a lawyer, but his ideas on ethics have certainly influenced the modern legal system. Aristotle believed in a general set of moral principles or maxims, which were called *nomoi*, or established law.[16] Nomoi were statutes that rational people, in a free society, would naturally find agreeable, but Aristotle did not believe the nomoi were the foundation for ethical action.[17] The true foundation, according to Aris-totle, is *phronesis*—practical wisdom.[18] Today, phronesis would be referred to as sound judgment, the ability to determine how to apply these laws, and when to depart from them, in particular situations. This is a much different approach to ethics than that of philosopher Immanuel Kant, who argued that ethical principles were categorical and must be adhered to regardless of the situation.[19] In contrast, Aristotle believed that the situation involved in any ethical decision was crucial; common sense agrees.[20] For Aristotle, all declared virtues, moral rules, and commandments are merely guideposts for judgment and reflection.

The centrality of judgment is also crucial for the practice of law. The law operates on the basic assumption that each particular situation can and must be studied; every case must be carefully examined on its own merits. Attention is given to the nuances of the context, for as Aristotle argued and experience verifies, context is crucial. In the case of murder, penalties differ depending on the circumstances.[21] Questions are asked: was it premeditated, or was it a crime of passion? The Roman dramatist Terence expressed this Aristotelian mind-set when he said: "The extreme rigor of the law is oftentimes extreme injustice."[22]

Only practical judgment can ensure that the letter of the law does not cloud the law's purpose. This was Aristotle's thesis, and it is also an assumed truth behind our legal system. And though legal practitioners often forget, it is also true of legal ethics. In the end, documents like the Model Rules or the Lawyer's Creed delineate sets of prohibited and favored conduct. The former includes minimum standard, mandatory prescriptions, and the latter proposes voluntary, aspirational ones.[23] But both documents prescribe rules. Aristotle would say these are a good start, but they are not enough to ultimately solve moral and ethical dilemmas.[24] One must apply these rules effectively in real situations that the rules do not mention. One must ask how the abstract rules inform the concrete reality.

This is a rare and complicated skill, argued Aristotle.[25] It is an acumen that involves not only intelligence but imagination, and above all, empathic knowledge of human nature. Good judgment is grounded on the rational insight that most people, very often, act irrationally. Practical wisdom requires one to understand the nuanced web of aversions, desires, and prejudices that drive human action.[26]

If this is true, and one cannot be truly engaged in the rational world without empathizing and syncing with the world around oneself, how is one to obtain such knowledge? It should be clear to us, as it was to Aristotle, that it cannot be learned from mere books, codes, or law school classes.[27] It must be gained from experience, from participating in imperfect situations among flawed men who act out the full range of their humanity, when the "better angels of our nature" cannot be summoned.[28] It is a kind of street smarts coupled with a genuine desire to do good. Outside of abstract discussions of legal ethics, there awaits the ethical lawyer an arena of demanding clients, not to mention ethically compromised allies and adversaries. When sent out as a lamb among the wolves, one must have the innocence of a dove and the cleverness of a snake.[29]

But Aristotle goes further in discussing how ethics should be learned. It is not enough to merely gain experience in the world of people. Because in this world, all too few are truly ethical. While gaining experience, one could easily be learning to act worse, not better. It stands to reason that one needs ethical role models.[30] Such role models should possess the practical wisdom necessary to navigate in potentially dirty water. The judgment these role models possess, that the rest of us desire to learn, is an insight which defies analysis. President John F. Kennedy observed that "[t]he essence of ultimate decision remains impenetrable to the observer—often, indeed, to the decider himself. . . . There will always be the dark and tangled stretches in the decision-making process—mysterious even to those who may be most intimately involved."[31] The role model's judgment must demonstrate "a self-reflective ability to . . . shift one's style of reasoning in response to situational demands."[32] The role model must be able and willing to constantly respond to a world in flux. They must have the will to marshal this ability not only for themselves, but for the common good. Considering this, it becomes clear that true ethical role models in the field of law, or any other profession, are scarce.

Choosing a lawyer who naturally encompasses such practical wisdom is a difficult task. The task is not challenging because the bar lacks historical or contemporary members who possess the necessary traits that Aristotle believed important. Fortunately, the bar was, and is, replete with these women and men. The difficulty lies in finding a role model whose development of practical wisdom can be traced and documented throughout his or her career, and whose career has relevance for today's lawyer. Further, the challenge is choosing an individual with a track record of making not only ethical decisions but also inspirational decisions. And above all else, this individual must be relatable. In essence, the best role model should be a "legal everyman" who nonetheless goes beyond the profession's ethical milieu. A first instinct is to choose a woman or man that might appear on the cover of *The American Lawyer,* a president of the ABA, or perhaps a U.S. Supreme Court justice who had a private practice before his well-touted judicial career. We decided on someone much different. While there are many examples of ethical lawyers past and present, few meet Aristotle's requirements as well as Abraham Lincoln.

Lincoln as a Role Model

The "[l]aw . . . is a 'compromise between moral ideas and practical possibilities.'"[33] This tension, between absolute moral principles and the relativity of situations, strongly intuited by Aristotle,[34] was a dichotomy personified by

(*Above*) *Lincoln the Lawyer,* a painting by Fletcher G. Ransom commissioned by the Chicago and Midland Railroad. (*Below*) *Lincoln the Circuit Rider,* a painting by Reynolds Jones commissioned by the Chicago and Midland Railroad.

Unless otherwise noted, illustrations are courtesy of the Frank and Virginia Williams Collection of Lincolniana.

Lincoln the Circuit Rider, a painting by Louis Bonhajo. (From the collection of the Abraham Lincoln Library and Museum, Lincoln Memorial University)

The first photograph of Lincoln—as a lawyer and congressman-elect.
(Daguerreotype by H. H. Shepherd, 1846)

Lincoln at age forty-five, after his 1854 Peoria speech railing against Senator
Stephen A. Douglas and his Kansas-Nebraska bill allowing for the extension of
slavery in the territories. (Photograph by Johan Carl Frederic Von Scheidau)

Lincoln in 1858, after the trial of Duff Armstrong, whom Lincoln represented. It was known as the "almanac trial"; Lincoln obtained an acquittal. (Photo by Abraham Byers, Beardstown, Illinois)

Lincoln's "particular friend," Ward Hill Lamon, who had a law partnership with Lincoln in Danville, Illinois. Appointed marshal of the District of Columbia, he served as President Lincoln's sometime bodyguard.

Illustration of the S. M. T. Tinsley Store. The law firms of Lincoln and Logan as well as Lincoln and Herndon had offices in this building.

The Lincoln and Herndon law office. (Drawing by Kate M. Hall)

John Todd Stuart, Lincoln's fellow veteran of the Black Hawk War, who encouraged Lincoln to study law. A fellow Whig, he made Lincoln his law partner—Lincoln's first.

Judge David Davis presided over the Eighth Judicial Circuit most of the twenty-four years of Lincoln's law practice. Judge Davis respected Lincoln so much that he would have him sit as judge in his absence. Davis was one of Lincoln's campaign managers for the Republican nomination in 1860. President Lincoln named him an associate justice of the U.S. Supreme Court in 1862.

Norman A. Judd was one of Illinois' most respected attorneys and served on Lincoln's campaign team at the Wigwam in Chicago.

Samuel H. Treat was Lincoln's fellow attorney, an Illinois Supreme Court justice during 1841–1845, and later a judge on the U.S. District Court.

The Lincolns' home at 8th and Jackson. (Etched and printed by Bernhardt Wall)

The Metamora House, where Lincoln would stay while in Woodford County. (Etched and printed by Bernhardt Wall)

The Metamora Courthouse, the site of the Melissa Goings murder trial in Woodford County, Illinois. Goings was accused of killing her abusive husband, and Lincoln defended her. The clerk's docket reveals that Lincoln advised Goings to flee when the trial went badly. She did, and the indictment against her was dismissed a year later. (Etched and printed by Bernhardt Wall)

The first Macon County Courthouse, where Lincoln practiced while on the Eighth Judicial Circuit. (Etched and printed by Bernhardt Wall)

The law office of Logan and Lincoln was on the third floor of this building in Springfield, Illinois, 1841–1843. (Etched and printed by Bernhardt Wall)

Tazewell County Courthouse in Pekin, Illinois. (Etched and printed by Bernhardt Wall)

Map of the Eighth Judicial Circuit district in Illinois, 1847–1853. (Courtesy of the Abraham Lincoln Presidential Library and Museum)

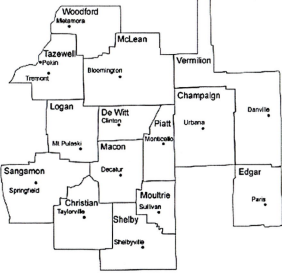

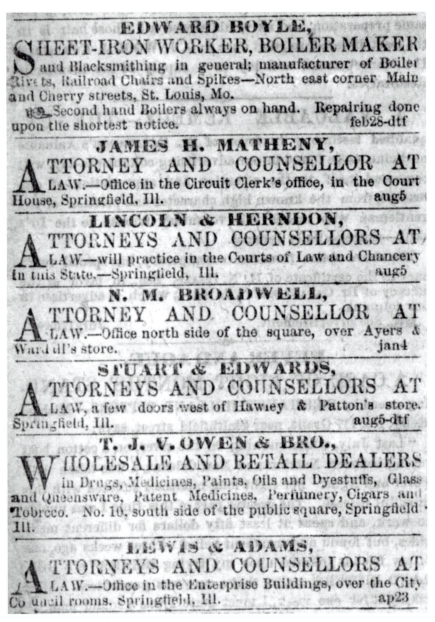

This advertisement for Lincoln's law firm ran almost daily in the Springfield, Illinois, newspaper. (From the collection of Roger Billings)

Abraham Lincoln. Throughout his life, Lincoln was thoroughly practical. Lincoln's legal practice was not driven by advocacy for the common man, as some have argued, or for big business, as others have claimed.[35] Lincoln defended the railroads, but he also defended workers who sued the railroads.[36] In the end, Lincoln was an advocate for his clients. Although he had a great interest in and ambition for politics, he was not overly political when it came to his law work—he chose to fight for people, as opposed to fighting for a particular ideology. At the same time, Lincoln possessed a Whig's desire for a smoothly functioning society, and he saw his practice as a contribution to that goal.[37]

But unlike many practical men, he buffeted his prudence with a strong, idealistic moral drive. In situations demanding clear, morally astute judgment, he was unbending while fighting for his beliefs without regard for the consequence. For example, on the issue of whether to implement the institution of slavery in new American territories, Lincoln, throughout his political career, adamantly refused to compromise.[38] And when it came to the preservation of the union, even at the cost of a terrible war that many believed could not be won, Lincoln did not entertain any compromises.[39] In these two cases, his clear sense of moral urgency outweighed all other concerns.[40]

This intellectual juxtaposition within Lincoln, constantly weighing idealism and pragmatism, mirrors a similar divide in Lincoln's character. On the one hand, he was stoic and incredibly self-disciplined.[41] On the other hand, he was a man of passion.[42] This split represents yet another reason why Lincoln is the perfect role model for lawyers: he was no saint.[43] He was ethical without being perfect, which means that despite the myth and majesty surrounding his name, he is relatable. Lincoln's flaws and worldly attributes add to his suitability as a role model because such imperfections make him relevant to people involved with the law, which, after all, is not a religion and does not ask for saintly guardians. The ethical lawyer aspires to contribute to the public good, but the law does not mandate that he feed the homeless, love his enemies, or sacrifice worldly ambition. Those virtues spring from men's faith and their hearts.

In one sense, Lincoln's practice, though successful, was typical for his day. The exercise of virtue and conscience did not prevent Lincoln from being a fierce advocate. He won many cases, of which many were very lucrative.[44] If alive today, Lincoln might be the equivalent of a senior partner at a large, prestigious, corporate law firm.[45] His practice was also thoroughly adapted to the realities of his day. Although the incredibly competitive environment of the current legal profession is often cited as a reason for today's ethical problems, Lincoln's practice was highly competitive as well.[46] He had to compete with a relatively large number of lawyers in his legal market.[47] He often had to take his practice on the road, touring through the circuit in a voracious attempt to solicit clients.[48] His practice mirrored the modern legal practice in that it included trials and tribulations.[49] He was forced to sue nineteen clients who refused to pay him.[50] He agonized over the decision to remain in a safe and comfortable practice or to join a blue-blood partnership in Chicago.[51]

Even though Lincoln's practice may be more typical than one might imagine, he may nonetheless strike many as an odd choice for a modern lawyer's ethical role model. One possible disadvantage to using Lincoln as a figure of inspirational study is that the reality of Lincoln the man is often replaced with the platonic form of Lincoln as a mythical hero. When history is mixed with myth, tall tales, and imagination, it is difficult to discern fact from fiction. Immortal Lincoln, the mythical log cabin president, certainly overshadows mortal Lincoln, the driven, practical, and honorable lawyer. Indeed, this former Lincoln is the object of a fascination so excessive and voracious it is almost inexplicable, despite his many accomplishments. More books have been written about Lincoln than any other figure in human history, except for Shakespeare, Jesus, and the Virgin Mary. He has been the subject of almost 15,000 works.[52]

Judging Lincoln through an Aristotelian perspective results in an interesting conclusion. Aristotle believed that a role model must be someone who can be emulated and understood; they must be real, tangible, or attainable. If Lincoln is to qualify as an Aristotelian role model, he must be rediscovered as a flawed man more ordinary than he is normally depicted. We can most easily find this quality in Lincoln the lawyer. In recent years, there has been a surge of scholarship dedicated to this often overlooked aspect of Lincoln's life. His legal career is now well documented. *The Law Practice of Abraham Lincoln: The Complete Documentary Edition* was published in 2000.[53] This state-of-the-art electronic collection of over 100,000 legal documents was the result of a ten-year project by the Illinois Historic Preservation Agency.[54] David Donald, an important Lincoln biographer, and one of the first to use the materials from the Lincoln Legal Papers project, referred to it as "perhaps the most important archival investigation now under way in the

United States."[55] Prior to this documentation, it was easier to use Lincoln's Honest Abe mantra to promote the profession and enrich his image than it was to see if his twenty-four years offered any real lessons to those interested in how he practiced law. However, it is by examining the everyday issues he faced that we not only can learn about him, but learn from him.

Another objection to using Lincoln as a role model for contemporary lawyers is that, of course, he is not at all contemporary, having lived over 150 years ago, when the American legal system was in its infancy. There is no doubt that the legal profession and the role of lawyers therein has undergone dramatic changes since Lincoln's day. The law has become far more complex and specialized. In the arena of professional standards, the ABA has created four different codes since Lincoln.[56] Specific areas of practice now have their own standards for conduct.[57] Yet despite the many changes in the law, and the many changes in its appurtenant professional standards, little else has changed in regard to legal ethics per se.[58] All of the codes now existing and those in existence since Lincoln express the same basic principles. At least six core duties of attorneys remain unchanged in the professional standards of the legal profession dating back eight hundred years to England: litigation fairness, competence, loyalty, confidentiality, reasonable fees, and public service.[59] When it comes to virtues like honesty and fairness, Lincoln's place in time does not hinder him from providing inspiration. Still, some will argue that the current profession offers different obstacles to ethical behavior than did Lincoln's.[60] This is partly true, but the important fact to consider is that Lincoln's time came with its own obstacles. In the legal profession, obstacles for ethical action abound; otherwise, ethics would not be so heavily discussed and fought for. Because these hindrances are always changing, their specifics are secondary. Far more important is learning, and being motivated, to overcome whatever particular obstacles stand between an individual and an ethical practice.

The fact that Lincoln lived in an age when the American legal landscape was young also provides us with an advantage. In the nineteenth century, legal regulation as we know it did not exist. No national consensus concerning ethical legal conduct existed, and, even if it had, there was no nationally sanctioned body to propose and endorse such a standard. Lawyers, by and large, were left to their own devices. When Lincoln acted ethically, it was on principle, not because he feared censure. Although worried about maintaining his reputation as a moral citizen, he had very little to fear in terms of malpractice suits, compared to today's attorneys, due to the lack of formal standards to be breached. He followed his own moral compass. This self-direction, unhindered by regulatory constraints, allows his ethical personality to come into clearer focus.

Finally, the sheer volume and range of Lincoln's practice allow him to stand out as an ideal legal role model. Lincoln practiced day in and day out for twenty-four years, with periodic sabbaticals to engage in the political realm. In his career, Lincoln practiced with three partners[61] and had a career that was by all accounts financially and professionally successful.[62] His career evolved over the years, and the need to constantly adapt to changes helped mold Lincoln's practical wisdom. At the outset of his career, he represented rural farmers in small cases. A typical case might have involved a cow that damaged a neighbor's crops, or the filing of a suit over a small promissory note.[63] Yet, over the years, Lincoln and his partners came to handle over 400 cases before the state's highest court, 340 cases in the U.S. Circuit and District Courts, and 2,400 cases in the Sangamon County Circuit Court.[64] In 1850, in a county with a large number of lawyers per capita, Lincoln was "involved in 18 percent of all cases brought before the Sangamon County Circuit Court."[65] In 1853, he was involved in 33 percent of all the cases in that county.[66] In addition to the work he did with his three partners, Lincoln personally took on several important cases that involved admiralty,[67] intellectual property,[68] real estate,[69] tax,[70] and political subdivision.[71] He had several cases involving the most powerful economic machine of the nineteenth century, the railroads.[72] In addition, Lincoln "was an attorney of record for four . . . cases before the United States Supreme Court."[73] All told, Lincoln and his partners handled over 5,600 cases.[74]

Lincoln and the Model Rules

Once the mythology has been appropriately addressed, it becomes clear that Abraham Lincoln the lawyer was simply an ordinary man dealing with the same unexceptional problems facing any contemporary attorney. While his trials became front-page news, his tribulations have been shared by his peers not only in the mid-nineteenth century, but in the twenty-first. Lincoln earned his reputation as an astute and ethical attorney by facing these tribulations over the course of many years. Without a code to abide by—voluntary or otherwise—Lincoln showed his legal descendants how honest attorneys should conduct themselves. His ethical fortitude produced within him the same type of aspirational drive that the voluntary, idealistic codes aim to instill within each of today's attorneys. Lincoln, guided only by his own moral compass, charted a course that today's lawyers have trouble finding, despite a cornucopia of codes, regulations, and standards at their fingertips.

When Lincoln was faced with difficult decisions, he relied on his conscience, whereas many of today's lawyers consult the Model Rules when in ethical doubt. But when we compare Lincoln's actions and behavior when mired in morally gray areas with those actions suggested by the Model Rules, a surprising commonality between Lincoln and modern attorneys becomes apparent. Although so much of the legal environment was different in Lincoln's day, the same cannot be said for the definition of ethical conduct. The aspirational principles, implicitly informing the Model Rules, though conspicuously omitted, were consistently evident in Lincoln's actions. Ironically, this astute moral quality did not result from Lincoln's desire to be a paragon of virtue. In fact, Lincoln did not see himself as aspiring beyond the black letter rules at all, for those rules did not exist at the time. He simply did what he thought a good lawyer should do. By linking some of the major Model Rules with documented cases and situations from Lincoln's practice, we can examine how Lincoln's actions would not only have complied with today's rules, but exceeded them. These cases, and their connection to contemporary standards of conduct, illustrated below, are not only instructive but, hopefully, inspiring to today's lawyer.

MODEL RULES 1.1 AND 1.3—COMPETENCE AND DILIGENCE

Two of the most fundamental of the Model Rules are, interestingly, also two of the most succinct. Rule 1.1 (or the "Competence Rule") states: "A lawyer shall provide competent representation to a client. Competent representation requires the legal knowledge, skill, thoroughness and preparation reasonably necessary for the representation."[75] In common parlance, a competent person is adequate, but not exceptional.[76] Several comments to the Competence Rule reinforce this view:

[2] A lawyer *need not necessarily* have special training or prior experience to handle legal problems of a type with which the lawyer

is unfamiliar. . . . A lawyer can provide *adequate* representation in a wholly novel field through necessary study.

. . .

[4] A lawyer may accept representation where the requisite level of competence can be achieved by *reasonable preparation.*

[5] Competent handling of a particular matter includes . . . *adequate* preparation.

[6] To maintain the requisite knowledge and skill a lawyer should keep abreast of changes in the law and its practice, engage in continuing study and education, and comply with all continuing legal education requirements to which the lawyer is subject.[77]

Given this commentary's focus on adequacy, it seems that complying with Rule 1.1 poses little difficulty. To someone unfamiliar with contemporary legal practice, the sixth comment appears to pose the greatest challenge. However, modern legal competence is defined by only the most minimal and easily followed standard; the Competence Rule, in many states, only demands fifteen hours of continuing legal education annually, which may include attending or teaching a course, writing a legal article, or self-study.[78] As any practicing attorney can attest, aspiring *beyond* competence requires much more than fifteen hours per year.

Model Rule 1.3 (or the "Diligence Rule") defines diligence in a similarly succinct fashion: "A lawyer shall act with reasonable diligence and promptness in representing a client."[79] Interestingly, Comment 2 to the Diligence Rule underscores the fact that the Competence and Diligence Rules are inextricably intertwined. The comment reads: "A lawyer's work load must be controlled so that each matter can be handled competently."[80] In other words, a lawyer must be diligent to maintain competence, and vice versa. Though this seems like an easily followed standard, it can pose a challenge to even the most renowned or successful attorneys.[81] Maintaining both diligence and a successful legal practice is a difficult juggling act, but with dedication and focus the balance can be achieved.

Lincoln's twenty-four years as a practicing attorney offer concrete examples of how one can aspire to and exceed the minimum definitions of competence and diligence provided in the Model Rules. As previously discussed, Lincoln achieved several notable professional successes.[82] Lincoln's desire to maintain and develop a thorough legal understanding is best illustrated by a case that, at first glance, seems hardly more than a footnote in his storied biography. Not only did Lincoln not win this case, he did not even argue it. The case was *McCormick v. Manny,* a seminal patent case in the nineteenth century.[83] Yet, by dutifully watching from the sidelines, he embodied a level of devotion to his continued legal education that dwarfs today's mandatory fifteen-hour minimum requirement.

In 1834, Cyrus H. McCormick invented a reaping machine that revolutionized the farming industry.[84] In 1854, McCormick sued John H. Manny for infringement of his patents.[85] This was an extremely important case, given that Manny was only one of several manufacturers who had begun to make reapers similar to McCormick's. Manny enlisted the services of George Harding, one of the most renowned patent lawyers at the time.[86] The case was set for Chicago, and Harding believed that retaining a local lawyer with a good reputation in the Chicago courts was pivotal to their case.[87] Manny and Harding chose Lincoln, with some reservation, to serve this role.[88] At the time of the *McCormick* case, Lincoln, although not attaining the national stature of the other attorneys involved, had established a successful legal practice.[89] Thus, he was excited and eager to be involved in such a prominent case.[90] To prepare himself for the trial, he poured himself into his work, including personal visits to Manny's factories.[91] Lincoln prepared to give the best and most important argument of his career in the *McCormick* case, and, still smarting from his recent defeat in the U.S. senatorial election of 1856, his morale and famous depression needed the boost.[92]

Nonetheless, as the trial date grew nearer, Lincoln's anticipation and excitement succumbed, as was frequently the case with him, to worry and embarrassment. First, Lincoln began to wonder why he had not received copies of any legal papers, as had been previously discussed with Harding's representatives who engaged his legal services as co-counsel.[93] Even more disheartening, the trial had moved from the familiar surroundings of Chicago to Cincinnati, and he learned about this transfer in the newspaper.[94] Disregarding this snub, Lincoln traveled to Cincinnati anyway. Upon his arrival in Cincinnati, Harding and the high-profile Philadelphia attorney Edwin M. Stanton, who had been added to the defense team, bluntly informed him that he would no longer be involved in the litigation at all.[95] In fact, Stanton regarded Lincoln as a country yokel, a "long armed baboon" who had no business being involved in such an important, complex case.[96] Underscoring their disrespect for Lincoln, Manny's defense team not only refrained from using any of Lincoln's pretrial work, they returned his trial briefs to Lincoln unopened. Finally, even though Lincoln was staying at the same hotel as Harding and Stanton, neither of the distinguished attorneys, according to Harding, "ever conferred with him, ever had him at our table, or sat with him, or asked him to our rooms, or walked to and from the court with him."[97] When Supreme Court justice John McLean, who presided over this case, invited counsel on both sides to his house for dinner, Lincoln was not included.[98] In short, Lincoln was harshly and unjustifiably rebuked by nearly everyone involved in *McCormick v. Manny.*

At first glance, *McCormick v. Manny* appears to show very little, if anything, about Lincoln's abilities as a lawyer, nor his ethical qualities. Lincoln never argued, nor did he even participate in, the case.[99] Yet the background details of the trial speak volumes. After suffering professional and personal disgrace, Lincoln made an unlikely decision. Instead of expressing his outrage and storming back to Springfield, he chose to stay for an entire week in Cincinnati and observe the trial.[100] After a week, he admitted that counsel on both sides, including Stanton, were indeed great lawyers. He concluded they were far better than he, and he aimed to learn from them.[101] Amid humiliating circumstances, he concerned himself with improving his lawyering ability and remained in Cincinnati despite the harsh rebuke from his former co-counsel.[102] He further commented that when he did go home, he was going to recommit himself to the study of law, and further his evolution as a lawyer.[103]

In addition to illustrating Lincoln's desire to foster his own knowledge of the law, this example also serves as a manifestation of the method through which Lincoln intended to build his legal knowledge: hard work. Lincoln never considered himself one of the premier legal scholars of his time, but he compensated for that by outworking his peers.[104] He once advised an aspiring lawyer that he should "[a]lways bear in mind that your own resolution to succeed, is more important than any other one thing."[105] "Work, work, work is the main thing," Lincoln counseled another.[106] Diligence, to Lincoln, meant more than following up in situations where, as in *McCormick v. Manny,* he otherwise would have been forgotten. Lincoln believed and showed that through sheer force of determination and will he could be a successful lawyer.

Lincoln's actions in this case demonstrate his humility, an unlikely attribute to be so fundamental to moving beyond competence. As in many high-profile professions, the bar breeds its share of arrogance. Being more than competent, as defined in the Competence Rule, however, is not based in the proper application of an attorney's superior skill and talent, but rather in the attorney's humble recognition of what he lacks. Without humility, he likely will not be driven to improve or study on his craft. Lincoln exemplifies the type of humility that is conspicuously absent from the Model Rules. Lincoln exhibited a raw will to progress, and from this will comes an impressive diligence.

Lincoln's oft-mentioned diligence was not born out of a Protestant work ethic that extols work for its own sake, but out of a passionate desire to advocate well. In fact, the determination and attention to detail required in legal work did not come naturally to Lincoln. He very often grew bored, his attention waned, and he "detested the mechanical work of the office."[107] Yet he forced himself to overcome these obstacles. A diary entry from one of Lincoln's colleagues expressed his steadfastness: "Spent the morning in the law library at work—dined at my boarding house. Lincoln put in many evenings there, coming from home around seven or eight o'clock and working until midnight. Another more important place of refuge when in need of solitude while preparing his more important cases was the office of his friend Governor Bissell, where, concealed in one of the recesses, he would think and write for hours."[108]

An excerpt from one of Lincoln's lectures offers a clear picture of how Lincoln might view the Competence Rule as intertwined with the Diligence Rule:

> I am not an accomplished lawyer. I find quite as much material for a lecture in those points wherein I have failed as in those wherein I have been moderately successful. The leading rule for the lawyer, for the man of every other calling, is *diligence*. Leave nothing for tomorrow, which can be done today. Never let your correspondence fall behind. Whatever pieces of business you have in hand, before stopping, do all the labor pertaining to it, which can *then* be done. When you bring a common lawsuit, if you have the facts for doing so, write the declaration at once. In business not likely to be litigated, make all examinations of titles and note them and even draft orders and decrees in advance. . . . And there is not a more fatal error to young lawyers, than relying too much

on speech making. If any one, upon his rare powers of speaking, shall claim an exemption from the drudgery of the law, his case is a failure in advance.[109]

Here we find Lincoln's simple calculus for moving beyond competence. From the first sentence, Lincoln expresses humility. This humility then spurs one to diligence. Attorneys learn from their mistakes and shortcomings. In this process, will power serves as the driving force, as opposed to raw talent or skill. Finally, Lincoln honestly faces the practical demands involved in moving beyond competence, the "drudgery," which attention to detail sometimes requires. The advice itself is not particularly striking, but therein lies its quality. Moving beyond competence does not require glamour or elegance, daring or esoteric knowledge—attributes often associated with excellence. It requires a quiet, modest mastering of the basics.

MODEL RULE 1.5—FEES

Throughout the history of the legal profession there is probably no greater source of consternation, skepticism, or fodder for pundits than the amounts of fees lawyers charge.[110] Thus, the Fees Rule has been and will be scrutinized and studied unlike many others, as the Fees Rule governs a subject that elicits a visceral reaction from clients and lawyers alike. With concerns similar to their clients, who do not want to be overcharged or treated unfairly by their attorneys, lawyers want to be paid fully and promptly for their services. The Reporter to the Ethics 2000 Commission poignantly observed that the Fees Rule "is likely to be controversial, no matter what we do."[111] "Its terms measure lawyers' conduct in almost every case, clients find unexpectedly high fees a distasteful surprise, and public criticism about excessive fees damage the reputation of all lawyers."[112]

The Fees Rule Defined

Whereas the aforementioned Competence and Diligence rules are two of the most concise Model Rules, Model Rule 1.5: Fees (Fees Rule) is substantially longer.[113] There are several subsections of the Fees Rule, each dealing with important circumstances pertaining to fees and billing methods. The crux of the Fees Rule is found in its detailed definition of reasonableness, which states:

(a) A lawyer shall not make an agreement for, charge, or collect an unreasonable fee or an unreasonable amount for expenses. The factors to be considered in determining the reasonableness of a fee include the following:

(1) the time and labor required, the novelty and difficulty of the questions involved, and the skill requisite to perform the legal service properly;

(2) the likelihood, if apparent to the client, that the acceptance of the particular employment will preclude other employment of the lawyer;

(3) the fee customarily charged in the locality for similar legal services;

(4) the amount involved and the results obtained;

(5) the time limitations imposed by the client or by the circumstances;

(6) the nature and length of the professional relationship with the client;

(7) the experience, reputation, and ability of the lawyer or lawyers performing the services;

(8) whether the fee is fixed or contingent.[114]

In addition to the detail devoted to the definition of reasonableness, the importance of the Fees Rule is further emphasized by the disproportionate level of treatment given to the Fees Rule by the comments, treatises, and commentaries when compared to the coverage given to the previously discussed Competence and Diligence rules.[115] For example, the Fees Rule has six times as many subsections as the Competence and Diligence rules have *sentences* combined.[116] Similarly, the treatment afforded to the Fees Rule provides an overwhelming amount of detail. Whereas the *Lawyer's Deskbook on Professional Responsibility* discusses the Competence and Diligence rules in eight pages each, the same treatise uses seventy-one pages to discuss and comment on the Fees Rule.[117] Despite this attempt to clarify and delineate the standard for a reasonable fee, Comment 1 to the rule addresses lawyers' need for certainty and informs them that there is none to be found: "The factors specified in (1) through (8) are not exclusive. Nor will each factor be relevant in each instance."[118] Clearly, the Fees Rule and its comments are written to ensure that a lawyer's fees are "reasonable under the circumstances."[119] Yet, the Fees Rule represents an inexact formula, with many elements used to determine a reasonable fee.

The above discussion focuses on the Fees Rule's subject matter; however, it may be more important to discuss the justifications behind it. Analysis of the Fees Rule leads one to wonder why such an exhaustive treatment of the amounts and methods by which lawyers can charge a client is needed. Is the ABA, comprised wholly of attorneys, seeking to protect itself? Or, on the other hand, did the drafters of the Fees Rule craft a subjective standard so that clients could be protected against unscrupulous lawyers? The answer is unclear. One could argue that the detailed scheme embodied in the Fees Rule protects the profession by giving attorneys a plethora of ways to justify their fees as being reasonable. Alternatively, the complex, enumerated structure of Model Rule 1.5(a) could be seen as a method to prevent unscrupulous lawyers from taking advantage of their clients by specifically listing several factors that should be considered when charging a fee. The bottom line is that the ABA would be as likely to take up arms against clients on behalf of attorneys as it would be likely to create a myriad of problems for its own constituents simply to simplify matters for their clients. Understandably, saddled with conflicting goals, the ABA's attempt to find a middle ground between protecting both its members and the public-at-large resulted in a continuation of the understandable, longstanding tension between attorneys and their clients over fees.

As the likely result of the competing interests behind the creation of the Fees Rule, the drafters of the Model Rules declined to favor either their constituents or their clients, and, instead, drafted a subjective, flexible standard based on the idea of reasonable fees. Yet, little has been settled since the Fees Rule was drafted. The tension between clients and lawyers over the amount of a "reasonable" fee still drives most discussions about legal fees.[120] Of course, the ABA and its members—whether they be solo practitioners, members of a law firm, or card-carrying members of the professionalism movement who are working to fill the aspirational void in lawyers' ethical conduct—rightfully insist on being paid fairly for their services. However, reaping the benefits of their work is not always an easy task for attorneys. The quality, difficulty, and novelty of legal work are difficult to evaluate, and, when coupled with a consumer base that has become aggressive in dealing with the legal profession, justifying legal fees to clients is always an unpleasant chore.

Thus, in light of the difficulty in justifying and collecting legal fees, a flexible standard, subject to multiple interpretations concerning the definition of a reasonable fee, seems to simply make life more difficult for attorneys and clients alike. An objective standard for determining legal fees—one which states that a divorce costs X and that a will costs Y—would appear to solve these problems; however, upon reflection and analysis the Fees Rule's definition of reasonableness is subjective for good reason.[121] An objective, inflexible standard can be used by lawyers or their clients to take advantage of the other. For example, if a will simply costs $1,000, an attorney could fleece his or her client by charging the reasonable $1,000 fee for a will that required merely thirty minutes of the lawyer's attention. Alternatively, a client could use the rule to their advantage by only paying $1,000 for a massive, complex will that took their lawyer four days to draft.

Whether or not a subjective standard is ideal, one fact shines through: a reasonable fee and a fair fee are not always synonymous. Any standard for determining the proper amount to charge for legal services must take this reality into account. Looking beyond the Fees Rule is often necessary because the black letter law alone only prohibits lawyers from charging and collecting an unreasonable fee, as the Fees Rule attempts to define reasonableness, and thus implies that a firm and its lawyers can charge *any* fee as long as the fee is below the unreasonable fee threshold. This hardly seems to fit in the spirit of the Model Rules, or at the least, would require those who want to aspire to move beyond mere compliance to reexamine how they charge clients for services. Such an analysis proves difficult for a variety of reasons and requires practical wisdom and a keen sense of fairness.

Lincoln and the Fees Rule

Fees represent the life blood of today's law firm, but it must be understood that fee collection was just as critical in Lincoln's time as it is now.[122] Yet, Lincoln often regarded legal fees in a different way than both his contemporaries and today's lawyers.[123] Lincoln charged what he believed to be fair fees to his clients, which, with respect to the issue of fee charging and collection, granted him a level of confidence that many other lawyers did not enjoy. He believed his fees were fair, without the aid of arbitrary or rigid standards. Therefore, he tended to be equally resolute when seeking to recover delinquent fees from his clients.[124] Because he felt his fees were inherently fair, he felt comfortable asking his clients for the fees he rightfully earned. He was willing to sue his clients to recoup these fees and suffer the consequences of doing so, including losing some of his clients.[125] To Lincoln, determining the correct amount of legal fees to charge in a particular case involved careful, critical analysis about his own legal work on a particular matter. This honest introspection, if systematically practiced by lawyers and applied in their firms, would promote a new level of openness between lawyers and their clients and greatly decrease the strife that necessarily follows the discussion of legal fees. Lincoln's decisions over the proper amount of fees to charge his clients involved a calculus beyond merely aligning his fees with those charged by his contemporaries for similar services. As was typical with Lincoln, his words *and actions* over the course of his career illustrated his uncanny understanding of the difference between a reasonable fee—the types of fees that the Model Rules dictate should be charged to clients—and a fair fee. Importantly, he also knew that fair fees are good for business.[126] Clearly, no one needs a legal consultant to know that a satisfied client is more likely to be a repeat client than one who feels taken advantage of.

As fees are important to all lawyers, including Lincoln, it is understandable that the subject of fees is a frequently discussed topic in biographies and analyses pertaining to Lincoln's legal career. Fees, to Lincoln, were more than grease used to keep his legal practice running; he viewed his fees as a barometer of his own value in the legal community.[127] This perspective caused one historian to proclaim that "[o]ne way to understand Lincoln's work as a lawyer is through his fees."[128] Lincoln identified the corrupting nature of fees and was not shy in warning that "an exorbitant fee should never be claimed."[129] Of course, a fee can be both exorbitant *and* reasonable under the current Fees Rule, but Lincoln's actions show that he completely disregarded that type of analysis.[130] To Lincoln, exorbitant yet reasonable fees were not always fair, and to Lincoln fairness always prevailed.

This section presents several concrete examples of Lincoln's approach to fees and fee collection, but first it is important to address several objections to using Lincoln's approach to fees to help guide today's lawyers. One objection is that the mechanics of billing, charging, and collecting fees are vastly different from methods used in Lincoln's time.[131] One notable example, mentioned above, is that Lincoln took notes for services when accepting an engagement. Of course, the fee note is now ancient history.[132] But the purpose for using Lincoln as a guide lies in his attitude and sensibility toward fees, not on his actual method for charging and collecting fees, which are obviously different from those used now.[133]

A justification for dismissing Lincoln's advice and admonitions about not overcharging the client is that Lincoln and his contemporaries were not engaged in constant and expensive attempts to lure clients and new attorneys into their fold. Lincoln did not have to pay $160,000 for a first-year associate with no experience. He also did not have to pay exorbitant rent in San Francisco or Chicago or purchase a skybox so his clients could eat sushi and drink Chardonnay while watching their favorite NFL team. Although contemporary firms must pay more for rent and associates, it does not follow that they are under more financial stress than the lawyers of Lincoln's day. Indeed, the contemporary law firm often possesses a degree of luxury and profit that lawyers in Lincoln's era could not have imagined. One cannot discuss Lincoln's life as a lawyer without understanding the economic pressures and realities of living in the mid-1800s: "Lincoln's legal practice was not confined to Sangamon County. No lawyer could make his living from the two terms that the circuit court met in Springfield each year, and Lincoln, like most of the other attorneys, traveled on the huge circuit that the judges were obligated to make going from one country seat to another and holding sessions that lasted from two days to a week."[134] Donald's analysis of Lincoln's travails sheds some light on the wholly different environment in which Lincoln operated. Imagine reviewing a document on horseback or in a carriage; then remember that Lincoln's frequent travels took much, much longer than today's relatively short jaunts to and from a distant county.[135] These realities of practicing law in Lincoln's era pervade every aspect of his life, marriage, and political and legal career and can hardly be discounted.

Another objection against fully accepting Lincoln's advice as pertinent in today's society is that today's legal environment is more competitive than at any other time. However, a close examination of Lincoln and his contemporaries reveals a very competitive legal environment with more than enough lawyers to service the area in which he practiced.[136] Accordingly, Lincoln's legal environment involved fierce competition for clients, and legal fees were small, even by historical standards.[137] Even if one adjusts Lincoln's fees to reflect their present-day value, the fees Lincoln charged for drafting a client's lease or for an argument before the Illinois Supreme Court were notably smaller than the present value of similar fees charged by today's attorneys.[138] For a majority of the cases Lincoln handled in his early career, the fee was $5.00,[139] and often the range was from $2.50 to $10.00.[140] Later in his career, with Herndon as his partner, a typical fee for representing a client in the circuit court ranged from $10 to $25.[141] In one case he collected a debt of $600; his fee was a meager $3.50—or 0.05 percent of the debt he collected.[142] Fee collection is difficult for today's lawyer, but it is important to note that the fees charged by Lincoln and his contemporaries represented a much smaller percentage of the value underlying the charge compared to today's lawyers' fees.[143]

Once these arguments against taking Lincoln's advice seriously are dismissed, one must look to his message. Lincoln made a career of letting his actions speak for him, but from time to time he chose to speak directly in order to get his message across. In one instance, Lincoln spoke on the impropriety of and corrosive effect of taking advance payment in a matter. In a lecture to students given in 1850, he admonished that "as a general rule, [you should] never take your whole fee in advance, nor any more than a small retainer."[144] Understanding the nature of men, Lincoln lectured that "when fully paid beforehand, you are more than a common mortal if you can feel the same interest in the case, as if something was still in prospect for you, as well as for your client. And when you lack interest in the case, the job will very likely lack skill and diligence in the performance."[145] This is an honest examination of the motivations behind lawyering in his era, and these forces are still at play in today's community as well. With respect to fees, Lincoln proved himself to be astutely prescient, rational, and practical, and he maintained this mind-set while practicing law in a harsh, competitive environment, void of any regulations to guide his hand.

Lesson Learned: Differentiating between Reasonable and Fair Fees
As was the case with the Diligence and Competence rules, Lincoln's actions and motivations with respect to fees embodied the type of introspective ethical thought process necessary to filling the aspirational void at the root of today's ethical crisis. Over a century and a half before the Fees Rule's inception, Lincoln's actions in relation to his fees traced and exceeded its standards. He made sure his clients' fees were fair—not merely reasonable under the circumstances—even if his clients could afford larger fees. Fairness was always paramount for Lincoln. Such a shining example is found in one of Lincoln's cases from 1856.[146] After practicing law for nearly twenty years, and only four years from being president of the United States, he was being

heralded as an attorney "at the head of his profession" in Illinois.[147] Lincoln was called upon to draft a lease for a client in Quincy, Illinois. Following the conclusion of this matter, the client, satisfied with Lincoln's work on the lease, sent him a check for $25.00.[148] Lincoln kept $15.00 and returned $10.00 with a note that said: "You must think I am a high price man. You are too liberal with your money."[149]

Another example is evident from Lincoln's treatment of the fee he received following the *McCormick v. Manny* fiasco discussed in the prior section.[150] As discussed, Lincoln was originally retained by a very tony and prominent Eastern law firm. Upon being retained, Lincoln received a $400 retainer and arranged a fee of $1,000.[151] After returning from his humbling experience in Cincinnati, where his services were neither needed nor wanted, Lincoln received the balance of his fee. He sent the fee back to his co-counsel, reminding them that his services had not been used and that he had provided no services of value and, accordingly, did not feel he had earned anything beyond the original payment.[152] Several days later the check was sent back to Lincoln with a note that the lawyers and their client felt he was still entitled to the large balance. The ever-practical Lincoln cashed the check.[153]

As Lincoln's career evolved, his clients became more sophisticated and capable of paying a healthy fee.[154] One of the best examples of his increasingly sophisticated and financially capable clientele—as well as of Lincoln's pristine ethical compass in the realm of fees—is evident in the *Illinois Central Railroad* case. The railroad industry represented one of the most powerful economic and political influences of the second half of the nineteenth century. Lincoln hungered for the challenges inherent in involvement in railroad work, whether he represented the railroad or its opponents.[155] Lincoln offered his services to each of the parties, and the railroad accepted, subject to a $250 retainer.[156]

Unlike in the landmark *Manny* case, Lincoln not only argued the case but received the top billing for this important decision. He was very excited to be involved, but the joy was fleeting. This landmark case, argued successfully by Lincoln, produced the largest legal fee of his career.[157] However, collecting the fee proved to be as arduous as the case itself. Lincoln's client stood victorious after a historic decision; yet, while pleased with the result of the case, the Illinois Central Railroad felt that Lincoln's proposed fee far exceeded the value of his services.[158] Lincoln's client refused his fee of $2,000, even though his victory had saved the railroad hundreds of thousands of dollars.[159] Whether one abided by the circumstances in 1856 or the calculus of the Fees Rule, Lincoln was entitled to a generous fee for his services. When Lincoln presented his client with a bill of $2,000, it was flatly rejected. One company official remarked, "[T]his is as much as Daniel Webster himself would have charged. . . . We cannot allow such a claim."[160] A disheartened Lincoln surveyed the market. He consulted with six other notable Illinois attorneys and submitted a revised bill for $5,000—250 percent of his original fee request.[161] Despite reaping the rewards of future tax savings, the railroad company was a new venture and argued that they lacked the cash flow to pay the bill. On that basis, the railroad again refused to pay. Lincoln sued and the court returned a verdict for the full amount of $5,000, less the retainer of $250.[162]

A couple of lessons can be learned from Lincoln's actions following the Illinois Central Railroad collection suit. In this case, Lincoln's inherent sense of fairness worked to his advantage. He was comfortable that he had presented a fair fee to his clients; in fact, Lincoln's original fee was beyond fair, it was generous. That sense of being fair with his client from the onset of the attorney-client relationship gave him the fortitude to stand his ground in the face of accusations of overcharging his client and even allowed Lincoln to reevaluate his position in order to secure an even larger fee.[163] Lincoln's sense of what is right did not hurt his reputation with his client or the powerful railroad industry. Shortly after Lincoln collected his fee he was retained to handle two important cases involving what taxes were to be paid by the Illinois Central Railroad to the state. Furthermore, reputedly, Lincoln was offered the position of general counsel to the New York Central Railroad in February 1860, on the occasion of his Cooper Union speech, for an annual retainer of $10,000.[164]

Lincoln believed that clients should be treated not just reasonably, but fairly. Further, he believed that fees were an essential extension of an attorney's desire to be fair.[165] Lincoln pursued his fees openly and aggressively for one main reason: he could fearlessly stand before a court and show that his fees accurately represented the value of his legal services. This represents a wholly different sentiment when compared to today's law firms, who are reluctant to expose their records to a court, even if this means forgoing certain fees.

Practicing law, whether in 1856 or 2009, requires a strong work ethic. Lincoln, like many of his predecessors, contemporaries, and successors, worked diligently for his clients. He demanded to be treated fairly in return. Whether it represented his business-oriented philosophy or resulted from his psychological background, Lincoln wanted his clients to compensate him for services performed, fully and promptly. In fact, Lincoln and his partners sued at least nineteen clients for delinquent fees throughout Lincoln's career.[166]

Similar lawsuits are very unusual today. On its face, the reason appears simple. Clients, once they have been sued by their former counsel, will often countersue, claiming malpractice or other claims. The firm's malpractice carrier or general counsel often will then tell the firm that it should not pursue the matter any further. In complete opposition to actions taken by Lincoln, firms often forgo their rightfully earned fees. However, there may be a darker reason that firms often choose not to pursue delinquent fees via litigation. Law firms may be hesitant to sue their clients for their fees because of the fear that, during the ensuing litigation, the court will ask the law firm to produce its billing records and other similar memoranda documenting the work performed on behalf of the client. As discussed throughout this chapter, Lincoln would *encourage* the court to look at his records and examine his efforts, which would likely show that Lincoln's fee was fair. Yet typically, today's law firms appear reluctant to share Lincoln's sentiment. This reluctance to allow the court and former client to examine its records is likely not due to the fear that some small administrative errors will be unearthed. Quite the contrary, firms appear terrified to reveal—or learn for the first time—that their records might be replete with either negligence or, far worse, systematic billing inconsistencies.

This is the conundrum facing today's firms, and it is a headache that Lincoln rarely suffered. Of course, these problems exist even for those who carefully adhere to the Fees Rule because certain clients do not hesitate to slow-pay or negotiate a reduced fee under any number of circumstances, including those where the client simply does not want to pay for services that were timely and properly performed. And, while it is true that lawyers today do not pursue their clients with the same zeal as they did in Lincoln's time, getting paid promptly and fully is a constant source of frustration and expense for many lawyers and law firms, especially for those firms that have clean hands, who are diligent in their billing practices, and whose fees accurately represent the value of their legal services.

While Lincoln practiced close to 150 years ago, one last act by Lincoln shows how well he understood the timeless concepts of equity and fairness with respect to fees. In a speech given in 1853 Lincoln stated: "Are, or are not the amount of labor, the doubtfulness and difficulty of the question, the degree of success in the result; and the amount of pecuniary interest involved, not merely in the particular case, but covered by the principle decided, and thereby secured, to the client, all proper elements, by the custom of the profession to consider in determining what is a reasonable fee in a given case?"[167] Here, Lincoln provides a roadmap to determine when a fee is appropriate in a given case, but, most importantly, the factors Lincoln identifies correspond with those factors identified in the Fees Rule:

Lincoln in 1853	*Model Rule 1.5*
The amount of labor involved	- 1.5(a)(1)—"the time and labor involved"
The doubtfulness of the question	-1.5(a)(1)—"the skill requisite to perform the legal service properly"
The difficulty of the question	- 1.5(a)(1)—"the novelty and difficulty of the questions involved"
The amount of pecuniary interest involved[168]	- 1.5(a)(3)—"the amount and the results obtained"[169]

Lincoln consistently embodied and espoused a set of ethical standards that, if described and written concisely, would likely mirror the Fees Rule in place today, and even aspire beyond it. In a microcosm, the examples presented earlier in this section highlight the differences between today's Fees Rule—touting reasonableness, defined as that which one can get away with, and the aspirational standard embodied by Lincoln, which emphasizes fairness. Lincoln walked the walk in the ethical realm and did so at a time when there was no professionalism movement, no Lawyer Creeds displayed prominently in the lawyer's office, and no black letter requirements that defined the minimal standards for reasonableness. Lincoln returned the portion of a fee that he deemed to be excessive, despite the fact that his client believed the fee to be reasonable. Embodying the essential principles of the professionalism movement, Lincoln held himself to a higher standard than that imposed upon him by his clients. Even though his clients could tolerate paying the full fee, Lincoln, if his work did not warrant such a fee, would attempt to return it. Compare this to his actions in the Illinois Central Railroad case, where Lincoln's sense of fairness drove him to ask for more, not less, compensation following a landmark and lucrative court victory. Whether his motives were to foster a continued relationship with the client or whether he was purely driven by his internal ethical compass is unknown. The critical point is that Lincoln looked not at what he *could* do; he did what he thought he *should* do. That, in a nutshell, is the difference between a fair fee and a fee that is not unreasonable. It is also the difference between the minimum standard set by the Fees Rule and aspiring beyond the rule.

Conclusion

The goal of this chapter has not been to persuade lawyers to model their behavior after Lincoln, or to ask themselves, when faced with an ethical dilemma, what Lincoln would do. The first problem with asking what Lincoln would do in a contemporary legal situation is that, quite simply, we do not know what he would do. We only know what he did. The second problem with asking this question is that Lincoln's practice should not be made into a kind of personified aspirational code of ethics. Codes and creeds, even if modeled after the decisions and actions of a particular person, betray the spirit of Aristotle permeating this article. Aristotle does not argue that we should learn from the decisions of ethical role models so that we can codify those decisions into some kind of guidebook or manual. He believed we should learn from ethical role models so that we can eventually make ethical decisions for ourselves, following our own judgment.

The ultimate purpose of looking to Lincoln is that he can remind us of self-evident truths nevertheless forgotten or ignored—the legal profession is made up of individuals, each one of them possessing deep responsibility, agency, and the ability for self-determination. Lawyers make decisions. They advise and provide counsel. Yet very often there is no single, obvious direction to take. At times there is not even a map. Lincoln calls to mind the presence of this forgotten possibility, and thus overlooked responsibility, because in his day the lack of a map was obvious. There was no national code of conduct, no national bar, virtually no regulations for lawyers of any kind.

In our day, regulations of conduct are ubiquitous, in both their mandatory and voluntary forms. The sheer volume of these regulations, and the obsession often given to them in legal and scholastic debates, obscures the simple fact that lawyers must often regulate themselves. The reason some lawyers act unethically, while still staying within the bounds of the minimum standards of conduct, may have little to do with bad intentions. Their behavior represents an attempt to avoid agency altogether, be it moral or immoral. By simply consulting the black letter guidelines of the Model Rule whenever an ethical dilemma arises, they avoid struggling with the dilemma at all. They fail to see it through the lens of their own judgment. They fail to approach it with a sense of their own agency. Behind this failure is an assumption that their profession allows them an ethically neutral innocence, a naive, childlike role in which all they need to do is dutifully serve their client without breaking the law.

In this chapter, we have examined Lincoln not so lawyers can be inspired to mimic him or in some way continue his legacy. In shedding light on the kind of lawyer Lincoln was, we can reflect on what kind of lawyers we are and imagine what kind of lawyers we want to be. Most importantly, we can discover that moving from the one to the other is always within our power.

Notes

1. Stephen Gillers, "Twenty Years of Legal Ethics: Past, Present, and Future," 20 *Geo. J. Legal Ethics* 321, 324 (2007).

2. Robert F. Dirnan, "Introduction to the Georgetown Journal of Legal Ethics," 1 *Geo. J. Legal Ethics,* 1, 1–2 (1987).

3. See Mary C. Daly, "Researching Professional Responsibility Issues," 180 *PLI/NY* 155, 119 (2008).

4. *Law. Manual on Prof'l Conduct* (ABA/BNA Supp. 2009).

5. Geoffrey C. Hazard Jr., W. William Hodes, and Peter R. Jarvis, *The Law of Lawyering* (3rd ed. Supp., Aspen Publishers, 2009).

6. Ronald D. Rotunda and John S. Dzienkowski, *Legal Ethics: The Lawyer's Deskbook on Prf'l Responsibility* (Thomson/West, 2008).

7. Thomas D. Morgan, *Lawyer Law: Comparing the ABA Model Rules of Professional Conduct with the ALI Restatement (Third) of the Law Governing Lawyers* (Center for Professional Responsibility, ABA, 2005).

8. See generally David Sweet, "Sacrifice, Atonement, and Legal Ethics," 113 *Yale L.J.* 219 (2003).

9. See generally Chenise Kanemoto, "Bushido in the Courtroom: A Case for Virtue-Oriented Lawyering," 57 *S.C. L. Rev.* 357 (2005).

10. See generally, ". . . In the Spirit of Public Service: A Blueprint for the Rekindling of Lawyer Professionalism," 112 *F. R. D.* 243 (1986).

11. See Nathan M. Crystal, "The Incompleteness of the Model Rules and the Development of Professional Standards," 52 *Mercer L. Rev.* 839 (2001). See generally "ABA Lawyer's Creed of Professionalism" (1988), in *Professional Responsibility Standards, Rules and Statutes,* 497–99 (John S. Dzienkowski, ed., West, 2007–2008 ed.).

12. "ABA Lawyer's Creed of Professionalism" (1988), supra note 11, §§ C.1, D.1, at 499.

13. Ibid. at 497–98.

14. M.W. Rowe, *Philosophy and Literature: A Book of Essays* 108 (Ashgate, 2004).

15. A. Le Roy Johnson, "An Introductory Study of Habit," in 55 *The Dental Cosmos: A Monthly Record of Dental Science* 603–6 (Edward C. Kirk, ed., S. S. White Dental Manufacturing Company, 1913).

16. James P. Sickinger, *Public Records and Archives in Classical Athens* 12 (Univ. of North Carolina Press, 1999).

17. David Carr, 2 *Moral Education: A Handbook* 353 (F. Clark Power et al., eds., Praeger, 2008).

18. Ibid.

19. Ibid. at 353–54.

20. Dennis P. Wittmer, "Ethical Decision-Making," in *Handbook of Administrative Ethics* 482 (2nd ed., Terry L. Cooper, ed., CRC Press, 2001).

21. See, e.g., Model Penal Code § 210.6 (2001) (stating that a defendant found guilty of murder shall receive a sentence for a felony in the first degree or the death penalty if a judge or jury determines it is appropriate).

22. Terence, *Heautontimorumenos* 50 (London, Oxford Co., 1777).

23. Compare "ABA Lawyer's Creed of Professionalism," *supra* note 11, at 497–99 (stating that a lawyer will do these things prescribed), with *Model Rules of Prof'l Conduct,* Rule 1.1, cmt. 6 (American Bar Association, 2008) (stating that a lawyer should not do the things proscribed).

24. See Aristotle, *The Nicomachean Ethics* 1.3[1094b30-1095] at 3, 1.4[1095b2-85] at 5, 10.9[1179b24-26] at 270 (David Ross, trans., Oxford Univ. Press, 1975) (1925) [hereafter cited as *NE*].

25. See Amélie Oksenberg Rorty, *Mind in Action: Essays in the Philosophy of Mind* 272–73 (Amélie Oksenberg Rorty, ed., Beacon Press, 1988); accord *NE, supra* note 24, 6.2 [2 1139b5-6] at 139.

26. Ibid.

27. See generally Ian Johnston, "Lecture on Aristotle's Nicomachean Ethics" (November 18, 1997), available at http://records.viu.ca/~johnstoi/introser/aristot.htm (accessed January 21, 2008).

28. Abraham Lincoln, First Inaugural Address (March 4, 1861), available at http://showcase.netins.net/web/creative/lincoln/speeches/1inaug.htm (accessed January 21, 2009).

29. Matthew 10:16 (New International Version).

30. Reinhold Niebuhr and Robin W. Lovin, 2 *The Nature and Destiny of Man* 302 (New York: Charles Scribner's Sons, 1941).

31. Theodore C. Sorensen, *Decision-Making in the White House: The Olive Branch or the Arrows,* xxix (Columbia Univ. Press, 2005).

32. Philip E. Tetlock, "Is It a Bad Idea to Study Good Judgment," *Political Psychology* 13 (1992).

33. Deborah L. Rhode, "Ethics in Practice" 1 (Stanford Public Law and Legal Theory Working Paper Series, Working Paper No. 2, 1999).

34. See Johnston, *supra* note 27. As Johnston explains, Aristotle writes in *Nicomachean Ethics*: "'[A] mean [is] defined by a rational principle, such as a man of practical wisdom would use to determine it.' This seems to be saying that our benchmark for understanding the mean should be a role model, a man of practical wisdom, someone recognized for his moral quality. As we shall see, this is an important principle (that our moral understanding must use role models), but at this stage it still leaves open what a person has to do to display practical wisdom. We might note, in passing, what Aristotle does not do here: he does not offer any sense that there is a theoretical route to understanding the doctrine of the mean. Whatever we are to make of this central tenet of his moral teaching, it is something practical, something acquired in the world of experience and daily living. It is not something we can pick up by private study."

35. See Brian R. Dirck, *Lincoln the Lawyer* 159–60 (Univ. of Illinois Press, 2007).

36. Ibid.

37. Ibid. at 160.

38. William Lee Miller, *Lincoln's Virtues: An Ethical Biography* 434 (Knopf, 2002).

39. Ibid. at 442–56.

40. See, for example, ibid. at 442–56 (detailing Lincoln's refusal to compromise in regard to the union) and 434 (outlining Lincoln's refusal to compromise on the extension of slavery).

41. Ibid. at 77–79 (providing an interesting example of Lincoln's stoicism). When Lincoln was a young man, he fell in love with the beautiful Matilda Ed-

wards. Lincoln had mentioned to confidants that he did not love Mary Todd, but nonetheless agonized over who to marry because he had previously promised Mary that he would marry her; and, regardless of the consequences, and despite his feelings, Lincoln wanted to keep his word. Ibid.

42. Ibid. at 76–77. (Lincoln's friend and partner, David Davis, commented that "Lincoln had a terribly strong passion for women, could hardly keep his hands off of them. And yet he had honor and a strong will, and these enabled him to put out the fires of his terrible passions. . . .")

43. Bishop Anthony Fisher, Auxiliary Bishop of Sydney, Australia, "Red Mass Homily: Can Lawyers Be Saints?," http://www.ad2000.com.au/ articles/2004/mar2004p3_1553.html (accessed January 21, 2009) (citing historical examples of lawyers who were canonized saints. "The early Church . . . knew many lawyer-saints. Cyprian, Ambrose, Jerome, Benedict, Thomas A. Becket and many others were all lawyers before they became clerics, monks, preachers and saints. Many more recent saints had a legal background, for example, Thomas More, Charles Borromeo, Peter Canisius, Francis de Sales, Alphonsus Ligouri and [Blessed] Frederick Ozanam. . . . All in all—and here's the surprising thing given the image in the popular culture—lawyers seem to be the most represented profession amongst the ranks of canonized saints after the professionally religious.").

44. See, for example, Mark E. Steiner, *An Honest Calling: The Law Practice of Abraham Lincoln* 72 (Northern Illinois Univ. Press, 2006) (noting that in one large case, Lincoln retained $5,000, a very considerable sum in those days).

45. Ibid. at 72. (Lincoln was, after all, involved in many cases of the railroads, the largest corporations of the time.)

46. See ibid. at 73.

47. Ibid. ("[A]n 1849 article in the Western Law Journal observed that 'the profession of the bar has a large number of members in proportion to the business, and that they are constantly increasing.' . . . A Virginia lawyer in 1853 echoed this complaint. Richard Hawes believed 'there is a super abundance of Lawyers, but a dearth of clients.'")

48. See Dirck, *supra* note 35, at 43–53.

49. See Steiner, *supra* note 44, at 161 (discussing Lincoln's discontent with the new, fast-paced style of lawyering demanded by corporate clients); see also Dirck, *supra* note 35, at 39 (describing Lincoln's battle with boredom); John J. Duff, *A. Lincoln, Prairie Lawyer* 325–32 (Rinehart, 1960) (describing one case where Edwin M. Stanton, a famous lawyer serving as Lincoln's co-counsel, became enraged when he found out that Lincoln had been retained to make the closing argument. Stanton insulted Lincoln, whom he considered to be a nobody, calling him a "long armed baboon." He also claimed "if that giraffe

appears in the case, I will throw up my brief and leave." Lincoln was told his services were no longer required).

50. See Steiner, *supra* note 44, at 71.

51. See ibid. at 167.

52. A worldwide catalogue search in 2002 found 14,985 books on Lincoln, making him the fourth-most popular subject of authors in world history after Jesus, Shakespeare, and the Virgin Mary. See Gerald J. Prokopowicz, *Did Lincoln Own Slaves?* (Pantheon, 2008).

53. *The Law Practice of Lincoln: The Complete Documentary Edition,* DVD-ROM (Martha L. Benner and Cullom Davis, eds., Univ. of Illinois Press, 2000).

54. Steiner, *supra* note 44, at 17.

55. Ibid.

56. Carol Rice Andrews, "Standards of Conduct for Lawyers: An 800-Year Revolution" 57 *SMU L. Rev.* 1385.

57. See ibid. at 1452–1453 (addressing the separate codes and standards applicable to entire legal practices or to the minutiae of a single lawyer's particular practice).

58. Ibid. at 1.

59. Ibid.

60. See generally Ethan S. Burger and Carol M. Langford, "The Future of Legal Ethics: Some Potential Effects of the Globalization and Technological Change on Law Practice Management in the Twenty-First Century," 15 *Widener L. J.* 267, 279–81 (2006) (suggesting solutions from decreasing billable hour requirements for lawyers so that more emphasis can be placed on ethics to integrating ethics into the substantive subjects being taught in law schools, instead of segregating ethics to a two-hour stand-alone course).

61. 1 Abraham Lincoln, *The Papers of Abraham Lincoln: Legal Documents and Cases* xxxiv–xxxvi (Daniel W. Stowell, ed., Univ. of Virginia Press, 2008).

62. Duff, *supra* note 49, at 228 (noting that at the end of Lincoln's law career, he was worth $15,000, a large sum at the time).

63. Dirck, *supra* note 35, at 59–60 (identifying Lincoln as primarily specializing as a "debt collection attorney." In his first year as a lawyer, 1837, sixty-five of Lincoln's ninety-one cases were debt collections. Five years later, 175 of 219 cases, nearly 80 percent, involved debt collection).

64. 1 Lincoln, *supra* note 61, at xxxvi.

65. David Herbert Donald, *Lincoln* 145 (Simon and Schuster, 1995).

66. Ibid.

67. See Steiner, *supra* note 44, at 8.

68. Dirck, *supra* note 35, at 87–91.

69. 1 Lincoln, *supra* note 61, at xxxiv.

70. Donald, *supra* note 65, at 154.

71. Dirck, *supra* note 35, at 148.

72. Ibid. at 91–92.

73. 1 Lincoln, *supra* note 61, at xxxix.

74. Steiner, *supra* note 44, at 71; accord 4 Lincoln, *supra* note 61, at 232.

75. *Model Rules of Prof'l Conduct,* Rule 1.1 (2008).

76. *Merriam-Webster's Collegiate Dictionary* 234–35 (10th ed., 1993).

77. *Model Rules of Prof'l Conduct,* Rule 1.1 (2008) (emphasis added).

78. American Bar Association, "ABA Model Rule for Continuing Legal Education with Comments," § 2, http://www.abanet.org/cle/ammodel.html (accessed January 21, 2009).

79. *Model Rules of Prof'l Conduct,* Rule 1.3 (2008).

80. Ibid., Rule 1.3, cmt. 2.

81. Charles B. Strozier, *Lincoln's Quest for Union* 141–42 (Basic Books, 1982) (noting that Lincoln "had no bookkeeping system to speak of, except his hat," and that after buying a new hat and thereby misplacing a client's letter, he apologized: "[W]hen I received the letter I put it in my old hat, and buying a new one the next day, the old one was set aside, and so, the letter lost sight of for a time." [internal quotations and citations omitted]).

82. See 1 Albert J. Beveridge, *Abraham Lincoln: 1809–1858,* at 584–605 (Scholarly Press, 1971) (describing two of Lincoln's well known, successful trials: the Illinois Central Railroad case and the *Effie Afton* case).

83. Ibid. at 575.

84. Ibid.

85. Duff, *supra* note 49, at 323–23.

86. 1 Beveridge, *supra* note 82, at 576.

87. See ibid. at 577; Donald, *supra* note 65, 186–86.

88. Ibid. at 577–78. See also Donald, *supra* note 65, at 185–86 (noting that Lincoln was not the first choice as the Chicago attorney, though Harding likely did not worry himself with Lincoln's engagement in this case, considering that he noted "in his superior Eastern way 'we were not likely to find a lawyer there who would be of real assistance in arguing such a case'").

89. Duff, *supra* note 49, at 297, 315 (describing the high repute in which Lincoln was held by Illinois judges and his latest victory in the McLean County tax case).

90. 1 Beveridge, *supra* note 82, at 578.

91. Duff, *supra* note 49, at 323; see also Donald, *supra* note 65, at 186.

92. Donald, *supra* note 65, at 178–85 (describing Lincoln's defeat in the elections of 1854); 1 Beveridge, *supra* note 82, at 524 (describing Lincoln's extreme melancholy after political defeats).

93. Donald, *supra* note 65, at 186.

94. Ibid.

95. Duff, *supra* note 49, at 323–24.

96. Ibid. at 323.

97. 1 Beveridge, *supra* note 82, at 580.

98. Ibid.

99. Ibid. at 583.

100. Ibid. at 580–81.

101. Ibid.

102. Ibid. at 580.

103. Ibid. at 582.

104. Strozier, *supra* note 81, at 139–41.

105. Ibid. at 140.

106. Ibid.

107. Dirck, *supra* note 35, at 39.

108. 1 Lincoln, *supra* note 61, at 12.

109. Ibid.

110. See, for example, Art Barnum, "Stripper's Private Dancing Lands DeKalb Lawyer in Hot Water," *Chicago Tribune,* September 19, 2008, available at http://www.chicagotribune.com/news/local/chicago/chi-lap-dance-lawyer-both-19-sep19,0,6962009.story (accessed January 21, 2009); Debra Cassens Weiss, "Judge Calls Fee Request 'Grossly Excessive,' Trims Nearly $1M," *ABA Journal* (2008), available at http://abajournal.com/news/judge_calls_fee_request_grossly_excessive_trims_nearly_1m/ (accessed January 21, 2009); Lawyer Jokes and Cartoons, Lawyers Fees Jokes, http://www.lawyer-jokes.us/modules/mylinks/viewcat.php?cid=14 (accessed January 21, 2009); Expert Law Website, "Law Laughs: Legal Fees," http://www.lawlaughs.com/money/legalfees.html (accessed January 7, 2009); accord Lisa G. Lerman, "A Double Standard for Lawyer Dishonesty: Billing Fraud Versus Misappropriation," 34 *Hofstra L. Rev.* 847, 848 (2006) (examining cases of dishonest lawyers); De Broglio Attorneys Website, "Why Legal Fees Are High," http://www.onlinelaw.co.za/content/index.cfm?navID=10&itemID=54 (accessed January 21, 2009).

111. Ankur Parekh and Jay R. Pelkofer, "Lawyers, Ethics, and Fees: Getting Paid under Model Rule 1.5," 16 *Geo. J. Legal Ethics* 767, 767 (2003) (citing "Reporter's Observations of Proposed Rule 1.5," Draft No. 2 [July 19, 1999]) (on file with *The Georgetown Journal of Legal Ethics*).

112. Ibid.

113. Compare *Model Rules of Prof'l Conduct,* Rule 1.5 (2008) (contains several parts and subparts), with *Model Rule of Prof'l Conduct,* Rule 1.1 (2008) (contains only two sentences) and *Model Rules of Prof'l Conduct,* Rule 1.3 (2008) (contains only one sentence).

114. *Model Rules of Prof'l Conduct*, Rule 1.5 (2008). (Subsections [b], [c], [d], and [e] of the Fees Rule—dealing with, respectively, communicating the fees to the client, situations wherein contingent fees are acceptable, two types of fees against public policy, and division of fees between lawyers in different firms—are not relevant to this paper's analysis of how lawyers should aspire beyond the Model Rules. Such rules, while important, serve primarily as complements to the Fees Rule's overarching goal: defining and prohibiting an unreasonable fee.)

115. *ABA Annotated Model Rules of Prof'l Conduct* 17–25, 41–47, 61–81 (5th ed., 2003) (illustrating the disproportionate treatment given Rule 1.5 compared with Rules 1.1 and 1.3); see also *Cases and Materials on the Rules of the Legal Profession* 47, 52, 249, 256–57, 259, 261, 315 (Robert F. Cochran Jr. and Teresa S. Collett, eds., West Publishing, 1996).

116. See *Model Rules of Prof'l Conduct*, Rule 1.1, 1.3, 1.5 (American Bar Association, 2008).

117. Rotunda and Dzienkowski, *supra* note 6, at 83–90, 122–29, 141–211.

118. *Model Rules of Prof'l Conduct*, Rule 1.5, cmt. 1 (2008); see also *Nat'l Info. Servs. v. Gottsegen*, 737 So. 2d 909, 98-528 (5th Cir. 1999) (listing ten factors "derived from" the Fees Rule, including the result obtained, responsibility incurred, importance of litigation, amount of money involved, extent and character of work performed, number of appearances made, intricacies of facts involved, counsel's diligence and skill, court's own knowledge, and counsel's legal knowledge, attainment, and skill).

119. See generally *Model Rules of Prof'l Conduct*, Rule 1.5, cmt. 1, 3 (2008).

120. See, for example, Parekh and Pelkofer, *supra* note 111, at 767, 769 (addressing the evolution of the Fees Rule and noting that the definition of reasonableness, and its use in the Fees Rule and its predecessor rule, remained ·at the forefront of the Fees Rule's evolution).

121. See *The Living Lincoln: The Man, His Mind, His Times, and the War He Fought* 69 (Paul M. Angle and Earl Schneck Miers, eds., 1995) (stating that Lincoln himself agreed that a strict, all-encompassing rule would be inappropriate. Lincoln wrote "[a]s to fees, it is impossible to establish a rule that will apply in all, or even a great many cases.") [hereafter cited as *Living Lincoln*].

122. See, for example, Donald, *supra* note 65, at 106–7 (discussing the difficulties of maintaining and supporting a family while traveling the circuit for twenty weeks each year).

123. Ibid. at 156 (noting that in the *McClean County* case, which Lincoln regarded as the "largest law question" of his time, Lincoln originally received a $250 retainer, then, once victorious in the suit, requested a $2,000 fee for his services and only raised this amount to $5,000 after consulting with six prominent Illinois attorneys).

124. Ibid. (pointing out that Lincoln brought suit against his own client, the Illinois Central Railroad, to recover a fee that was 250 percent larger than the client intended and 2,000 percent more than his retainer, and, because the fee was fair, "[t]he action did not interrupt his amicable relationship with the Illinois Central Railroad, which he continued to represent in numerous subsequent cases").

125. See ibid. (showing that Lincoln enjoyed a continued relationship with his client due to the fact that his fee, which was markedly higher than his client wanted to pay, was indeed fair).

126. Ibid.

127. Ibid. at 104 (quoting Lincoln lecturing that fees are "important far beyond the mere question of bread and butter involved").

128. Strozier, *supra* note 81, at 145.

129. *Living Lincoln, supra* note 121, at 144–45. (Lincoln followed up on this advice by suggesting to these prospective lawyers that they "[s]ettle the amount of fee and take a note in advance. . . . Never sell a fee note. . . . It leads to negligence and dishonesty. . . .")

130. Donald, *supra* note 65, at 148; *Microtek Med., Inc, v. 3M Co.,* 942 So. 2d 122, 131 (Miss. 2006) (holding that a fee of $223,031.09 was reasonable where the attorney's time, effort, lost employment opportunity, and hourly rate were taken into account).

131. 4 Lincoln, *supra* note 61, at 232 (Lincoln exchanged legal services for goods with local craftsmen); see also Harry J. Lambeth, "Practicing Law in 1878," in *Readings in the History of the American Legal Profession* 164 (Dennis R. Nolan, ed., Univ. of South Carolina Press, 1980).

Legal fees a century ago varied as they do today. A minimum fee schedule adopted by the Bar Association of the District of Columbia in 1873 suggested these fees: Arguing a cause in the Superior Court of the District of Columbia, $50; circuit court trials, $25; police court, $10; written contract or deed, $10; printed contract, $5; preparing a will, $25; examination of title abstract, $25; collections, 10 percent up to $5,000, more than $5,000, 10 percent on the first $5,000 and 5 percent on the excess.

132. See generally 2 Edward M. Thornton, *A Treatise on Attorneys at Law* § 446 (Edward Thompson, 1914) (explaining a fee note).

133. See ibid. (explaining that a fee note is in the "nature of an indemnity contract and, as a general rule, the promisee can recover thereunder only such sums as he has actually and necessarily expended or become liable for on account of the default of the promisor, and then only when they are reasonable, and proven to be so . . .").

134. Donald, *supra* note 65, at 73.

135. Ibid. at 104–6 (detailing the extent to which life on the circuit was difficult, crowded, and exhausting).

136. Steiner, *supra* note 44, at 73 ("In 1830, Illinois had 73 lawyers among its population of 157,445 [1:2,156]; by 1840, lawyers numbered 429 and the population 476,183 (1:1,110). The population had grown 300 percent; the number of lawyers, nearly 600 percent. In 1850, Illinois had one lawyer for every 1,042 people.").

137. Donald, *supra* note 65, at 73. Donald noted that "Springfield was a town full of lawyers, and all were obligated to charge modest fees." He also noted that their clients, despite paying small fees, offered to compensate Lincoln and his partner by, among other things, "making a coat" and "giving Lincoln board for $6.00."

138. There are numerous ways to determine the value of a sum of money over time. Popular methods are to follow the consumer price index, the consumer bundle, or the value of unskilled labor. While each method is of course viable, there are instances where the use of one is more appropriate than another. The authors could have chosen to use the value of unskilled labor for this chapter. See Samuel H. Williamson, Measuring Worth Web site, "Six Ways to Compute the Relative Value of a U.S. Dollar Amount, 1774 to Present," http://www.measuringworth.com/uscompare/# (accessed January 21, 2009). Instead, the authors use the method of determining value described in *The Law Practice of Abraham Lincoln* (*supra* note 53), reference section, "Monetary Conversion." Under that method, $5 in either 1842 or 1860 dollars is approximately $100 in 1999 dollars.

139. See ibid.

140. Donald, *supra* note 65, at 185–87.

141. Ibid. at 104.

142. Ibid. at 148.

143. See 1 Beveridge, *supra* note 82.

144. *Living Lincoln, supra* note 121, at 143.

145. Ibid. at 143–44.

146. Donald, *supra* note 65, at 148.

147. Ibid. at 151 (quoting an Illinois journalist, who continued that "though he may have his equal, it would be no easy task to find his superior.").

148. Ibid. at 138.

149. *Living Lincoln, supra* note 121, at 193 (adding that "Lincoln cherished the right of the professional man to set his own fees.").

150. Ibid., at 19–22.

151. Donald, *supra* note 65, at 185–87.

152. Ibid. at 186.

153. Ibid.

154. Compare ibid. at 70–74 (discussing the early days of Lincoln's law practice and his typical clientele), with ibid. at 155–58 (noting that, while Lincoln still represented clients with small matters, he increasingly found himself in legal matters of great consequence).

155. Lincoln correctly identified this case as one of the most important of his time. The background facts involved the State of Illinois chartering the Illinois Central Railroad, which the state granted an exemption from all taxation, contingent on the company paying the state an annual "charter tax." Though clearly advantageous to both the state—searching for economic growth—and to the new railroad ventures, several counties saw the deleterious ramifications of the lack of additional income to their tax bases. The authorities for McLean County understood the economic importance of the tax exemption and assessed a levy on the Illinois Central Railroad property, asserting that the Illinois legislature lacked the authority to exempt the railroad from county taxes.

156. Ibid.

157. *The Lincoln Reader* 179 (Paul M. Angle, ed., Rutgers Univ. Press, 1947).

158. See ibid., at 156.

159. Ibid.

160. Ibid.

161. Ibid.

162. Ibid.; Lincoln, *supra* note 61, at 410.

163. See Donald, *supra* note 65, at 156; Lincoln, *supra* note 61, at 409–12.

164. Duff, *supra* note 49, at 318.

165. *Living Lincoln, supra* note 121, at 144–45.

166. Lincoln, *supra* note 61, at 412 (having only two suits dismissed, Lincoln won seventeen favorable judgments, with an average award of $69.76).

167. 2 *Collected Works of Abraham Lincoln* 398 (Roy P. Basler, ed., Rutgers Univ. Press, 1953).

168. Ibid.

169. *Model Rules of Prof'l Conduct,* Rule 1.5(a) (2008).

Lincoln's Legal Ethics

The Client Correspondence

Roger Billings

The *Law Practice of Abraham Lincoln* project has opened a new window into Abraham Lincoln's life. The project contains around 100,000 documents about Lincoln's legal career, all available online. There are 5,600 of his cases, representing his practice of law from A to Z, or more accurately, from adoption to usury.[1] One of the least explored aspects of his practice is his legal ethics and how they stack up against the modern rules.[2]

In Lincoln's day very little was written about attorney-client relations, which are the focus of today's Model Rules of Professional Conduct. Instead, ethics was a synonym for the word "morality." Some examples illustrate the difference between the ethics of morality and the ethics of the lawyer-client relationship. As early as 1836, David Hoffman's influential book, *A Course of Legal Study,* moralized that the ideal lawyer should not plead the statute of limitations against an honest debt.[3] Hoffman might have found Lincoln immoral because he did not hesitate to use the statute of limitations to defend his debtor clients, and he also did not hesitate to use other technicalities if they would win a case.[4]

Another example of the confusion between morality and legal ethics was the refusal of some lawyers to represent owners of fugitive slaves. Salmon P. Chase of Cincinnati believed it was immoral to represent slaveowners; instead, he represented runaway slaves in court when their owners sued to recover them. He did so much pro bono work of this kind that he became known as the "attorney general for runaway negroes."[5] Lincoln was not so moralistic. He noted that slaveowners' rights were in the Constitution. Once he even represented a slaveowner, and when he did so he was in compliance with the modern ethics rule, which says, "A lawyer's representation of a client . . . does not constitute an endorsement of the client's . . . social or moral views. . . ."[6] Lincoln's representation of a slaveowner might have conflicted with his personal belief that slavery was evil, but it did not conflict with an ethics rule. Lincoln believed in representing clients with all the tools the law allowed. Ethics rules say that "A lawyer . . . should take whatever lawful and ethical measures are required to vindicate a client's cause. . . ."[7] In other words, "The lawyer should represent a client zealously within the bounds of the law" whether or not the client's cause is popular.[8]

Frontier courtrooms where Lincoln practiced did not have the formality of today's courtrooms. A story from a tiny Illinois courtroom illustrates the easy-going camaraderie among lawyers. The attorneys were gathered around a table when they noticed that Lincoln's friend and fellow lawyer, Ward Hill Lamon, had a big tear in the seam of his pants exposing his backside. One lawyer got the idea of passing around a piece of paper on which the lawyers would pledge some money to pay for a new pair of pants. When the paper came to Lincoln, Lincoln wrote, "I decline to contribute to the end in view."[9]

The judge who presided in that courtroom was David Davis—one of Lincoln's best friends and the man who organized Lincoln's nomination for president at Chicago on May 18, 1860.[10] The friendship was so close that Lincoln appointed Davis a justice of the U.S. Supreme Court in 1862.[11] The relationship between Lincoln and Davis brings to mind the ethics rule in the Model Code of Judicial Conduct, "A judge shall not . . . consider . . . communications made to the judge outside the presence of the parties or their lawyers. . . ."[12] Did Lincoln and Davis break this rule, which is referred to as the "ex parte communication" rule?[13] For years Davis and Lincoln were just two lawyers who rode the Eighth Judicial Circuit together, stopping each week at a different county courthouse.[14] In 1848, Davis was elected judge of the circuit, and for the next twelve years Lincoln practiced before him.[15] Now they were in the relationship of lawyer and judge, but their friendship kept growing, as is evidenced by a letter of Davis to Lincoln dated August 30, 1860:

Bloomington, Ill.

Aug. 30, 1860

Dear Lincoln,

The Davenport case was not decided at Danville—I intended to decide it but adjourned the court for the Chicago convention. Have not been back since.

> I am very sorry of the postponement of your fees but they will
> have to be deferred until after the Danville court—The court is not
> until after the election—My mind is now wholly unfit to investigate
> any law case requiring thought. . . .
>
> [Signed] D. DAVIS[16]

Davis is apologizing to Lincoln for being too exhausted to rule on a case, because he knows Lincoln is waiting for his fee. The adjournment to the Chicago convention Davis mentions refers to the convention where Lincoln would be nominated by the Republicans.[17]

Another letter also gives strong indication of the close relationship. In this letter Davis, while a sitting judge, seems to be handling client business for Lincoln:

> Springfield, Illinois
>
> March 28, 1856
>
> My Dear Sir—Mr. Lincoln had examined the questions
> presented in the statement of facts very thoroughly—and herewith
> enclosed is his opinion.
>
> I have read the opinion and examined some of the authorities.
> I am thoroughly persuaded that he is correct and that the Courts
> must sustain the views he takes. If any litigation grows out of the
> matter I would unhesitatingly recommend that Mr. Lincoln be sent
> for.
>
> His charge for the examination and opinion is $100—which
> you can send to me for him—if you so desire and I will procure a
> receipt from him and send to you. I have been holding Court here
> for two weeks—will get through tomorrow—shall see Rachel or you
> at Bloomington in April.
>
> Truly your friend
>
> [Signed] D. DAVIS[18]

Given that Lincoln and Davis traveled together on the prairie and stayed at the same hotels, it is possible that at some time they indulged in ex parte communications about a pending case and that they would have violated the ethics rule.[19] A hint of impropriety comes from a contemporary lawyer, Henry Clay Whitney, who wrote that "while several of us lawyers were together, including Judge Davis, Lincoln suddenly asked a novel question of court practice, addressed to no one particularly, to which the Judge . . . replied, stating what he understood the practice should be. Lincoln thereat laughed and said, 'I asked that question, hoping that you would answer. I have that very question to present to the Court in the morning, and I am glad to find out that the court is on my side.'"[20] David Davis's biographer concludes, however, that Davis was scrupulously impartial with his favorite and in fact decided more cases against Lincoln than for him.[21]

The lawyers Lincoln practiced with had primitive offices by today's standards. There were no secretaries, no paralegals, no file cabinets, no computers, not even typewriters. Everything was written by hand. Even the law library was sparse.[22] Transportation to county courts on the Eighth Judicial Circuit was by horseback until the 1850s, when jolting train rides were available.[23] Lincoln's primary filing system was to put documents inside his stovepipe hat. He also left important papers in a stack in the corner of his office. David Donald says that as a result Lincoln and his partner "were constantly looking for misplaced letters and documents, and there were times when they had to confess frankly that papers were 'lost or destroyed and cannot be found. . . .'"[24] The people he represented were poorly educated and the client letters were often ungrammatical. In contrast, Lincoln's work product as an attorney was clear and well-written. Consider a few opinion letters:

To John D. Swallow

[c. June 15, 1854]

Both your questions are the same. After you sold and deeded your property to Edmons, for a consideration which is worthless and fraudulent, any person who buys or takes a mortgage from Edmons, without *Notice* of the fraud, will hold the property against you; but whoever buys or takes a mortgage *after* your Bill is filed, is conclusively presumed to have had *notice* of the fraud, and therefore can have no better right against you than Edmonds himself had. This is the whole law of the case.

Yours truly
A. LINCOLN[25]

Hon: H. E. Dummer—   Springfield
My dear Sir: Feb. 8, 1860
    I have examined and considered the question propounded in your letter accompanying copy of contract in relation Lard Tanks, apparatus &c, and my opinion is that Messrs H. C. Chadsey & Co, would, as a general proposition, have the right to continue to use the Tanks, apparatus &c, which they have on hand.

    The reason why I say "*as a general proposition*" is that I fear the particular phraseology of their contract, deprives them of it. The language of the contract is so explicit, and so oft repeated, that the right to use, "shall be until the expiration of said patent" that I fear it will be held that by their contract, they can not have the benefit of the extension.

    Much may be said on the other side; and I only mean to say that in my mind the question, on the phraseology of the contract is doubtful, and perhaps is worth trying.

Yours as ever
A. LINCOLN[26]

Joseph Means   Springfield,
Dear Sir   May 11. 1858
    The statements made within, if true are evidence of *fraud* on the part of the executor in selling the land. Fraud by the principles of law, invalidates everything. To get rid of this sale, a bill in chancery is to be filed, charging the fraud, and then, if the fraud can be *proved,* the sale will be set aside. This is all that can be said. Any lawyer will know how—to do it.

Yours &c
A. LINCOLN[27]

The quality of Lincoln's prose in legal documents and in letters to clients is impressive. Historians overlook them and analyze only the presidential letters and speeches, but Lincoln's legal documents reveal that he was also a good draftsman before he became president. Just the same, he was capable of making mistakes. Bear in mind that Illinois lawyers had no bar association, there was no requirement for attending law school (or any school for that matter), and there were no written ethics rules to follow.[28] Lincoln himself wrote down a few of his personal rules in the famous "Notes for a Law Lecture."[29] What Lincoln wrote was an early version of ethics rules. It is interesting to see whether Lincoln lived up to his own principles.

The first rule he proclaimed in his "Notes for a Law Lecture" was that lawyers should "Discourage litigation." He said, "Persuade your neighbors to compromise whenever you can."[30] There is no direct counterpart to that statement in the Model Rules, but it is accepted wisdom that lawyers should avoid going to court whenever possible. In the nineteenth century, when commentators were first starting to write about legal ethics, there were a number of people who argued that lawyers should seek to avoid lawsuits as an ethical matter. Of course, this sprang from the common law idea that fomenting lawsuits was bad: champerty, barratry, and maintenance were the common law crimes of those who sought to stir up and profit from lawsuits. Today the rules tell us that the lawyer has a duty to keep the client informed,[31] and that the client gets to decide whether to settle,[32] but that the lawyer may refer to nonlegal factors in counseling the client.[33] Taken together, these rules make clear that lawyers must counsel clients about the benefits and costs of litigation and then let them decide.[34]

Lincoln easily passes his own test. John Lupton of *The Papers of Abraham Lincoln* project writes that Lincoln preferred to settle a case rather than go to trial. Lincoln's friend Judge David Davis, before whom Lincoln practiced for many years, tells us that Lincoln hated long trials and was fond of settlements. A clerk who read law in Lincoln's office said, "I have heard him tell would-be clients again and again—You have no case; better settle."[35] Lupton says about 33 percent of Lincoln's cases were dismissed, many of them because they settled.[36]

One means of resolving a dispute is through arbitration. Arbitration is popular today; it was also popular in Lincoln's day, and he took advantage of it many times. He and opposing counsel would ask the court to appoint a panel of three arbitrators. Lincoln himself was appointed an arbitrator at least three times.[37] In addition Lincoln was a mediator. A client named Abram Bale hired Lincoln to sue the firm of Wright and Hickox, which had not paid Bale for $1,000 worth of "good, merchantable, superfine flour." After he dutifully filed suit Lincoln wrote a letter to Bale, advising him to settle. He said, "I sincerely hope you will settle it. I think you *can* if you *will*, for I have always found Mr. Hickox a fair man in his dealings." Lincoln then told Bale that as to his fees, "I will charge nothing for what I have done, and thank you to boot." He reassured Bale, "By settling, you will most likely get your money sooner; and with much less trouble and expense."[38]

Lawyers are always alert to a conflict of interest.[39] There was no written ethics rule on conflicts in Lincoln's Illinois, but there was an unwritten conflicts rule, as Lincoln recognizes in this letter:

R. E. Williams, Esq.   Springfield,
Dear Sir   Aug: 15.1857.

Yours of the 12th. in relation to a suit of Bakewell vs Allin, was received a day or two ago. I well remember the transaction; but as Bakewell will need no lawyer but you, and as there is likely to be some feeling, and both the parties are old friends of mine, I prefer, if I can, to keep out of the case. Of course I will not engage against Mr. Bakewell.

Yours truly
A. LINCOLN[40]

In another letter Lincoln reassured his client, Mason Brayman, who was counsel for a railroad, that he would not take a case against the railroad. He wanted Brayman to be confident that he was aware of conflicts of interest. An old man wanted Lincoln to sue the railroad for breach of a promise to make fences, but Lincoln told Brayman not to worry, "as I have sold myself out to you."[41] The letter reads in part:

Springfield, March 31.1854
M. Brayman, Esq.
Dear Sir,
I write this to inform that the people, (or some of them) of McLean and DeWitt county, through whose farms the I. C. R. R. passes are complaining very much that the Co. does not keep its covenants in regard to making fences—An old man from DeWitt was down here the other day to get me to bring a suit on the account; but as I have sold myself out to you, I turned him over to Strait, who, I understand, will bring the suit—A stitch in time may save nine in this matter—

A. LINCOLN[42]

In his "Notes for a Law Lecture" Lincoln said, "The matter of fees is important. . . . An exorbitant fee should never be claimed . . . never take your whole fee in advance. . . . Settle the amount of the fee and take a note in advance. . . . Never sell a fee note."[43] Lincoln's recommendation for modest fees and collection of them only after legal services are rendered anticipates the modern rule. The Ohio Rules of Professional Conduct say that "A lawyer shall not make an agreement for, charge, or collect an illegal or clearly excessive fee."[44] The rule is found in similar form in all states. Some biographers have written that Lincoln charged such modest fees that other lawyers believed he was depressing the market! In one of his best known fee letters Lincoln wrote:

> Mr. George P. Floyd   Springfield, Illinois
>   February 21, 1856
> Dear Sir: I have just received yours of 16th, with check on Flagg &
> Savage for twenty-five dollars. You must think I am a high-priced
> man. You are too liberal with your money.
>   Fifteen dollars is enough for the job. I send you a receipt for
> fifteen dollars, and return to you a ten-dollar bill. Yours truly,
>   A. LINCOLN[45]

There is doubt that Lincoln's fees were any lower than those of other lawyers. Albert Woldman, an excellent biographer of Lincoln's career, wrote that "for the most part [his fees] were normal and compared favorably with the compensation received by other lawyers of the same region."[46] One thing is certain: once a fee was negotiated, Lincoln did not allow himself to be denied it, as the following letter shows:

> Andrew McCallen   Springfield, Ills
>   July 4, 1851
> Dear Sir:
>   I have news from Ottawa, that we *win* our Galatin & Saline
> county case. As the dutch Justice said, when he married folks "Now,
> vere ish my hundred tollars"
>   Yours truly
>   A. LINCOLN[47]

Lastly, a rule Lincoln proclaimed in his "Notes for a Law Lecture" is "Never let your correspondence fall behind."[48] Lincoln freely admitted that his law practice was often interrupted by politics and he apologized to clients and colleagues for his absence.[49] Neglect of clients is one of the most common problems that lead to ethics violations. A typical ethics rule today says, "A lawyer shall act with reasonable diligence and promptness in representing a client."[50] No Supreme Court ethics committee was supervising lawyer conduct in Lincoln's day, however, and Lincoln often began letters with a comment on his tardiness. He could well have been the subject of complaints to a bar association ethics committee had he been in practice today.

In 1838, Lincoln's second year of practice, we find the first of many letters where Lincoln begs his client's pardon for neglecting business. Here is what he wrote the client.

Levi Davis   Springfield
Dear Sir: March 15— 1838
        We received yours of the 2nd. Inst. by due course of mail, and have only to offer in excuse for not answering it sooner, that we have been in a great state of confusion here ever since the receipt of your letter; and also, that your clients can not suffer by the delay. The suit is merely instituted to quiet a title. . . .
        We beg your pardon for our neglect in this business; if it had been important to you or your client we would have done better.
                                Yours sincerely
                                STUART & LINCOLN[51]

Recall that Lincoln stored legal documents inside his stovepipe hat. In 1850 he wrote this letter:

Richard S. Thomas   Springfield
Dear Thomas: June 27. 1850
        I am ashamed of not sooner answering your letter, herewith returned; and, my only apologies are, first, that I have been very busy in the U.S. court; and second, that when I received the letter I put it in my old hat, and buying a new one the next day, the old one was set aside, and so, the letter lost sight of for a time. . . .
                                Yours as ever,
                                A. LINCOLN[52]

Using the same language in two successive letters, Lincoln suggests that he is a little slow.

E. W. Bakewell, Esq   Springfield,
Dear Sir: Augt. 1. 1850
    I have at last found time to draw up a Bill in your case. Inclosed you have it . . .

                A. LINCOLN[53]

Hon: William Martin: Springfield,
                          Feb: 19. 1851
    The Legislature having got out of the way, I at last find time to attend to the business you left with me on behalf of the Alton and Sangamon Railroad Company. . . .

                A. LINCOLN[54]

Sometimes Lincoln explained that he was too busy in the courts. In the following letter he admits that he missed a chance to get a corporate charter from the state legislature for his client.

Hon. John A. Rockwell.   Springfield, Ill., Feby. 15, 1853.
My dear Sir: I have failed to get your Coal Mining Charter. Being very busy in the Courts when your letter reached me, I let a few days slip before attending to it. A little more than a week before the close of the Session, I got a Bill for the Charter howsoever into the Senate, which Body it passed in about five days. It then went to the H.R. and was lost for want of time. . . .
    If you continue to desire it, I will get it passed at the next Session—it being borne in mind that at a *called* Session the door may not be opened for such business.
                    Your obt. Servant,
                    A. LINCOLN[55]

The following letter is a candid admission that the reason for neglect of business was politics.

Messrs. Sandford, Porter & Striker   Springfield,
New York   March 10— 1855
    Gentlemen: Yours of the 5th. is received; as also was that of
15th. Decr. Last, inclosing bond of Clift to Pray. When I received the
bond, I was dabbling in politics; and, of course, neglecting business.
Having since been beaten out, I have gone to work again. . . .
Very Respectfully
A. LINCOLN[56]

After a certain number of years the law says it is too late to file suit, and
this law is called the statute of limitations. Every lawyer knows that one of
the biggest malpractice nightmares is letting the statute of limitations run
before filing a client's lawsuit. Lincoln had a healthy respect for the statute,
as this letter shows:

To Elihu N. Powell   Springfield
Dear Powell: Feb. 15. 1856
    When you wrote me from Chicago about our Aspinall case,
I had done nothing with it. But being thereby stirred up, I looked
into it, and took fright, lest the Statute of Limitations had matured
against it, since the papers were in my hands. To make sure, if it had
not, that it should not, I brought the suit at once in our Sangamon
Circuit Court, —not knowing where Aspinall lives, so as to sue in
the Federal court. . . .
A. LINCOLN[57]

Lincoln lived up to his reputation for honesty in the practice of law. His
stovepipe hat filing system and his love of politics, however, forced him to
the brink of neglecting clients' business.

Notes

This essay was originally published in slightly different form in the *Northern
Kentucky Law Review* 36, no. 2, and is reprinted here by permission.
    1. *The Law Practice of Abraham Lincoln: Complete Documentary Edition,*
DVD-ROM (Martha L. Benner and Cullom Davis, eds., Univ. of Illinois Press,
2000), available at http://www.lawpracticeofabrahamlincoln.org.

2. See generally *Model Rules of Professional Conduct* (2007).

3. David Hoffman, *A Course of Legal Study* (1817), quoted in Mark E. Steiner, *An Honest Calling: The Law Practice of Abraham Lincoln* 135 (2006).

4. Ibid.

5. Frederick J. Blue, *Salmon P. Chase: A Life in Politics* 40 (1987).

6. Doris Kearns Goodwin, *Team of Rivals: The Political Genius of Abraham Lincoln* 92 (2005); *Model Rules of Professional Conduct,* Rule 1.2(b) (2007).

7. *Model Rules of Professional Conduct,* Rule 1.3(1) (2007).

8. See *Massachusetts Rules of Professional Conduct,* Rule 1.3, quoted in Stephen Gillers and Roy D. Simon, *Regulation of Lawyers* 50 (2008).

9. *Abe Lincoln Laughing: Humorous Anecdotes from Original Sources by and about Abraham Lincoln* 72 (P. M. Zall, ed., 1995).

10. Willard L. King, *Lincoln's Manager: David Davis* 195, 111–26 (1960).

11. Ibid. at 192–96.

12. *Model Code of Judicial Conduct,* Rule 2.9 (2008).

13. *Black's Law Dictionary* 296 (8th ed., 2004).

14. King, *supra* note 10, at 71–98.

15. Ibid. at 61.

16. *The Law Practice of Abraham Lincoln, supra* note 1, *Davenport v. Sconce & Don Carlos,* Document ID 94154.

17. See generally Benjamin P. Thomas, *Abraham Lincoln* 208, 214 (1952) (Knopf, 1976).

18. *The Law Practice of Abraham Lincoln, supra* note 1, *Dillingham v. Fisher,* File ID L02512, Document ID 4171.

19. See King, *supra* note 10, at 71–98.

20. Henry C. Whitney, *Life on the Circuit with Lincoln* 146 (1892); see also Henry Clay Whitney interview with William H. Herndon (c. 1887), in *Herndon's Informants: Letters, Interviews and Statements about Abraham Lincoln* 647 (Douglas L. Wilson and Rodney O. Davis, eds., 1998).

21. King, *supra* note 10, at 91.

22. See generally Frederick Trevor Hill, *Lincoln the Lawyer* 19–26 (1906).

23. King, *supra* note 10, at 71.

24. David Herbert Donald, *Lincoln* 103 (1995).

25. 2 *The Collected Works of Abraham Lincoln* 219 (Roy P. Basler, ed., 1953), available at http://quod.lib.umich.edu/l/lincoln/.

26. 3 *The Collected Works of Abraham Lincoln, supra* note 25, at 517.

27. 2 *The Collected Works of Abraham Lincoln, supra* note 25, at 446.

28. Steiner, *supra* note 3, at 37–40, 131–36.

29. 2 *The Collected Works of Abraham Lincoln, supra* note 25, at 81.

30. Ibid.

31. *Model Rules of Professional Conduct,* Rule 1.4 (2007).

32. *Model Rules of Professional Conduct,* Rule 1.2 (2007).

33. *Model Rules of Professional Conduct,* Rule 2.1 (2007).

34. E-mail from John M. Bickers, Professor of Law, Salmon P. Chase College of Law, to Roger Billings, Professor of Law, Salmon P. Chase College of Law (October 1, 2008) (on file with the author).

35. Allen D. Spiegel, *A. Lincoln, Esquire: A Shrewd, Sophisticated Lawyer in His Time* 41–42 (2002).

36. Ibid. at 42.

37. *The Law Practice of Abraham Lincoln, supra* note 1, Henry for the use of *Logan v. Spear,* 11/1842, assumpset, File ID L03425; *Saltonstall v. Saltonstall et al.,* 03/1857 partition, fee dispute, File ID L01820; *Webster v. Rhodes & Angell,* 04/1856, File ID L00982; see generally *Model Rules of Professional Conduct,* Rule 2.4 (2007). (In Model Rule 2.4 there are rules for a "Lawyer Serving as Third-Party Neutral." That is a rather awkward phrasing, but the rule authorizes lawyers to be arbitrators.)

38. *The Law Practice of Abraham Lincoln, supra* note 1, Lincoln to Abraham Bale, Feb. 22, 1850, Document ID 94155.

39. See *Model Rules of Professional Conduct,* Rules 1.7, 1.9, 1.18 (2007).

40. 2 *The Collected Works of Abraham Lincoln, supra* note 25, at 413.

41. *The Law Practice of Abraham Lincoln, supra* note 1, Abraham Lincoln to Mason Brayman, Document ID 130031.

42. Ibid.

43. 2 *The Collected Works of Abraham Lincoln, supra* note 25, at 82.

44. *Ohio Rules of Professional Conduct,* Rule 1.5(a).

45. *The Collected Works of Abraham Lincoln, supra* note 25, at 332–33.

46. Alfred A. Woldman, *Lawyer Lincoln* 212–13 (1936).

47. 2 *The Collected Works of Abraham Lincoln, supra* note 25, at 106.

48. Ibid. at 81.

49. Steiner, *supra* note 3, at 26–29.

50. *Ohio Rules of Professional Conduct,* Rule 1.3.

51. 1 *The Collected Works of Abraham Lincoln, supra* note 25, at 116.

52. 2 *The Collected Works of Abraham Lincoln, supra* note 25, at 80.

53. Ibid. at 91.

54. Ibid. at 98.

55. Ibid. at 190–91.

56. Ibid. at 308.

57. Ibid. at 331.

Lincoln and the Kentuckians

Placing Lincoln in Context with Lawyers and Clients from His Native State

Christopher A. Schnell

Abraham Lincoln was born in and spent the first seven years of his life in Kentucky.[1] In 1816, his father, Thomas Lincoln, moved his family north across the Ohio River from what was then Hardin County, Kentucky, and settled on a wooded, 160-acre claim in what was then Perry County, in southern Indiana.[2] Lincoln later attributed his father's move north to his dislike of slavery and his failed efforts to establish a clear title to land: disadvantages that plagued many yeomen farmers in early Kentucky.[3] In migrating north of the Ohio River, the Lincolns joined thousands of other pioneers of the Upland South moving into the so-called Old Northwest during the early decades of the nineteenth century.[4] There, they sought cheap federal land on which to practice subsistence (or pre–market economy) agriculture.[5] Soon, relatives from Kentucky joined the Lincolns in Indiana, settling on nearby claims and establishing a small community of security and exchange.[6] This sort of pattern migration characterized the great exodus north and west from the Upland South to the new territories or states of Indiana, Illinois, Missouri, and Iowa.[7] In early 1830, Thomas Lincoln sold his farm and again moved his family, including twenty-one-year-old Abraham, to establish a farm in Macon County in central Illinois.[8]

By the 1830s, central Illinois contained a mix of settlers from both the North and South. Settlers from the Upland South (Kentucky, Tennessee, Virginia, and the Carolinas) represented the largest group of immigrants.[9] The Lincolns settled on land in a part of Macon County on the north side of the Sangamon River, alongside a "Yankee" settlement.[10] Kentuckians were the first large immigrant group to take up residency in Illinois, first settling in southern Illinois, then, during the 1830s, settling further north, colonizing the fertile soil of central Illinois.[11] In 1850, the first year the federal census recorded nativity, male, native-born Kentuckians were the second largest immigrant group in Illinois, and the largest single immigrant group in central Illinois.[12] They settled east to west across central Illinois; in the Sangamon valley, in the west and center; and along the Embarrass and Vermilion rivers in the east: a region that composed the heartland of Lincoln's law practice.[13]

Using nativity as a guide, central Illinois in 1850 was a crossroads of the country.[14] Northerners spread south from Chicago and northern Illinois to encroach on central Illinois.[15] Southerners moved south to north, halting as far north as the military tract in western Illinois and the Sangamon valley of central Illinois.[16] Settlers from the Mid-Atlantic and Ohio also settled in central Illinois.[17] Despite this diversity, the majority of the population in central Illinois, as late as 1850, was born in Kentucky.[18] Native-born Kentuckians were the core population in several of the counties that formed the Eighth Judicial Circuit, Lincoln's home circuit. These counties included Sangamon (his home county) and McLean, in the central part of Illinois, and Vermilion and Edgar, on the Indiana border in the east-central part of the state.[19]

From this, it is natural enough to form a corollary that because of the preponderance of native-born Kentuckians in central Illinois, Lincoln's clients were also mostly from Kentucky. A sampling of Lincoln's clients supports this corollary. Ten of Lincoln's twenty-nine most frequent clients were either native Kentuckians or had lived there for a substantial amount of time before moving to Illinois. Those ten clients were involved in 26 percent of the cases represented in the study. Thus, approximately one-third of Lincoln's top clients were born in or had lived in Kentucky, and these clients gave him about one-quarter of his caseload from his top clients.[20]

Settlers from the Upland South brought their cultural and economic models with them and implanted them in Illinois. Likewise, settlers from other regions brought with them their own ways of doing things.[21] These cultural differences affected, in small ways, Lincoln's law practice. Yeoman farmers from the Upland South populated the countryside surrounding Lincoln's homes, first when he lived in New Salem and later after he moved to Springfield. While subsistence farming gave way to increased farm production for market under steadily maturing economic conditions during the 1830s and 1840s, old habits died slowly, so many of Lincoln's clients were farmers of small holdings with little means. Characteristic of this agriculture-based economy, Lincoln's law practice included a great deal of small debt collection, property law, and inheritance law. Urban settlement also characterized the 1830s and 1840s as more and more single men left farming for work as artisans, mechanics, merchants, or in nascent industries in town. A small minority, like Lincoln, left the farm to engage in training for a limited spectrum of professions. Most of these men apprenticed themselves for a brief period before starting out on their own, usually in a new location, perhaps a growing place like Springfield. As such, many of Lincoln's colleagues and clients were small businessmen and members of the professional class from Kentucky. Lincoln also labored to meet the needs of his urban clients, and this is reflected in the wide variety of debt collection and contract law in his law practice.[22]

While many clients and lawyers who were transplanted Kentuckians may have been predisposed to hire or conduct business with Lincoln because of his roots, nativity probably had very little to do with his success as a lawyer. By necessity Lincoln had to take all comers to foster his practice; this openness brought him into contact with a broad spectrum of transplanted people. It did not make business sense to exclude from his practice, because of sectional prejudices, the greedy "hawk billed yankee," as he once referred to a creditor from Chicago.[23] Nor could he afford to refuse the cases involving $5 fees or clients who had little personal wealth, such as those from the Upland South who had not advanced much beyond subsistence farming. This openness benefited his political career as well as provided him with a high volume of clients throughout his twenty-four years as a lawyer.[24]

Kentuckians who were professionals or businessmen figured heavily among Lincoln's friends and associates during the early years of his residence in Illinois, in both New Salem (1831–1837) and after he moved to Springfield in 1837. Lincoln's one-time employer, county surveyor Thomas M. Neale, studied law in Kentucky before moving to Sangamon County, where he served as a justice of the peace in addition to his official duties.[25] One of Springfield's founders, Elijah Iles, came from Kentucky to Illinois with a stock of goods to sell. When his mercantile business languished, he speculated in land, and he profitably purchased one-quarter of the land that would later become Springfield.[26] Dr. Richard F. Barret, a leader among Springfield's Whigs and an occasional client of Lincoln's, was born in Green County, Kentucky, where he began his medical practice before moving to

Springfield in 1833.[27] Beyond Sangamon County, Lincoln encountered Kentuckians among the leaders in communities throughout central and southern Illinois. This can be seen by looking at the attendees of the 1847 state constitutional convention. Included among this elective body were at least twenty-eight delegates who called Kentucky their native state, the most delegates from a single state. Half of these native Kentuckian delegates were either lawyers or physicians.[28]

During the early decades of the nineteenth century, Louisville and Lexington were economic and cultural centers for the West, and many of Lincoln's colleagues and clients from the entrepreneurial and professional classes were trained and educated in Kentucky before establishing themselves in Illinois. Merchandise and merchants from Louisville began arriving in the Illinois marketplace during the 1830s. Lexington exported to Illinois many learned men and professionals trained at Transylvania University.[29] According to Horace Holley, who became president of Transylvania University in 1820, "This whole Western country is to feed my seminary, which will send out lawyers, physicians, clergymen, statesmen . . . who will make the nation feel them."[30]

Although most lawyers learned their craft through apprenticeship or self-education, many of Lincoln's colleagues at the bar were well educated.[31] Transylvania, early on, had a law department, one of only two west of the Appalachians during the middle decades of the nineteenth century.[32] At least twelve lawyers and judges with whom Lincoln worked attended Transylvania for a liberal arts education or for legal education.[33] Some attorneys, like Lincoln's friend John J. Hardin, emerged from their Kentucky home with a degree from Transylvania and settled in Illinois to practice law.[34] Most, however, were residents of Illinois who were drawn to Transylvania to obtain a higher education, whereupon they returned to Illinois to practice law. Quincy, Illinois, attorney Orville Hickman Browning, a longtime friend of Lincoln's, attended Augusta College in his native Kentucky before coming to Illinois.[35]

John Todd Stuart had a lasting influence on Lincoln's career as a lawyer. Stuart was born in Walnut Hills, Kentucky, the son of a Presbyterian minister.[36] He was well educated, having attended Centre College, in Danville, Kentucky, and studied law in a Richmond, Kentucky, law office.[37] In 1828 he moved north to Springfield, Illinois, where he began to practice law.[38] A few years later, in 1832, Stuart met Lincoln while they were both serving in a

Sangamon County militia company that took part in the Black Hawk War.[39] After they were discharged from duty, both men traveled home together and Stuart suggested Lincoln take up the study of law.[40] A few years later, Lincoln borrowed law books from Stuart to begin his self-education in law, and in 1837 Stuart took Lincoln as his junior partner.[41] As such, Lincoln's legal education was more full-time employment than apprenticeship, and after Stuart went to Congress in 1839, Lincoln took over as the lone member of the firm.[42] With Stuart, Lincoln had the advantage of an established and growing clientele, and he was able to avoid the sparse practice faced by many aspiring lawyers.[43] Indeed, it would have been unlikely for Lincoln to have succeeded in a place like Springfield, a steadily growing state capital, without being sponsored by an established member of the local bar like Stuart. The firm was busy, and, in addition to their work in the crowded Sangamon County Circuit Court, Lincoln visited some, or occasionally all, of the courts of the circuit to gather more clients.[44] Still, lucrative appellate work was sparse, and most likely their federal practice was minimal. With Stuart in Washington, or deeply involved in running for office, the practice suffered, and in early 1841 they amicably ended their partnership.[45]

Stephen Trigg Logan was born in Kentucky, where he received his education and served a legal apprenticeship with his uncle.[46] When he moved to Springfield in 1832, he commenced the practice of law and only three years later became judge of the First Judicial Circuit.[47] He later resigned this post to return to the practice of law, and in 1841 he joined with Lincoln in a partnership that would last until 1844.[48] During these years Lincoln apparently learned much about law, as it was Logan who later reminisced that "Lincoln's knowledge of law was very small when I took him in."[49] As Logan's junior partner, Lincoln benefited much from his large clientele and vast legal knowledge.[50] While they were partners, Lincoln became more active in the Illinois Supreme Court and in the federal courts. In the division of labor, Lincoln traveled the circuit while the senior partner tended to business at home.[51] Logan's political ambitions were more muted than Stuart's, and as a result he was a much more active lawyer and the firm prospered.[52]

In 1844, when Logan wanted to take on his son as a partner, Lincoln broke away and formed a partnership with a younger lawyer.[53] This time he joined with William Henry Herndon, who was born in Kentucky but came to Springfield at a young age with his father.[54] In the early 1840s he studied law in the Logan & Lincoln law office.[55] Lincoln took Herndon in as a junior partner, and it was Lincoln's turn to help a younger member of the bar get started.[56] The partnership worked out so well that even after Herndon exhibited excellent skills as a lawyer, he remained on as Lincoln's partner until the latter left for Washington in 1861. As with his earlier partnerships, Lincoln attended courts on the circuit, but he also did much of the trial work in the federal courts and appellate work before the Illinois Supreme Court.[57] Herndon managed the office, conducted research, and received walk-in clients.[58] He also attended to probate matters and maintained the firm's cases in nearby Menard County after the state legislature removed it from the Eighth Judicial Circuit.[59] Like Stuart and Logan before him, Herndon was an ardent Whig, but he represented perhaps a younger point of view on the political questions of the day.[60] During the 1850s Herndon was much more vocal about his antislavery feelings than the politically savvy Lincoln ever allowed himself to be publicly.[61] Herndon, acting alone, represented fugitive slaves in two habeas corpus hearings in Springfield during the 1850s.[62]

Lincoln's Kentucky family and friends influenced his law career by affording him both business and, at times, grief. Joshua Fry Speed was perhaps Lincoln's closest friend and confidant. When Lincoln first arrived nearly penniless in Springfield from New Salem, he took Speed's offer to share sleeping quarters above the store Speed co-owned.[63] Their friendship lasted even after Speed returned to his native Louisville in the early 1840s. Speed, who had arrived in Springfield in 1835, sold his part of a dry goods partnership and left several accounts in the hands of the Logan & Lincoln partnership for collection.[64] In cash-poor Illinois, most mercantile firms either took agricultural goods as payment or gave credit to conduct sales.[65] In taking goods as payment, these firms often served as clearinghouses for market produce in the years before cheap rail and river transportation.[66] Likewise, by offering credit, these firms served their clients as a proto-bank, in advance of reliable banking institutions.[67] Speed's firm largely gave credit in the form of promissory notes bearing 10 percent interest.[68]

When Speed sold out, his partner agreed to assign to him full interest in several unpaid notes.[69] These notes went to Logan & Lincoln for collection and led, eventually, to fifteen litigated cases in which they represented Speed's interests.[70] Speed's collection work typified the sort of work Lincoln would continue to do throughout his career in law. In court, Lincoln and his partners sued debtors using a wide variety of remedies, including such actions as assumpsit, debt, or, in an uncontested case, petition and summons, a speedy, creditor-friendly action borrowed directly from Kentucky law.[71]

As Lincoln became more established among Springfield's professional elite, a benefit of his partnership with Stuart, he came to know Ninian W. Edwards, the leading Whig lawyer in Springfield during the early 1840s.[72] Edwards was the son of Ninian Edwards, a Kentuckian and early governor of Illinois.[73] The younger Edwards was born in Frankfort, Kentucky, and studied law at Transylvania University.[74] While there, he met Elizabeth Todd, the daughter of an influential and well-to-do Lexington businessman, and they soon married.[75] Edwards moved to Illinois to begin practicing law, but later established himself as a merchant in the budding prairie town of Springfield.[76] He soon thereafter met Lincoln while campaigning for the legislature.[77] The Edwardses soon became the leading family of Springfield, and Elizabeth began inviting her sisters in Lexington to visit her and enjoy the society of the young town.[78] Lexington, once the cultural hub of the West, was in decline, and Elizabeth's many siblings began to migrate away from Kentucky. In a sort of chain migration, several of her sisters joined Elizabeth at her home in Springfield over the next few years.[79] During this time, Lincoln, with the encouragement of friends, fitfully entered the Edwardses' social circle, and it was there that Lincoln met Mary Todd, one of Elizabeth's immigrant sisters.[80]

Mary Todd Lincoln was the most influential Kentuckian in Lincoln's life. Other than a lifelong dislike of Lincoln's partner William Herndon, Mary had very little influence over her husband's law practice. Their marriage cemented the separation of Abraham's professional and domestic spheres.[81] Even before marriage, he had always maintained a law office, a dedicated space for business separate from his sleeping quarters with Speed or other friends.[82] Separating work from home was still a fairly new concept among lawyers during the early decades of the nineteenth century, and after they wed the Lincolns continued to meet with this middle-class, domestic rule.[83] To Mary, Abraham ceded all power over domestic doings.[84]

After they married in 1842, Lincoln entered a world further from his humble beginnings and closer to the middle-class ideal to which so many other young lawyers like him aspired.[85] From her he learned rudimentary social skills and refinements he lacked because of his rough frontier upbringing and rustic, self-made adulthood.[86] As one scholar noted, Mary provided Lincoln with "a marriage-long course in middle-class etiquette."[87] As unlike as they were in appearance and background, they shared an intellectual bond and a deep streak of ambition. In marriage they complemented each other in a variety of ways, so that they led, according to Mary, "eminently peaceful" domestic lives.[88] As Lincoln became more successful in law and politics he moved further from the frontier ideal of manhood and closer to the still developing Victorian ideal, an ideal which required the social skills and personal refinements Mary brought to the marriage. While Lincoln would never iron out his rough edges, much to Mary's sometimes volatile chagrin, he became more middle class with help from his wife.[89] Their collective ambition helped to ensure that he would succeed in his professional calling.[90]

The marriage also brought Lincoln new connections to his native state, and, as one scholar has noted, for the rest of his life Lincoln was "awash in a sea of Todds."[91] Lincoln's marriage to Mary also brought debt collection work from his father-in-law's Lexington business. Furthermore, in 1843 Lincoln represented Robert Todd in *Todd v. Ware,* litigation arising from a contract Todd signed to purchase land in Sangamon County. Ware stipulated that Todd had to pay off his promissory notes with "current" banknotes. Todd made the first two payments with paper currency printed by the State Bank of Illinois, a failing institution in Springfield. When he tried to pay the balance with the same paper a few months later, after the bank had failed, Ware refused the payment since the value of the bank's paper had declined so far. After a year of litigation, the Sangamon County Circuit Court sided with Ware and ordered Todd to pay the contract off with currency on par with banknotes issued by banks in Kentucky, Missouri, and Indiana. Although Lincoln lost this case, his father-in-law deeded the land to his family in Springfield, including Abraham and Mary.[92]

Robert Todd asked Lincoln and Edwards to collect some debts on behalf of his Lexington-based cotton manufacturing firm. The firm maintained a slave-operated factory in Sandersville, Kentucky, and a wholesale business in Lexington, and they sold their products to several merchants in Illinois. When some of these merchants could not pay, Lincoln and Edwards were called upon to collect. In 1853, four years after Todd's death, his former business partners, Oldham & Hemingway, sued Lincoln and Edwards for payment on two promissory notes that had allegedly been given to them by Robert Todd to collect during the 1840s.[93] The surviving members of the firm sought to prove that Lincoln and Edwards had collected the debts on behalf of the firm yet never paid the firm its due.[94] Lincoln was greatly troubled by the case, and when he wrote his attorney in Lexington he found it "difficult to suppress my indignation towards those who have got up this claim against me."[95] Perhaps suspecting that his litigious brother-in-law Levi O. Todd was behind the lawsuit, he fumed that, "This matter harasses my feelings a good deal," and complained that the time needed to find evidence in the case would cost him time away from his active law practice.[96] Despite being busy with work on the circuit, Lincoln doggedly found evidence in his favor and wrote several times to his lawyer, assuring him that despite any claim made under oath he would "*disprove* it."[97] Eventually, the plaintiffs dismissed their case when Lincoln produced the necessary evidence to show that he had never collected the debts, either because they were never sent to him in the first place or because the debtors were too destitute to warrant process. Lincoln did admit to obtaining $50, a fractional amount on one claim, but Robert Todd had allowed him to keep the proceeds for his trouble.[98]

When Robert Todd died in 1849, he left a will and a modest estate to his widow and fourteen children.[99] One of Mary's siblings successfully challenged the will because it was only signed by one witness, causing the estate to be tied up in litigation for several years.[100] In the end, Mary and Lincoln had to pay money back into the estate to equalize the distributions based on the court's judgment.[101] Apparently they had received more money or property than several other heirs.[102] Lincoln and Edwards alternately represented the Springfield Todds in this litigation through correspondence with their Lexington attorney, George B. Kinkead.[103] After their father's death, the Todd siblings also tried to nullify one of Robert Todd's land conveyances, claiming the deed was defective. This and other similar protracted schemes inspired by Lincoln's in-laws kept the Lincolns in Lexington's Fayette County Circuit Court throughout much of the 1850s.[104]

Lincoln's most notorious Kentucky client was Robert Matson, a planter who owned property both in Bourbon County, Kentucky, and in Coles County, Illinois. He owned a few slaves who worked on his Kentucky farm, and at some point after establishing his "Black Grove" farm in Coles County in 1836, he began using slave labor there as well. Matson was a member of an entrepreneurial family that spread west from Bourbon County to Illinois, western Kentucky, Missouri, and Texas. During the War of 1812 he served as a lieutenant in his brother's militia company and fought bravely at the River Raisin. He was a staunch Henry Clay Whig and served in the Kentucky House of Representatives. Matson had a creative business sense, perhaps even of such a quality as to make him unique in his unfettered times, and he scrambled his whole life in the attempted creation of wealth. His scheme in Coles County was just part of this effort.[105]

At first, he made a show of rotating slaves between his farms in a nod to Illinois law, which prohibited slavery but allowed slave owners to move their property through the state. As long as Matson could argue his slaves were technically in transit he could get away with his scheme. Unfortunately for Matson, he lived in an area heavily populated by yeoman farmers from the Upland South who had moved north to get away from slavery. Eventually, locals caught on to Matson's charade, and when his slave Jane Bryant emancipated herself and her four children in mid-August 1847 and showed up at a local abolitionist's home, she found support for her efforts.[106]

Illinois law required African Americans to certify their free status with their county of residence. Since Jane and her children were not certified, they were assumed to be fugitives from labor, and at Matson's request the county sheriff arrested them. Abolitionists Hiram Rutherford and Gideon Ashmore, a local doctor and a tavern keeper, respectively, hired attorneys and applied for a writ of habeas corpus. Matson, in turn, also hired attorneys, including Lincoln, in order to fight in court for the return of his slaves. Four of the five attorneys known to have participated in the case were Kentucky natives.[107]

Upon arriving in the Coles County seat of Charleston in time for the hearing, Lincoln was approached by Rutherford to represent him, since Matson was also pursuing civil penalties against Rutherford and Ashmore, of $500 per slave (the maximum fine allowed under Illinois law for harboring fugitive slaves).[108] Reluctantly, Lincoln informed Rutherford of his having been previously retained by Matson.[109] During the habeas corpus hearing Lincoln argued that the Bryants were in transit, they were going back to Kentucky and were thus rightfully Matson's property.[110] Illinois courts were bound to honor the Kentuckian's rights under the doctrine of interstate comity. The judges, however, ruled in favor of the Bryants and gave them their freedom.[111] Chief Justice of the Illinois Supreme Court William Wilson concluded that Matson had held the Bryants in a condition of slavery for over two years at Black Grove, and in doing so he had manumitted them from service under the Illinois Constitution.[112] The right of rendition in the U.S. Constitution, the supporting federal fugitive slave law, and subsequent federal court rulings all concluded that a fugitive from labor must escape from the state in which he or she owed service into another state.[113] The Bryants never escaped from Kentucky, they were brought voluntarily by their master into Illinois.[114] In doing so he forfeited any federal protection, and, by all but establishing their residency on Illinois soil for two years, Matson perhaps unknowingly freed his slaves under a provision of the Illinois Constitution.[115]

Matson moved back to Kentucky and started a new farm operation in Fulton County after marrying his longtime housekeeper and overseer. He still owned several slaves who worked his farms, and he also employed them in the building of a local railroad venture. The other Kentuckians in this story, the Bryants, fared less well. Jane and her children left the United States not long after they gained their freedom. Representatives of the American Colonization Society prevailed upon them to emigrate to Liberia along with hundreds of other freed slaves. So it was that early the following year Jane and her family, along with her freedman husband, Anthony, all left New Orleans for Liberia on a ship chartered by the Colonization Society. Sometime later an African American minister from Springfield, Illinois, visited Liberia and spoke with Anthony. Reverend Ball found Anthony distraught over his family's destitute circumstances in the new African republic, and Bryant begged Ball to work for their return to the United States. There is no further information about the fate of the Bryant family.[116]

What was Lincoln's attitude toward these representatives of Kentucky, both the Bryants and Matson? Lincoln had well-formed, negative opinions about slavery by 1847; some of his strongest feelings came from seeing it in person while visiting the South. However, he also had a lot in common politically with Matson and certainly had high opinions about Kentuckians of the Matson stripe. They were largely men with whom Lincoln worked as a lawyer, worked for as a lawyer, and looked up to as politicians. In taking up Matson's cause, Lincoln challenged his personal aversion to slavery because Matson asked him to; Matson retained Lincoln before Rutherford had a chance to request his services.[117] Lincoln did not discriminate among clients seeking his services and held himself professionally dedicated to his clients no matter the issue. It also appears, however, he wished to see this vital issue well argued in court.[118] Because he was close to both judges involved, he understood from them the unusual nature of this case. The Bryant case, a habeas corpus hearing before a county circuit court, was not only unusual for the fact that two judges presided, but because an opinion was to be issued and published in a national law journal. All involved in the case, the lawyers and the judges, intended this case to stand as precedent—a bellwether of the Illinois courts' attitude toward the growing slavery question.[119]

While the legal issue of slavery rarely surfaced in Lincoln's law practice (Lincoln himself only participated in three such cases), he did share his feelings about slavery with his legal brethren. Reminiscences by two lawyers with whom Lincoln traveled the circuit, John T. Stuart and Theophilus Lyle Dickey, both of whom were born and educated in Kentucky, contain evidence that Lincoln struggled with the politically charged issue.[120]

Stuart and Lincoln debated the issue on horseback while traveling the circuit.[121] The debate concluded with Stuart declaring that soon everyone would be either abolitionists or Democrats.[122] Lincoln answered that if such were the case, his mind was made up: "the Slavery question can't be compromised."[123] Stuart also made his choice, and they steadily followed separate political paths thereafter.[124] Stuart eventually won a seat in Congress in 1862, endorsed as a Democrat and a critic of Lincoln administration policies, including the preliminary Emancipation Proclamation.[125]

Judge Dickey also maintained a critical view of antislavery rhetoric. While sharing a hotel room in Bloomington, Illinois, during the mid-1850s, Lincoln and Dickey debated the night away, arguing over the future of slavery in the United States.[126] Finally, Dickey went to bed, and when he woke in the morning he found Lincoln had not slept at all and had continued to brood over the question until morning. Without missing a beat, Lincoln continued the debate and insisted that it was "not possible for slavery to continue to exist in the nation." By 1858, Dickey, a lifelong Henry Clay Whig, left Lincoln's political sphere and joined with the Democrats out of fear that the Republican Party was dominated by abolitionists.[127] While Lincoln clearly respected both of these lawyers, and probably even respected their conservative views on emancipation, he broke with his fellow Kentuckians over the morality of slavery. The slavery issue separated him from many of the lawyers and judges that he knew and respected throughout his career.[128]

The Civil War all but tore the Todd family in half, and two of Lincoln's brothers-in-law fought and died for the Confederacy.[129] Mary's brother-in-law Hardin Helm, a Confederate brigadier general, died at Chickamauga.[130] While Lincoln and Joshua Speed's strong friendship of the late 1830s and early 1840s faded with time and distance, the slavery issue also helped to form a wedge between them.[131] Speed, himself a slaveholder, was not an active slavery advocate, but he could not bring himself to accept Lincoln's movement toward emancipation.[132] Despite these political differences, Speed actively worked in support of the Union in Kentucky during the

Civil War and served as Lincoln's confidant on political conditions in the commonwealth.[133]

In Illinois, Lincoln was sometimes referred to as a Kentuckian, even after he had been in the state for twenty-five years. Indeed, in notes for a speech he intended to deliver to Kentuckians in 1861 (but never did), he referred to himself as a Kentuckian.[134] During the years Lincoln practiced law, however, he developed into his own man, shedding some of the traditional Kentucky motifs that made him popular among his Illinois friends and colleagues. Over time he moved steadily away from the quiet acceptance of slavery exhibited by so many moderate Kentuckians, a process that ended with the passage of the Thirteenth Amendment.

Notes

This essay was originally published in slightly different form in the *Northern Kentucky Law Review* 36, no. 2, and is reprinted here by permission.

1. Kenneth J. Winkle, *The Young Eagle: The Rise of Abraham Lincoln* 10 (Dallas, Tex: Taylor Trade Publishing, 2001).

2. Ibid. at 10–11.

3. Ibid.; Louis A. Warren, *Lincoln's Youth: Indiana Years, Seven to Twenty-One, 1816–1830,* at 13 (Indiana Historical Society, 1991) (1959).

4. Winkle, *supra* note 1, at 10.

5. Ibid. at 13; Warren, *supra* note 3, at 20.

6. Winkle, *supra* note 1, at 13.

7. John Mack Faragher, *Sugar Creek: Life on the Illinois Prairie* 49–51 (New Haven, Conn.: Yale Univ. Press, 1986).

8. Winkle, *supra* note 1, at 22.

9. Ibid. at 24.

10. Ibid. at 26.

11. Douglas K. Meyer, *Making the Heartland Quilt: A Geographical History of Settlement and Migration in Early-Nineteenth-Century Illinois* 142–43 (Carbondale, Ill.: Southern Illinois Univ. Press, 2000).

12. Ibid. at 141.

13. Ibid. at 143–44; For maps of the Eighth Judicial Circuit during the years Lincoln practiced law, see the reference section in *The Law Practice of Abraham Lincoln: Complete Documentary Edition,* DVD-ROM (Martha L. Benner and Cullom Davis et al., eds., Univ. of Illinois Press, 2000), available at www.lawpracticeofabrahamlincoln.org.

14. Meyer, *supra* note 11, at 141.

15. Ibid. at 143; Winkle, *supra* note 1, at 24.

16. Meyer, *supra* note 11, at 143–44.

17. Ibid. at 144, 166–68; Winkle, *supra* note 1, at 25.

18. Meyer, *supra* note 11, at 143.

19. Ibid., especially map at 143.

20. See the "Peers and Clients" section in "Statistical Portrait" and corresponding biographies, all in the reference section in *The Law Practice of Abraham Lincoln, supra* note 13.

21. Faragher, *supra* note 7, at 44–51; Meyer, *supra* note 11, at 98–99.

22. See James E. Davis, *Frontier Illinois* 247–81 (Indiana Univ. Press, 1998); and Winkle, *supra* note 1, at 30–55; For the variety of legal actions in Lincoln's law practice, see the "Legal Actions" section in "Statistical Portrait," in the reference section in *The Law Practice of Abraham Lincoln*, DVD-ROM, *supra* note 13; and 1 *The Papers of Abraham Lincoln: Legal Documents and Cases* xxxiii–xlii (Daniel W. Stowell et al., eds., Charlottesville: Univ. of Virginia Press, 2008).

23. Letter from Abraham Lincoln to John T. Stuart (December 23, 1839) (on file with the Abraham Lincoln Presidential Library and Museum), available at http://ilhpa.hpa.state.il.us/alplm/docs/200192.xml.

24. See Mark E. Steiner, *An Honest Calling: The Law Practice of Abraham Lincoln* 70–74 (Northern Illinois Univ. Press, 2006).

25. Benjamin P. Thomas, *Lincoln's New Salem* 74, 118 (Southern Illinois Univ. Press, 1987) (1954).

26. Winkle, *supra* note 1, at 31–32.

27. 1 *Encyclopedia of the History of St. Louis, A Compendium of History and Biography for Ready Reference* 106–7 (William Hyde and Howard L. Conard, eds., Southern History Co., 1899).

28. "Appendix: Biographical Sketches of Officers and Members of the Constitutional Convention," in *The Constitutional Debates of 1847* (Trustees of the Illinois State Historical Library, vol. 14, Constitutional Series, vol. 2, Arthur C. Cole, ed., 1919).

29. See Richard C. Wade, *The Urban Frontier: Pioneer Life in Early Pittsburgh, Cincinnati, Lexington, Louisville, and St. Louis* 198, 233–36 (Univ. of Chicago Press, 1959).

30. Ibid. at 235.

31. Steiner, *supra* note 24, at 31.

32. Ibid. at 29–30.

33. See biographies of Orville Hickman Browning, Ninian W. Edwards, Thomas Ford, Joseph Gillespie, James Haines, John J. Hardin, Gustavus P.

Koerner, Josiah Lamborn, Thomas A. Marshall, Nathaniel Pope, David Prickett, Jesse B. Thomas Jr., and Richard Yates in 4 *The Papers of Abraham Lincoln: Legal Documents and Cases, supra* note 22, at 337, 347, 349–50, 351–52, 353, 354, 361–62, 362, 366–67, 372–73, 374, 380, 386.

34. Steiner, *supra* note 24, at 30.

35. 4 *The Papers of Abraham Lincoln: Legal Documents and Cases, supra* note 22, at 337.

36. 4 *The Papers of Abraham Lincoln: Legal Documents and Cases, supra* note 22, at 377.

37. Ibid.

38. Ibid.

39. Ibid. at 378.

40. Ibid.

41. William H. Townsend, "Stuart and Lincoln," 17 *A.B.A. J.* 82, 83 (1931).

42. Ibid.; 4 *The Papers of Abraham Lincoln: Legal Documents and Cases, supra* note 22, at 378.

43. 4 *The Papers of Abraham Lincoln: Legal Documents and Cases, supra* note 22, at 378.

44. Townsend, *supra* note 41, at 82, 83.

45. 4 *The Papers of Abraham Lincoln: Legal Documents and Cases, supra* note 22, at 378.

46. Ibid. at 364.

47. Ibid.

48. Ibid.

49. Paul M. Angle, "Stephen T. Logan Talks about Lincoln," 12 *Lincoln Centennial Ass'n Bull.* 3 (September 1, 1928).

50. Ibid.

51. Ibid.

52. 4 *The Papers of Abraham Lincoln: Legal Documents and Cases, supra* note 22, at 364; William H. Townsend, "Logan and Lincoln," 19 *A.B.A. J.* 87, 87–90 (1933).

53. 4 *The Papers of Abraham Lincoln: Legal Documents and Cases, supra* note 22, at 364.

54. Ibid. at 356.

55. Ibid.

56. Ibid.

57. David Donald, *Lincoln's Herndon* 45–47 (Knopf, 1948).

58. Ibid. at 45.

59. Ibid.

60. 4 *The Papers of Abraham Lincoln: Legal Documents and Cases, supra* note 22, at 356.

61. Ibid.

62. Donald, *Lincoln's Herndon* , *supra* note 57, at 105–7.

63. 1 *The Papers of Abraham Lincoln: Legal Documents and Cases, supra* note 22, at 251–52.

64. Ibid.

65. Ibid. at 251.

66. Ibid.

67. Ibid.

68. Ibid. at 252–53.

69. 1 *The Papers of Abraham Lincoln: Legal Documents and Cases, supra* note 22, at 252.

70. Ibid.

71. Ibid. at 251–58.

72. Stephen Berry, *House of Abraham: Lincoln and the Todds, a Family Divided by War* 25 (Houghton Mifflin, 2007).

73. Ibid.

74. Ibid.

75. Ibid.

76. Ibid. at 26.

77. Ibid. at 27.

78. Berry, *supra* note 72, at 29–30.

79. Ibid.

80. Ibid. at 32–33; 1 *The Papers of Abraham Lincoln: Legal Documents and Cases, supra* note 22, at 347–48.

81. Jean H. Baker, *Mary Todd Lincoln: A Biography* 132 (Norton, 1987).

82. Christopher A. Schnell, *Stovepipe Hat and Quill Pen: The Artifacts of Abraham Lincoln's Law Practice* 8 (2002).

83. Ibid.

84. Baker, *supra* note 81, at 132–33.

85. Ibid. at 133.

86. Ibid. at 132–33.

87. Ibid. at 132.

88. Ibid.

89. Ibid. at 132–33.

90. Baker, *supra* note 81, at 130–33.

91. Berry, *supra* note 72, at ix–x.

92. 1 *The Papers of Abraham Lincoln: Legal Documents and Cases, supra* note 22, at 301–37.

93. Ibid. at 357.

94. Ibid.

95. Letter from Abraham Lincoln to George B. Kinkead, Attorney (May 27, 1853) (published in William H. Townsend, *Abraham Lincoln, Defendant: Lincoln's Most Interesting Lawsuit* 8 [1923]).

96. *The Law Practice of Abraham Lincoln, supra* note 13, Letter from Abraham Lincoln to George B. Kinkead, Attorney (September 13, 1853) Document ID 137244, File ID L05934.

97. Ibid., Letter from Abraham Lincoln to George B. Kinkead, Attorney (July 6, 1853), Document ID 137242, File ID L05934.

98. 2 *The Papers of Abraham Lincoln: Legal Documents and Cases, supra* note 22, at 371; See Berry, *supra* note 72, at 45 (discussing Levi's "litigiousness").

99. Berry, *supra* note 72, at 41; William H. Townsend, *Lincoln and His Wife's Home Town* 205–6 (Bobbs-Merrill, 1929).

100. Berry, *supra* note 72, at 41; Townsend, *supra* note 99, at 206.

101. Berry, *supra* note 72, at 42.

102. Ibid.

103. Townsend, *supra* note 99, at 206.

104. Ibid. at 206–48; see also *Edwards et al. v. Parker et al.* (File ID L05936), *Parker v. Richardson et al.* (File ID L05935), *Todd et al. v. Edwards et al.* (File ID L05938), *Todd et al. v. Wickliffe* (File ID L05933), *Todd et al. v. Wickliffe* (File ID L05932), *Todd v. Oldham et al.* (File ID L05940), and *Todd v. Todd et al.* (File ID L05939), in *The Law Practice of Abraham Lincoln*, DVD-ROM, *supra* note 13.

105. 2 *The Papers of Abraham Lincoln: Legal Documents and Cases, supra* note 22, at 1.

106. Ibid. at 2–3.

107. Ibid. at 3, 5, 9–10.

108. Ibid. at 7.

108. Steiner, *supra* note 24, at 113.

110. 2 *The Papers of Abraham Lincoln: Legal Documents and Cases, supra* note 22, at 18; "In the Matter of Jane, A Woman of Color" 5 *West. L. J.* 202, 202–6 (1848).

111. 2 *The Papers of Abraham Lincoln: Legal Documents and Cases, supra* note 22, at 18; "In the Matter of Jane," *supra* note 110, at 206.

112. 2 *The Papers of Abraham Lincoln: Legal Documents and Cases, supra* note 22, at 18; "In the Matter of Jane," *supra* note 110, at 206.

113. 2 *The Papers of Abraham Lincoln: Legal Documents and Cases, supra* note 22, at 18; "In the Matter of Jane," *supra* note 110, at 204–5.

114. 2 *The Papers of Abraham Lincoln: Legal Documents and Cases, supra* note 22, at 18; "In the Matter of Jane," *supra* note 110, at 202.

115. 2 *The Papers of Abraham Lincoln: Legal Documents and Cases, supra* note 22, at 18; "In the Matter of Jane," *supra* note 110, at 206.

116. 2 *The Papers of Abraham Lincoln: Legal Documents and Cases, supra* note 22, at 27.

117. Steiner, *supra* note 24, at 113.

118. See ibid.

119. For an excellent discussion of why Lincoln represented Matson, see ibid. at 103–36.

120. The three cases were *Bailey v. Cromwell & McNaghton* (File ID L01213), *Ex parte Warman* (File ID L05867), and *In re Bryant et al.* (File ID L00714), in *The Law Practice of Abraham Lincoln, supra* note 13.

121. *Herndon's Informants: Letters, Interviews, and Statements about Abraham Lincoln* 64, 519 (Douglas L. Wilson and Rodney O. Davis, eds., Urbana: Univ. of Illinois Press, 1998).

122. Ibid. at 64, 482, 519.

123. Ibid.

124. 21 *American National Biography* 78 (John A. Garraty and Mark C. Carnes, eds., New York: Oxford Univ. Press, 1999).

125. Ibid.

126. See *Herndon's Informants, supra* note 121, at 504.

127. Ibid. at 643.

128. Letter of William Pitt Kellogg to James R. B. Van Cleave, Secretary of Lincoln Centennial Association (February 8, 1909) (on file with Abraham Lincoln Presidential Library and Museum); Leonard Swett, "In Memoriam, T. Lyle Dickey," *Proceedings in the Supreme Court of Illinois at its September Term, 1885, at Ottawa, with Addresses before the Illinois State Bar Association and United States Circuit Court,* at 32–33 (Springfield, Ill.: H. W. Rokker, 1887).

129. Berry, *supra* note 72, at xi.

130. Ibid.

131. See David Herbert Donald, *"We Are Lincoln Men": Abraham Lincoln and His Friends* 55–62 (New York: Simon and Schuster, 2003).

132. Ibid. at 61.

133. Ibid. at 58–60.

134. 2 *The Collected Works of Abraham Lincoln* 379 (Roy P. Basler et al., eds., New Brunswick, N.J.: Rutgers Univ. Press, 1953); 4 ibid. at 200.

Part Three

The Washington Years

Abraham Lincoln as Practical Constitutional Lawyer

Mackubin Thomas Owens

There is an old saying that goes, "Everybody talks about the weather, but no one does anything about it." The same could be said about scholars of constitutional law. They may argue about nuances of the Constitution, but for the most part these debates are of interest only to other constitutional lawyers.

Those who practice constitutional law do, of course, have some impact on how the Constitution is read. But it is rare for a lawyer of any kind to have a major impact on the Constitution itself. One lawyer who did was Abraham Lincoln. Indeed, no one other than the Framers of the Constitution themselves had a greater impact on the document than Lincoln. In fact, Lincoln's contributions may exceed those of the framers of the document in that, faced by an unprecedented crisis, he saved the Constitution—and with it republican government. As Daniel Farber has remarked, "to call the Civil War a constitutional crisis is almost a misuse of words, like calling Pearl Harbor a military setback. In the Civil War, the Constitution was placed under pressure that it had never seen before and has not seen since."[1]

To understand what Lincoln accomplished, it is necessary to recognize just exactly what it was that Lincoln believed he was saving. It was not simply "the Union." It was not even simply "the Constitution." For Lincoln, the Constitution was principally a framework for sharing power within a *republican government*. *This* was the real thing he aimed to preserve, because only republican government was capable of protecting the liberty of the people.

Lincoln believed the foundation for such a government to be the Declaration of Independence. The Declaration asserts that since "all men are created equal," a legitimate government derives its "just powers from the consent of the governed." It is the principles found in the Declaration of Independence that authorize "the people" to "ordain and establish" a Constitution. Such a Constitution establishes a government the power of which is limited by its purpose: securing the God-given rights of life, liberty, and the pursuit of happiness. Thus the Constitution is the *means* of implementing a republican government capable of protecting the equal natural rights of all.

Lincoln articulated the relationship between liberty and republican government on the one hand and the Constitution on the other in a fragment that he probably composed in 1860, perhaps as the basis for some speeches he gave in New England. Here Lincoln observes that, as important as the Constitution and union may be, there is "something back of these, entwining itself more closely about the human heart. That something, is the principle of 'Liberty to all'" as expressed in the Declaration. With or without the Declaration, Lincoln continues, the United States could have declared independence, but "*without* it, we could not, I think, have secured our free government, and consequent prosperity."[2]

Lincoln refers to the Declaration's principle of liberty for all as a "word 'fitly spoken,' which has proved an 'apple of gold' to us. The Union and the Constitution, are the picture of silver, subsequently framed around it," not to conceal or destroy the apple "but to adorn, and preserve it. The picture was made for the apple—not the apple for the picture. So let us act, that neither picture, [n]or apple, shall ever be blurred, or broken."[3] In other words, republican liberty was the real thing to be preserved by saving the union and the Constitution.[4]

The *means* to preserve the *end* of republican government were dictated by *prudence*. According to Aristotle, prudence is concerned with deliberating well about those things that can be other than they are (means). In political affairs, prudence requires the statesman to be able to adapt universal principles to particular circumstances in order to arrive at the means that are best, given existing circumstances.[5] For Lincoln to achieve the end of preserving the union and thereby republican liberty, he had to choose the means necessary and proper under the circumstances. Aristotle calls prudence the virtue most characteristic of the statesman. It is through the prism of prudence that we must judge Lincoln's actions during the War of the Rebellion.

There are two categories of constitutional issues raised by the War of the

Rebellion. The first concerns federalism, the theory concerning the "nature of the Union and the states." This debate lies at the heart of the issue of secession.

The second category involves the power of the executive in the conduct of war or response to domestic insurrection: i.e., "the breadth of the president's independent power to pursue the national interest, the scope of civil liberties during national emergencies, and the collision between the imperatives of national survival and the rule of law."[6]

Secession

Lincoln faced an emergency that indeed threatened to break the "picture of silver," and with it the "apple of gold." The crisis he faced was unprecedented. Insurgents, arguing that the Constitution itself provided for breaking up the union, initiated a rebellion "too powerful to be suppressed by the ordinary course of judicial proceedings."[7] Lincoln could have responded as his predecessor, James Buchanan, did, by claiming that while secession was illegal, so was military intervention to stop it.[8] But to merely enforce simple legality would have led to the complete destruction of the union. Alternatively, he could have accepted a compromise that essentially would have given the slave states what they wanted—for example, the Crittenden plan to extend the 36°30' Missouri Compromise line (which applied only to territories carved out of the Louisiana Purchase) to the Pacific coast.

But Lincoln believed his constitutional responsibility required him to hold the country together and convey it to his successor as the founders intended—as one indivisible union. This included the possible use of force. As he told his private secretary, John Nicolay, before his inauguration, "The necessity of keeping the government together by force [was an] ugly point." But "the very existence of a general and national government implies the legal power, right, and duty of maintaining its own integrity."[9]

Lincoln's first task was to offer a constitutional argument against secession. Most Southerners contended that there was a constitutional right to secede.[10] According to this view, the sovereignty of the states was prior to that of the union. By ratifying the Constitution, the states had delegated some functions and powers to the federal government, but gave up no sovereignty. Since the states had ratified the Constitution by convention, they could "de-ratify" it by the same process.

The most comprehensive articulation of the view that Southern secession was a legitimate constitutional act is found in *A Constitutional View of the Late War between the States*, written by Alexander Stephens, vice president of the Confederacy, published shortly after the war. Echoing John C. Calhoun, Stephens's defense of the right of secession is based on two major premises.[11] The first is that the United States was a federal union of states that individually retained undivided sovereignty. "The absolute Sovereignty of these original States, respectively," wrote Stephens, "was never parted with by them in that or any other Compact of Union ever entered into by them."

The second premise is a corollary of the first—that because the states were sovereign, they retained a constitutional right to secede. In this view, the union was a league, akin to a treaty organization like NATO. Members of a league accede to a league without giving up their sovereignty and may therefore secede at their pleasure. Furthermore, Stephens claimed, all presidents from Jefferson to Lincoln had acknowledged the right of secession.

Lincoln believed that there could be no constitutional process that permits a majority within a state lawfully to nullify the acts of the federal union within the boundaries of its delegated powers. There can be no right to destroy the Constitution. As he told Nicolay, "the right of a State to secede is not an open or debatable question.... It is the duty of a President to execute the laws and maintain the existing Government. He cannot entertain and proposition for dissolution or dismemberment."[12]

In his July 4, 1861, speech to Congress in special session, Lincoln called the claim that "any state of the Union may, *consistently* with the national Constitution, and therefore *lawfully* and *peacefully*, withdraw from the Union without the consent of the Union or any other State" an "ingenious sophism."[13] But Lincoln was not an innovator when it came to this issue. Nearly every statesman from the founding period on had previously made this point. These are the same individuals that Stephens claims recognized the right of secession. Whence the source of the disagreement?

The first problem is that the meaning of federalism changed during the founding era. Calhoun and Stephens used "federal" in the pre-American founding sense of a loose compact among separate and sovereign political entities. But the American constitutional experience had transformed the meaning of federal. As James Madison observed, the Americans had created a system of government "without precedent ancient or modern," one that although "wholly republican" was "partly federal, partly national."

So complete was this transformation that even the opponents of the Constitution, the so-called Anti-Federalists, embraced the new meaning, recognizing, as much as the Federalists, that rather than a league, the union constituted a nation that could not be torn asunder at the pleasure of its component parts.

That the American republic was both federal and national was the dominant view among statesmen of the antebellum period. For instance, in his reply to Calhoun on February 16, 1833, Daniel Webster observed that the state conventions, including that of South Carolina, did not accede to a league or association when they approved the Constitution, but ratified and confirmed that Constitution as a form of government.[14]

Andrew Jackson made the same point in his proclamation to the people of South Carolina during the nullification crisis. The Constitution, said Jackson, derives its whole authority from the people, not the states. The states "retained all the power they did not grant. But each State, having expressly parted with so many powers as to constitute, jointly with the other States, a single nation, cannot, from that period, possess any right to secede, because such secession does not break a league, but destroys the unity of a nation."[15] And Madison, who presumably knew something about the constitutional theory of the American founding, was horrified by the idea that the coordinate sovereignty retained by the states, as stated in the Tenth Amendment, implied the power of nullification, interposition, or secession.[16]

Lincoln argued that the union created the states, not the other way around, and that therefore the states had no other legal status than that which they held in the union.[17] The Revolutionary generation universally understood the *separation* of thirteen colonies from Great Britain and the *union* among them to have been accomplished simultaneously. Colonial resolutions called for both independence and union. According to Jefferson and Madison in 1825, the Declaration of Independence constituted an "act of Union of [the] States."[18]

The Articles of Confederation, a document that begins and ends with the assertion that the union is perpetual, was an unsuccessful attempt to govern the union created by the Declaration of Independence. It failed because the central government lacked the necessary power to carry out its obligations. The Constitution was intended to rectify the problems of the Articles—to create "a more perfect Union." As George Washington wrote in his letter transmitting the Constitution to Congress, "In all our deliberations . . . we kept steadily in our view that which appears to us the greatest interest of every true American, the consolidation of our Union, in which is involved our prosperity, felicity, perhaps our national existence."[19]

After the war, Alexander H. Stephens, vice president of the Confederacy, claimed that the right of secession had been widely accepted before 1860. For instance, Stephens invoked Lincoln himself in support of his thesis regarding the right of secession. He cited Lincoln's assertion in a speech of January 12, 1848, that "any people, any where, being inclined and having the power, have the right to rise up and shake off the existing Government, and form a new one that suits them better. . . . Any portion of such people that can, may revolutionize, and make their own of so much of the territory as they inhabit."[20]

But Stephens was being disingenuous. Lincoln was not invoking a *constitutional right* to destroy the union but the *natural right* of revolution, an inalienable right clearly expressed in the Declaration of Independence which Lincoln never denied. As he said in his First Inaugural of 1861, "This country, with its institutions, belongs to the people who inhabit it. Whenever they shall grow weary of the existing government, they can exercise their *constitutional right* of amending it, or their *revolutionary right* to dismember or overthrow it." But the people's right to revolution is in tension with the president's constitutional "duty . . . to administer the present government, as it came into his hands, and to transmit it, unimpaired by him, to his successor."[21]

Again, Lincoln was merely reiterating the commonly accepted political opinions of his predecessors. In the aforementioned "Proclamation regarding Nullification," Jackson said, "secession, like any other revolutionary act, may be morally justified by the extremity of oppression; but to call it a *constitutional right* is confounding the meaning of terms" (emphasis added).[22] But despite claiming to be the true heirs of the American founding, the seceding states never invoked the right of revolution that Jackson, Webster, Lincoln, and others acknowledged. Why not?

The main reason was that while the founders understood the right of revolution to be an inalienable natural right of individuals antecedent to political society, Calhoun, the architect of the theory of state sovereignty used to justify secession expressly repudiated the idea of individual inalienable natural rights. Calhoun dismissed the fundamental idea of the American founding—that "all men are created equal"—as the "most false and dangerous of all political errors."[23] Given the large slave population of the South, this denial of the inalienable natural rights of individuals, including the right of revolution, was no doubt prudent.

For Lincoln, secession constituted a repudiation of republican government as understood by the founders. For Calhoun, sovereignty was not a characteristic of individuals, but of collective political bodies. Individual rights, such as they were, were prescriptive, not natural. If Calhoun was right, then the founders were wrong.

For the founders, the purpose of government was to protect the equal natural rights of all. They understood these rights to be antecedent to the creation of political society and government. The just powers of government are derived from the consent of the governed who possess the equal natural rights that republican government is supposed to protect. While the people never relinquish their right to revolution, in practice, this natural right is replaced by free elections, the outcome of which are determined by majority rule.

When the states ratified the Constitution of 1787, they pledged that they would accept the results of elections conducted according to its rules. In violation of this pledge, the Southern states seceded because they did not like the outcome of the election of 1860. Thus, secession was the interruption of the constitutional operation of republican government, substituting the rule of the minority for that of the majority. Indeed, as William Freehling has argued, the supposed right to break up the government when the minority does not get its way is really nothing but blackmail.[24]

In his July 4 address to Congress, Lincoln observed that the American "experiment" in popular government had passed two of three tests—the successful *establishing* and the successful *administering* of it. One test remained. Could popular government in America *maintain* itself against a "formidable internal attempt to overthrow it"? It had yet to be proved, said Lincoln, that ballots were "the rightful and peaceful successors to bullets" and that "when ballots have fairly and constitutionally decided, there can be no successful appeal back to bullets."[25]

It is interesting to note that had secession been permitted to stand, the breakup of the union likely would have continued. Where that dynamic would have led is suggested by the fact that in January 1861 Fernando Wood, the Democratic mayor of New York City, recommended that the city secede from the state of New York and establish itself as a "free city."[26]

Lincoln believed that his constitutional obligations did not permit him to acquiesce in secession, unless it was authorized by those who had chosen him to be president. The people, not the chief magistrate, can "fix terms for the separation of the States." The duty of the executive "is to administer the present government, as it came into his hands, and to transmit it, unimpaired by him, to his successor."[27]

The War Power of the Executive

As Geoffrey Perret has observed, Lincoln "create[d] the role of commander in chief,"[28] but he did not create his war power out of whole cloth. Lincoln believed that the power he needed to deal with the rebellion was a part of the executive power found in the Constitution. As he wrote to James Conkling in August 1863, "I think the Constitution invests its commander-in-chief, with the law of war, in time of war."[29] In addition to the commander in chief clause, he found his war power in the clause of Article II requiring him to "take care that the laws be faithfully executed," and in his presidential oath "to preserve, protect, and defend the Constitution of the United States."

Some constitutional scholars (for example, Edward Corwin and Raoul Berger) have rejected Lincoln's claim that the commander in chief clause and the "faithfully execute" clause provide an inherent presidential war power.[30] But these scholars seem to take their constitutional bearings from normal times, during which the rights of the people are secure and the legislature, which expresses the will of the people, is the main instrument of majoritarian representative government. During normal times, the president, although he possesses his own constitutional source of power, primarily executes the laws passed by Congress.

But in times of extraordinary emergency, the principle that *salus populi est suprema lex* (the safety of the people is the highest law) trumps all other considerations and justifies extraordinary executive powers. As Thomas Jefferson observed in a letter to Caesar A. Rodney, "in times of peace the people look most to their representatives; but in war, to the executive solely . . . to give direction to their affairs, with a confidence as auspicious as it is well-founded."[31]

This of course is the "prerogative" described by John Locke as the power of the executive "to act according to discretion for the public good, *without the prescription of the law and sometimes even against it.*"[32] Since the fundamental law that the executive ultimately must implement is to preserve society, it is "fit that the laws themselves should in some cases give way to the executive power, or rather to *this fundamental law of nature and government, viz. that as much as may be, all members of society are to be preserved.*"[33]

The prerogative is rendered necessary by the fact that laws arising from legislative deliberation cannot foresee every exigency. For the safety of the republic, the executive must retain some latitude for action. Jefferson expressed the spirit of the prerogative in a letter to John B. Colvin. Responding to Colvin's question concerning "whether circumstances do not sometimes occur, which make it a duty in officers of high trust, to assume authorities beyond the law . . . ," Jefferson wrote:

> A strict observance of the written law is doubtless one of the highest duties of a good citizen, but it is not the highest. The laws of necessity, of self preservation, of saving our country when in danger, are of higher obligation. To lose our country by a scrupulous adherence to written law, would be to lose the law itself, with life, liberty, property and all those who are enjoying them with us; thus absurdly sacrificing the ends to the means. . . . It is incumbent on those only who accept of greatest charges, to risk themselves on great occasion, when the safety of the nation, or some of its very high interests are at stake.[34]

Lincoln made the same point in his speech to Congress in special session after Fort Sumter in defense of his suspension of the writ of habeas corpus:

> The whole of the laws which were required to be faithfully executed were being resisted, and failing of execution in nearly one third of the States. Must they be allowed to finally fail of execution, even had it been perfectly clear that by the use of the means necessary to their execution some single law, made in such extreme tenderness of the citizen's liberty, that practically it relieves more of the guilty than of the innocent, should to a very limited extent be violated? To state the question more directly: are all the laws but one to go unexecuted, and the Government itself to go to pieces, lest that one be violated? Even in such a case, would not the official oath be broken

if the government should be overthrown, when it was believed that disregarding the single law would tend to preserve it?[35]

Lincoln did not believe he had violated the law, because Article I of the Constitution states that the privilege of the writ of habeas corpus may be suspended "when, in cases of rebellion or invasion, the public safety may require it."

Some scholars have taken issue with the idea that the prerogative should form a part of constitutional government. Sanford Levinson, for example, asks if the powers implied by the prerogative, as understood by Lincoln, "mean, in effect, that it is impossible for Presidents to violate their constitutional oath, so long as they are motivated in their conduct by the sincere desire to maintain 'free government' against those whom they view as its enemies, foreign or domestic?"[36]

Lincoln answered in the affirmative. An emergency power is useless unless it is sufficient to meet the emergency. Since the magnitude and the character of the emergency determine the extent of the necessary power, the president is in the best position to determine how much power he needs. In revoking General David Hunter's emancipation order in South Carolina, Lincoln stated that the decision to free slaves would depend on his determination that such a step "shall have become a necessity indispensable to the maintenance of the government." The exercise of such a power, he continued, "I reserve to myself."[37] In September 1862, Lincoln declared that an emancipation proclamation was part of his power as commander in chief, which gave him "a right to take any measure which may best subdue the enemy."[38]

But Lincoln's emphasis on preserving republican government taught him, as it should teach us, that the prerogative is limited by the will of the people, which "constitutionally expressed, is the ultimate law for all. If they should deliberately resolve to have immediate peace even at the loss of their country, and their liberty, I know not the power of the right to resist them. It is their own business, and they must do as they please with their own."[39]

In addition, Lincoln entertained no doubt that any extraordinary powers were limited to the duration of the emergency and not applicable to normal times. His reply to Erastus Corning and a group of New York Democrats who had criticized his war measures is also the proper response to Professor Levinson:

I can no more be persuaded that the Government can constitutionally take no strong measures in time of rebellion, because it can be shown that the same could not lawfully be taken in time of peace, than I can be persuaded that a particular drug is not good medicine for a sick man, because it can be shown not to be good for a well one. Nor am I able to appreciate the danger apprehended by the meeting [of the New York Democrats] that the American people will, by means of military arrest during the Rebellion, lose the right of Public Discussion, the Liberty of Speech and the Press, the Law of Evidence, Trial by Jury, and Habeas Corpus, throughout the indefinite peaceful future, which I trust lies before them, any more than I am able to believe that a man could contract so strong an appetite for emetics during temporary illness as to persist in feeding upon them during the remainder of his healthful life.[40]

Lincoln faced other dilemmas as a war president. One was the dual nature of the conflict: it was both a war and a domestic insurrection. As argued above, Lincoln believed that the states could not legally secede and that, accordingly, the Confederacy was a fiction. Thus he had to be careful lest the steps he took be construed as recognizing the Confederacy. This applied to his decision to blockade Southern ports, traditionally a measure taken against a belligerent, and to congressional passage of acts confiscating Rebel property. Indeed, his concerns about the constitutionality of the two confiscation acts passed by Congress and the fact that they implied recognition of the Confederacy led him to treat emancipation as a war measure.

Emancipation and the Constitution

Emancipation was certainly a controversial issue during the Civil War, and its constitutional basis remains often misunderstood even today. To understand Lincoln's actions with regard to ending slavery, it is necessary to recognize that until the passage of the Thirteenth Amendment to the Constitution the federal government had no authority over the institution of slavery where it existed. It had always been a matter left to the individual states. Lincoln made this point during his First Inaugural:

Apprehension seems to exist among the people of the Southern States, that by the accession of a Republican Administration, their property, and their peace, and personal security, are to be endangered. There has never been any reasonable cause for such apprehension. Indeed, the most ample evidence to the contrary has all the while existed, and been open to their inspection. It is found in nearly all the published speeches of him who now addresses you. I do but quote from one of those speeches when I declare that "I have no purpose, directly or indirectly, to interfere with the institution of slavery in the States where it exists. *I believe I have no lawful right to do so*, and I have no inclination to do so. [emphasis added][41]

His recognition of the fact that the federal government had no authority over the institution of slavery where it existed led him to endorse a proposed amendment to the Constitution "to the effect that the federal government, shall never interfere with the domestic institutions of the States, including that of persons held to service. To avoid misconstruction of what I have said, I depart from my purpose not to speak of particular amendments, so far as to say that, holding such a provision to now be implied constitutional law, I have no objection to its being made express, and irrevocable."[42] As a good lawyer, he realized that he could accept such an amendment because no such federal power existed in the first place.

Of course, Lincoln firmly believed that Congress did have the authority to prohibit the extension of slavery into the federal territories. Allen Guelzo has argued persuasively that Lincoln believed that if he could prevent the expansion of slavery and prevail upon slave state legislatures to accept gradual, compensated emancipation (funded by Congress), he could shrink slavery, making it uneconomical and placing it back on the eventual road to extinction that he believed the founders had envisioned.

The outbreak of war derailed the original version of his grand scheme, but even after the war began, Lincoln reasoned that the combination of military success against the Confederacy and compensated emancipation in the loyal slave states would lead to the collapse of the Confederacy, which had staked its hopes on eventually incorporating the so-called border states.[43]

But neither condition came to pass: Lincoln's proposals for compensated emancipation were rejected by the border states, and the Army of the Potomac under General George McClellan was driven back from Richmond after coming close to capturing it. Lincoln concluded that he did not have the time to pursue his preferred legislative strategy in the border states and that therefore something stronger and more precipitous was needed to bring the war to a successful conclusion.

There were several other alternatives for ending slavery favored by radical Republicans in Congress: treating fugitive slaves under federal control as "contrabands of war"; confiscation; and martial law emancipation. But Lincoln believed that all of these alternatives were unconstitutional and open to legal challenge.[44]

For instance, the application of confiscation and contraband—as these terms were understood in international law—to escaped slaves placed Lincoln in a quandary concerning the status of the Confederacy, because both could be understood to bestow upon it belligerent status. This was at odds with Lincoln's insistence that the states of the Confederacy could never legally leave the union. On the other hand, if the war was only a domestic rebellion, as Lincoln held, then confiscation of slave contraband violated the constitutional prohibition against bills of attainder.

A similar problem arose with the use of martial law to effect emancipation. For this reason Lincoln revoked the emancipation that General John C. Fremont proclaimed in Missouri at the beginning of the war. Lincoln believed that to invoke emancipation for *political* rather than for *military* reasons, as Fremont was doing, was unconstitutional.[45]

Guelzo observes that Lincoln did everything he could to keep emancipation out of the federal courts, fearing that if the federal judiciary under Roger Taney ever took up emancipation, the court would become in effect the guarantor of slavery, setting back the prospect for all future emancipation just as Dred Scott had set back the effort to prevent the expansion of slavery into the territories.[46] The fact that the Prize Cases, which essentially affirmed the legality of the Union's conduct of the war, were decided by a vote of only 5–4 in the midst of the war seems to confirm Lincoln's decision.[47]

Indeed, it was possible that even after a successful war to subdue the rebellion, a slaveholder whose property had been seized in this manner could sue successfully in federal court. "[O]nce the war emergency was over," writes Guelzo, "the federal dockets would fill up with appeals that either attacked [martial law emancipation] proclamations as unconstitutional or denied that specific cases really fell within the definitions of the proclamation."[48]

Given the failure of Union arms by the fall of 1862, the rejection of compensated emancipation by the loyal slaves states, and his concerns about the legality of martial law emancipation and the application of confiscation and contraband to escaped slaves, Lincoln decided to deal with slavery under his authority as commander in chief. Thus after Lee's invasion of Maryland was turned back at Antietam, Lincoln issued a preliminary Emancipation Proclamation on September 22 that gave the Confederates one hundred days to submit to the Union or face the prospect of immediate emancipation. It was strictly a war measure. The time had come, as he wrote to Cuthbert Bullitt, to stop waging war "with elder-stalk squirts, charged with rose water."[49]

As a war measure, emancipation struck at both the war-making potential of the Confederacy and the Southern social system. But Lincoln rejected calls by the radical Republicans to expand the scope of emancipation. While Lincoln believed that, as the Corning letter illustrated, war and rebellion "created a new constitutional sphere" within which the executive possessed "all of the war powers necessary to deal with the emergency," he rejected the idea that those powers constituted a blank check.[50]

For instance, when secretary of the treasury Salmon Chase admonished Lincoln to issue an executive order expanding the scope of the Emancipation Proclamation to those parts of Virginia and Louisiana not originally covered, Lincoln replied:

The original proclamation has no constitutional or legal justification, except as a military measure. The exemptions were made because the military necessity did not apply to the exempted localities. Nor does that necessity apply to them now any more than it did then. If I take the step must I not do so, without the argument of military necessity, and so, without any argument, except the one that I think the measure politically expedient, and morally right? Would I not thus give up all footing upon constitution or law? Would I not thus be in the boundless field of absolutism? . . .[51]

In this, as in all of his acts, he appealed to the Constitution. A war measure is applicable only during a time of war. Ending slavery for good would require a constitutional amendment.

Lincoln had to proceed with emancipation according to the dictates of prudence. Accordingly, he was denounced by the conservatives as moving too fast and by the radicals as moving too slowly. For instance, he enraged the radicals soon after the war began by reversing Fremont's emancipation proclamation in Missouri.

Second, allowing it to stand might antagonize the loyal slave states, providing them an impetus to join the Confederacy. As he continued in his letter to Orville Browning, "I think to lose Kentucky is nearly to the same as to lose the whole game. Kentucky gone, we cannot hold Missouri, nor, as I think, Maryland. These all against us, and the job on our hands is too large for us."[52]

Vigilance and Responsibility: Civil Liberties in Wartime

The most controversial element of Lincoln's war presidency is his treatment of civil liberties.[53] Even many defenders of Lincoln argue that he overstepped constitutional bounds by declaring martial laws, arbitrarily arresting civilians and trying them by military tribunal, and shutting down opposition newspapers. After the war, the Supreme Court criticized many of these measures in *Ex parte Milligan*.

The dilemma that a president faces in time of emergency was expressed by James Madison in a letter to Thomas Jefferson: "It is a melancholy reflection that liberty should be equally exposed to danger whether the government have too much or too little power." Lincoln addressed this dilemma during his speech to a special session of Congress after Fort Sumter. "Is there," he asked, "in all republics, this inherent, and fatal weakness? 'Must a government, of necessity, be too *strong* for the liberties of its own people, or too *weak* to maintain its own existence?'"[54]

Throughout the history of the American republic, there has been a tension between two virtues necessary to sustain republican government: *vigilance* and *responsibility*.[55] Vigilance is the jealousy on the part of the people that constitutes a necessary check on those who hold power, lest they abuse it. As Thomas Jefferson wrote, "it is jealousy and not confidence which prescribes limited constitutions, to bind those whom we are obliged to trust with power."[56]

But while vigilance is a necessary virtue, it may, if unchecked, lead to an extremism that incapacitates a government, preventing it from carrying out even its most necessary and legitimate purposes: for example, providing for the common defense. "Jealousy," wrote Alexander Hamilton, often infects the "noble enthusiasm for liberty" with "a spirit of narrow and illiberal distrust."[57]

Responsibility, on the other hand, is the prudential judgment necessary to moderate the excesses of political jealousy, thereby permitting limited government to fulfill its purposes. Thus in *Federalist* 23, Alexander Hamilton wrote that those responsible for the nation's defense must be granted all of the powers necessary to achieve that end.[58] Responsibility is the virtue necessary to govern and to preserve the republic from harm, both external and internal. The dangers of foreign and civil war taught Alexander Hamilton that liberty and power are not always adversaries, that indeed, the "vigor" of government is essential to the security of liberty.

Lincoln's actions as president during the Civil War reflected his agreement with this principle. Due to the unprecedented nature of the emergency created by the rebellion, Lincoln believed that he had no choice but to exercise broad executive power. Lincoln addressed the issue of civil liberties in wartime in the aforementioned letter to Erastus Corning, who had sent him the resolutions of the Albany Democratic Convention.[59] His arguments remain applicable today.

The Albany Democrats had expressed loyalty to the union but had censured the Lincoln administration for what it called unconstitutional acts, such as military arrests of civilians in the North. To the Albany Democrats' claim that they supported the use of "every constitutional and lawful measure to suppress the rebellion," Lincoln replied that he had "not knowingly employed . . . any other" in the past, nor did he intend to in the future.

The Albany Democrats invoked the safeguards and guarantees for the liberties of citizens under the Constitution, observing that they "were secured substantially to the English people after years of protracted civil war, and were adopted into our Constitution at the end of the revolution." Lincoln replied that their point would have been stronger had they said that "these safe-guards had been adopted and applied during the civil wars and during our revolution, rather than after the one and at the end of the other." "I, too," said Lincoln, "am devotedly for them after civil war, and before civil war, and at all times, 'except when, in cases of rebellion or invasion, the public safety may require' their suspension."

Lincoln then argued that those who wished to destroy the Constitution were relying on the fact that "the government would, in great degree, be restrained by the same Constitution and law from arresting their progress."

If anything, Lincoln continued, he had waited too long to implement emergency measures. "[T]horoughly imbued with a reverence for the guaranteed rights of individuals, I was slow to adopt the strong measures which by degree I have been forced to regard as being within the exceptions of the Constitution, and as indispensable to the public safety."

The core of Lincoln's argument was that the courts of justice were incompetent to handle cases arising out of a vast emergency. Suspension of habeas corpus is the constitutional provision that applies in such cases. The drafters of the Constitution, he continued, understood that there were emergency instances in which "men may be held in custody whom the courts, acting on ordinary rules would discharge." Habeas corpus does not discharge those proved to be guilty of a defined crime. The Constitution permits its suspension "that men may be arrested and held who cannot be proved to be guilty of defined crime, 'when in cases of rebellion or invasion the public safety may require it.'" This is because in times of emergency, arrests must sometimes be made not for what has been done, but to prevent things that probably would be done.

Lincoln pointed out that a number of still high-ranking Confederates, whose sentiments were then known, were in the power of the government when the rebellion broke out. Had they been seized, the rebellion would have been weaker. But none of them had committed a crime defined in law, and so would have been discharged on the basis of habeas corpus if the writ had been permitted to operate. "In view of these and similar cases, I think I shall be blamed for having made too few arrests than too many."

The Albany Democrats had called the arrests of civilians in areas where the rebellion did not exist unconstitutional. Lincoln replied that the Constitution made no such distinction. His actions, he continued, were constitutional *wherever* the public safety required them, whether to prevent the rebellion from spreading, to prevent mischievous interference with raising and supplying the armies necessary to suppress the rebellion, to restrain agitators who sought to encourage desertion—in other words, his actions were "equally constitutional at all places where they will conduce to the public safety, as against the dangers of rebellion or invasion."

The Albany Democrats criticized the arrest and trial by military tribunal of the antiwar Ohio Democratic congressman Clement Vallandigham merely for his words. But Lincoln replied that Vallandigham was encouraging desertion from the army, upon which the nation was depending to save the union. He noted that the Albany Democrats supported the suppression of the rebellion by force. But this depended on an army, and one of the biggest problems armies faced was desertion, an act so serious that it was punished by death. "Must I shoot a simple-minded soldier boy who deserts, while I must not touch a hair of a wily agitator who induces him to desert?"

Lincoln said that if he were wrong on the question of his constitutional power, his error was in believing that certain actions that were not constitutional in the absence of rebellion or invasion became constitutional when those conditions exist—in other words, "that the Constitution is not in its application in all respects the same in cases of rebellion or invasion involving the public safety, as it is in times of profound peace and public security."

As noted above, Lincoln argued that the means appropriate for an emergency are not appropriate for normal times. A sick man is given medicine that would not be good for a well one. Lincoln's argument here is quintessentially prudential.

Conclusion

Don Fehrenbacher once observed that Lincoln has been described by historians as a dictator far more than any other president.[60] This is true not only of those who criticize him, but also of those who praise him. But if Lincoln was a dictator, he was one unlike any other in history. Dictatorship is characterized by unlimited, absolute power, exercised in an arbitrary and unpredictable manner, with no regard for political legitimacy. A dictator does not go out of his way to respect legal limits as Lincoln did, despite his belief that the emergency required special measures. In addition, a dictator is not subject to the pressures of public opinion, congressional constraint, and party competition that Lincoln faced during his war presidency. Finally, a dictator does not risk an election in the midst of an emergency, especially one that he thinks he might lose.

Fortunately for Lincoln and the country, the constitutional framework of the United States made it possible for the sixteenth president to suppress the rebellion without assuming dictatorial powers. This is a tribute to the founders.

Throughout history, war has been the great destroyer of free government. It seems always to have been the case that the necessities, accidents, and passions of war undermine liberty. The forces that contributed to the collapse of free government in Germany, Russia, China, and Japan in the twentieth century are the same ones that destroyed the possibility of free government among the ancient Greeks, as catalogued by Thucydides in his history of the Peloponnesian war. The United States, in contrast, has remained free while fighting numerous wars, both major and minor, both declared and undeclared, both hot and cold, during the republic's two hundred-plus years.

This unprecedented ability of the United States to wage war while still preserving liberty is the legacy of the American founders, who created institutions that have enabled the United States to minimize the inevitable tension between the necessities of war and the requirements of free government.[61] To his everlasting credit, Lincoln understood and took advantage of these institutions during the time of greatest stress on the American polity. In doing so, he established the precedents that have guided his successors in their attempt to keep the United States both safe and free.

Notes

1. Daniel Farber, *Lincoln's Constitution* (Chicago: Univ. of Chicago Press, 2003), 1.

2. Fragment, "The Constitution and Union" [1860?], in *The Collected Works of Abraham Lincoln*, ed. Roy Basler, 9 vols. (New Brunswick, N.J.: Rutgers Univ. Press, 1953), 4:169, hereafter cited as *CWL*.

3. Proverbs 25:11 (KJV). "A word fitly spoken is like apples of gold in pictures of silver."

4. A number of writers have commented on the importance of this fragment for understanding Lincoln's actions as war president. See Herman Belz, *Lincoln and the Constitution: The Dictatorship Question Reconsidered* (Fort Wayne, Ind.: Louis A. Warren Lincoln Library and Museum, 1984), 19–20; and Walter Berns, "Constitutional Power and the Defense of Free Government," in *Terrorism: How the West Can Win*, ed. Benjamin Netanyahu, 154 (New York: Farrar, Straus, and Giroux, 1986).

5. Aristotle, *Nicomachean Ethics*, Book V.

6. Farber, *Lincoln's Constitution*.

7. "Proclamation Calling Militia and Convening Congress," April 15, 1861, *CWL*, 4:332.

8. James Buchanan, "Last Annual Address," in Edward McPherson, *The Political History of the United States during the Great Rebellion, 1860–1864*

(reprint; New York: Da Capo, 1972), 49–50. Cf. "Opinion of Attorney-General Black upon the Powers of the President," in ibid., 51–52.

9. Nicolay Memorandum of November 15, 1860, in *With Lincoln in the White House: Letters, Memoranda, and Other Writings of John C. Nicolay, 1860–1865*, ed. Michael Burlingame, 10 (Carbondale: Southern Illinois Univ. Press, 2000).

10. For the Confederate view, see Alexander Stephens, *A Constitutional View of the Late War between the States*, 2 vols. (Philadelphia: National Publishing Company, 1868); Jefferson Davis, *The Rise and Fall of the Confederate Government* (New York: D. Appleton and Company, 1881), 1:86–198; J. L. M. Curry, "Legal Justification of the South in Secession," in *Confederate Military History* (Atlanta: Confederate Publishing Company, 1899 [reprinted by the Archive Society, 1994]), 1:8–58. For the contrary view, see, Harry V. Jaffa, *A New Birth of Freedom* (Lanham, Md.: Rowman and Littlefield, 2000), especially chapter 7.

11. John C. Calhoun, "Exposition and Protest," December 19, 1828, and "The Fort Hill Address: On the Relations of the States and the Federal Government," July 26, 1831, in *Union and Liberty: The Political Philosophy of John C. Calhoun*, ed. Ross M. Lence, 311–400 (Indianapolis: Liberty Fund, 1992); Stephens, *A Constitutional View*, 1:83.

12. Nicolay memorandum of December 13, 1860, in Burlingame, ed., *With Lincoln in the White House*, 16–17.

13. Message to Congress in Special Session, July 4, 1861, in *Abraham Lincoln: His Speeches and Writings*, ed. Roy Basler, 603 (New York: Da Capo, n.d.), hereafter cited as *AL*. Since this collection is more accessible than the *CWL*, I will cite *AL* whenever possible.

14. Daniel Webster, "The Constitution Not a Compact between Sovereign States: A Reply to John C. Calhoun," February 16, 1833, *Works of Daniel Webster* (Boston: Little, Brown, 1854), 3:448–505.

15. Andrew Jackson, "Proclamation regarding Nullification," December 10, 1832, http://www.teachingamericanhistory.org/library/index.asp?document=843.

16. James Madison, "The Nullification Heresy: Letter to the *North American Review*," August 28, 1830, in *The Mind of the Founder: Sources of the Political Thought of James Madison*, ed. Marvin Meyers, 532–44 (Indianapolis: Bobbs-Merrill, 1973). Cf. James H. Read, "Madison's Response to Nullification," in *James Madison: Philosopher, Founder, and Statesman*, ed. John Vile, William Pederson, and Frank Williams, 269–83 (Athens: Ohio Univ. Press, 2008).

17. Lincoln understood the creation of the union to have occurred in 1776, not 1787. Lincoln's theory of the union is laid out in his First Inaugural Address,

March 4, 1861, and his Address to Congress in Special Session, July 4, 1861, *AL,* 582–86 and 603–6.

18. "From the Minutes of the Board of Visitors, University of Virginia, 1822–1825: Report to the President and Directors of the Literary Fund (extract)," March 4, 1825, in *Jefferson: Writings,* ed. Merrill Peterson, 479 (New York: Library of America, 1984).

19. George Washington, Letter to Congress, September 17, 1787, in *The Records of the Federal Constitution of 1787,* ed. Max Farrand, 2:667 (New Haven, Conn.: Yale Univ. Press, 1966).

20. Stephens, *A Constitutional View of the Late War between the States,* 1:520.

21. *AL,* 586–87.

22. Andrew Jackson, "Proclamation regarding Nullification," December 10, 1832, http://www.teachingamericanhistory.org/library/index.asp?document=843.

23. John Calhoun, "Speech on the Oregon Bill," June 27, 1848, in Lence, ed., *Union and Liberty,* 565–66.

24. William Freehling, *Prelude to Civil War: The Nullification Controversy in South Carolina, 1816–1836* (New York: Oxford Univ. Press, 1965); William Freehling, *The Road to Disunion: Secessionists at Bay, 1776–1854* (New York: Oxford Univ. Press, 1990); and William Freehling, *The Road to Disunion: Secessionists Triumphant, 1854–1861* (New York: Oxford Univ. Press, 2007). The attempted dissolution of the union in 1860 and 1861 was the final act in a drama that had been under way since the 1830s, only this time the blackmailers' bluff was called. In 1833, the minority threatened secession over the tariff. The majority gave in. In 1835, it threatened secession if Congress did not prohibit discussions of slavery during its own proceedings. The majority gave in and passed a "gag rule." In 1850, the minority threatened secession unless Congress forced the return of fugitive slaves without a prior jury trial. The majority agreed to pass the Fugitive Slave Act. In 1854 the minority threatened secession unless the Missouri Compromise was repealed, opening Kansas to slavery. Again, the majority acquiesced rather than see the union smashed.

But the majority could only go so far in permitting minority blackmail to override the constitutional will of the majority. At the Democratic Convention in Charleston, held in April 1860, the majority finally refused the blackmailers' demand—for a federal guarantee of slave property in all U.S. territories. The delegates from the Deep South walked out, splitting the Democratic Party and ensuring that Lincoln would be elected by a plurality.

There are two ironies here. The first is that the real "secession" was that of the South from the Democratic Party. The resulting split in the Democratic Party was instrumental in bringing about the election of Lincoln, which the South then used as the excuse for smashing the union. The second is that the South's demand at Charleston, far from having anything to do with States' rights, was instead a call for an unprecedented expansion of federal power.

25. *AL*, 608.

26. "Mayor Wood's Recommendation of Secession of New York City," http://www.teachingamericanhistory.org/library/index.asp?document=435.

27. First Inaugural, *AL*, 587.

28. Geoffrey Perret, *Lincoln's War: The Untold Story of America's Greatest President as Commander in Chief* (New York: Random House, 2004), xiii.

29. Abraham Lincoln to James Conkling, August 26, 1863, *AL*, 721.

30. Edward Corwin, *Total War and the Constitution* (New York: Knopf, 1947); and Raoul Berger, *Executive Privilege: A Constitutional Myth* (Cambridge: Harvard Univ. Press, 1974).

31. Thomas Jefferson to Caesar A. Rodney, in *Jefferson: Writings*, 1218.

32. John Locke, *Second Treatise of Civil Government*, various editions, chapter XIV: "Of Prerogative," sec. 160 (emphasis added).

33. Ibid., sec. 159 (emphasis added).

34. Thomas Jefferson to John Colvin, in *Jefferson: Writings*, 1231–1233.

35. "Message to Congress in Special Session," *AL*, 600–601.

36. Sanford Levinson, "Abraham Lincoln as Constitutionalist: The Decision to Go to War," unpublished manuscript.

37. "Proclamation Revoking General Hunter's Order of Military Emancipation of May 9, 1862," May 19, 1862, *CWL*, 5:222.

38. "Reply to Emancipation Memorial Presented by Chicago Christians of All Denominations," September 13, 1862, *CWL*, 5:421.

39. Response to a Serenade, October 19, 1864, *AL*, 761.

40. Abraham Lincoln to Erastus Corning and Others, June 12, 1863, *AL*, 705.

41. Abraham Lincoln, First Inaugural Address, March 4, 1861, *AL*, 580.

42. Ibid., 587.

43. Allen Guelzo, *Lincoln's Emancipation Proclamation: The End of Slavery in America* (New York: Simon and Schuster, 2004). On Confederate war aims, see Alexander Stephens, Speech at Savannah, March 21, 1861, http://www.teachingamericanhistory.org/library/index.asp?document=76. Cf. Joseph Harsh, *Confederate Tide Rising: Robert E. Lee and the Making of Southern Strategy, 1861–1862* (Kent, Ohio: Kent State Univ. Press, 1998), 5–10.

44. Guelzo, *Lincoln's Emancipation Proclamation*, 29–59.

45. To Orville Browning, September 22, 1861, *AL*, 613.

46. Guelzo, *Lincoln's Emancipation Proclamation*, passim.

47. For an excellent and complete account of Lincoln and the Supreme Court in wartime, see Brian McGinty, *Lincoln and the Court* (Cambridge: Harvard Univ. Press, 2008).

48. Guelzo, *Lincoln's Emancipation Proclamation,* 54.

49. Abraham Lincoln to Cuthbert Bullitt, July 28, 1862, *AL,* 650.

50. Guelzo, *Lincoln's Emancipation Proclamation,* 198.

51. Abraham Lincoln to Salmon P. Chase, September 2, 1863, *CWL,* 6:428–429.

52. Abraham Lincoln to Orville Browning, September 22, 1861, *AL,* 614.

53. In addition to Farber, chapters 7 and 8, see, for example, J. G. Randall, *Constitutional Problems under Lincoln,* rev. ed. (Urbana: Univ. of Illinois Press, 1951); Paul Finkelman, "Civil Liberties and the Civil War: The Great Emancipator as Civil Libertarian," *Michigan Law Review* 91, no. 6 (1993): 1353–1365; Mark E. Neely Jr., *The Fate of Liberty: Abraham Lincoln and Civil Liberties* (Oxford: Oxford Univ. Press, 1991); and the Hon. Frank J. Williams, "Abraham Lincoln, Civil Liberties, and the Corning Letter," *Roger Williams University Law Review* 5, no. 2 (spring 2000): 319–38.

54. James Madison to Thomas Jefferson, October 17, 1788; Lincoln, "Message to Congress in Special Session," *AL,* 598.

55. See Karl-Friedrich Walling, *Republican Empire: Alexander Hamilton on War and Free Government* (Lawrence: Univ. Press of Kansas, 1999), 6–12.

56. Draft of the Kentucky Resolution, October 1798, *Jefferson: Writings,* 454.

57. Alexander Hamilton to James Duane, September 3, 1780, in *The Papers of Alexander Hamilton,* ed. Harold G. Syrett and Jacob E. Cooke, 2:404 (New York: Columbia Univ. Press, 1961).

58. *Federalist,* No. 23, 149–51.

59. *AL,* 699–708.

60. Don Fehrenbacher, "Lincoln and the Constitution," in *The Public and Private Lincoln: Contemporary Perspectives,* ed. Cullom Davis, 127 (Carbondale: Southern Illinois Univ. Press, 1979).

61. On this topic, see Walling, *Republican Empire.*

President Lincoln

The International Lawyer

William D. Pederson

Abraham Lincoln's innate ability and tenacity were consistently underestimated prior to his election as president and even while he served. Similarly, most historians have significantly underestimated Lincoln's contributions to foreign affairs and international law during the Civil War.[1] The flawed assumption that Lincoln could not possibly possess the background knowledge necessary for foreign affairs or international law was based partly on the fact that he was a self-taught frontier lawyer who never left the continental United States. To those who considered themselves socially and educationally superior to Lincoln, his very appearance confirmed their negative conclusions. Contrary to those judgments, this chapter argues that the legacy of America's sixteenth president in international law is commensurate with his other epic accomplishments—preserver of the union, the Great Emancipator, and the magnanimous reconciler. Indeed, his keen political instincts honed through legal training enabled Lincoln to listen to others who had the benefit of foreign travel and broader experiences, to glean lessons from those perspectives, and ultimately to achieve a unique legacy for the United States in international law.

For purposes of analysis and discussion, the chapter is organized into three sections. First is a presentation of Lincoln's formal legal advisers, consisting primarily of a trio of cabinet members, Secretary of State William Seward, Secretary of War Edwin Stanton, and Attorney General Edward Bates. Neither Lincoln nor his inner circle legal team succumbed to the danger of group think. Indeed, they consulted others, as the next section of the chapter shows. The second section discusses several incidents involving international law and Lincoln's deft political maneuvering that prevented

European powers from declaring war on the United States and recognizing the Confederacy. Moreover, the Lincoln administration forged a new precedent in international humanitarian law during armed conflict. The final portion of the chapter offers some tentative conclusions regarding Lincoln's behavior as an international lawyer.

Lincoln's Legal Advisers

By the twentieth century, American presidents had the luxury of an institutionalized executive branch of government. Staff included an international law adviser with a separate law library housed in the Department of State. In addition, legal teams from the departments of defense and justice have been available to modern presidents. Bureaucratic structure notwithstanding, presidents still have to choose between adherence to a narrow or a broad interpretation of customary international and treaty law. With the president resides the burden of finding legal and political interpretations that, in his judgment, adhere to the spirit and practice of America's democratic traditions.

Ironically, research suggests that presidents with the most legal experience tend to become rigid or passive, characteristic of the worst chief executives. In contrast, those with the least formal legal experience—even none at all—tend to possess active and flexible personalities, characteristic of America's greatest presidents.[2] The major exception to this pattern of the best presidents having the least legal experience is Lincoln. But, significantly, Lincoln also ran for political office earlier in his career than any of the other lawyer-presidents. He sought elective office even before he was admitted to the bar. This behavior suggests that Lincoln had already recognized his calling to the political arena, where he could work on public policy issues rather than engage in the practice of law. Years later, when he was presented with the opportunity to hold one of the best lawyer positions in the corporate world, he unhesitatingly turned it down in favor of the riskier road of running for president. Lincoln spent most of his adult life seeking political office, undaunted by frequent elective defeats. Like many politicians, he used the law as a springboard to politics.

Lincoln was a self-taught lawyer whose practice focused on state and local matters, but he also was aware of international law.[3] Even though he emerged from the frontier, Lincoln was surprisingly well versed about world events, collecting his information from newspapers he read avidly and individuals of diverse backgrounds that he engaged in conversations. His trait of seeking to hear various perspectives, especially from those with conflicting views, served him well as president. His own cabinet, members of the Congress, and the public all provided him with opinions to consider. Lincoln set a prudent precedent for subsequent historic-minded presidents, like John F. Kennedy, who in tragic irony was assassinated one hundred years after Lincoln. Among the many parallels that can be drawn between Lincoln and Kennedy, who carried one of Lincoln's lesser known quotes in his pocket, was the astute leadership tactic of listening to voices beyond formal advisers. Throughout the protracted Civil War, Lincoln practiced the wisdom of seeking opinions beyond those of his cabinet. A century later, when faced with the escalating Cuban Missile Crisis, Kennedy behaved similarly and effectively by eliciting and weighing diverse perspectives that informed his own judgment.[4] Kennedy's mature judgment in the Cuban Missile Crisis contrasts sharply with the Bay of Pigs fiasco earlier in his presidency. Just as Lincoln had done during the Civil War, Kennedy, during the Cuban Missile Crisis, sought then mulled wisdom from often competing points of view. Their leadership suggests that these presidents understood better than their respective political rivals and critics the depth of the democratic process intrinsic in America's historic experiment.

William H. Seward (1801–1872), as the secretary of state in Lincoln's cabinet, also served as his primary international law adviser. Admitted to the bar in 1822, fourteen years before Lincoln began his own law practice, Seward had traveled abroad extensively in Europe, the Middle East, and Canada. Before the Civil War, he had met regularly with the royalty and political leaders of Great Britain, Italy, and Belgium, as well as with Pope Pius IX, all of whom shared Seward's view that he would become the next president of the United States, rather than dark-horse hopeful Abraham Lincoln.[5] Seward made two tactical blunders. He underestimated Lincoln. And he overidentified with Europe, advocating that the United States build a European-model empire by acquiring colonies. After he was appointed secretary of state, his imperialistic values initially undercut his usefulness to Lincoln. On April 1, 1861, he suggested that the United States start a war with France or Spain as a means of rekindling the South's patriotism for the union.[6] Put off by Seward's advice, Lincoln turned to Charles Sumner

(1811–1874), the chairman of the Senate's foreign relations committee. The chairmanship was a natural fit for the Harvard-educated Sumner, who had traveled abroad, was fluent in several languages, and knew international law, eventually teaching international law at Harvard for a brief period. His law degree had been guided by the great Supreme Court justice Joseph Story. Sumner provided counterbalance to Seward's initially more aggressive approach. Over time, Seward moderated his views and became Lincoln's closest cabinet secretary, a relationship fostered in part by their mutually affable personalities. However, Lincoln continued to consult Sumner.

Complementing Seward was Edwin M. Stanton (1814–1869), Lincoln's second secretary of war who briefly had been James Buchanan's assertive last attorney general. He then became a legal adviser to Simon Cameron, Lincoln's short-term first secretary of war. When Stanton was appointed as secretary of war on January 13, 1862, it was with the backing of cabinet rivals Seward and Secretary of the Treasury Salmon P. Chase. Each saw Stanton as a potential ally.

Stanton had the most extensive legal experience among Lincoln's formal advisers, having practiced before the U.S. Supreme Court. His stern personality, shaped by a series of personal tragedies, acted as a foil to Seward's affable disposition. A workaholic and loyal pragmatist, Stanton was determined to win the war. He was ably assisted by Joseph Holt, who Lincoln made the first judge advocate of the army on September 3, 1862. Holt had served with Stanton at the end of the James Buchanan administration. The Kentucky-born Holt came to work closely with both Stanton and Lincoln. In 1864, the president offered Holt the position of attorney general, which he turned down, instead remaining as judge advocate general until 1875. Stanton's team also included William Whiting, a solicitor, whose *The War Powers of the President* (1862) influenced the administration.

Lincoln's chief constitutional lawyer was his attorney general, Edward Bates (1793–1869). Like Seward, Bates was first licensed to practice law at age twenty-one. In 1821 he became the first attorney general of the new state of Missouri. The oldest and most conservative member of Lincoln's legal team, Bates was loyal to Lincoln. He held the distinction of being able to separate his personal and political views. Bates could back policies even if personally opposed to them.

Compared to members of his legal team, Lincoln had substantially less experience in international law and had not traveled abroad. Still, he often demonstrated prudence superior to theirs in the international arena. He understood that the American Civil War was fundamentally a constitutional crisis involving issues of both constitutional and international law. He relied on both his legal and political judgment in approaching the thorny constitutional and international issues.

Civil War Incidents Involving International Law

Lincoln was Stanton's senior by five years, although both had become lawyers in 1836. Stanton had moved from Ohio to Pennsylvania, then to the nation's capital, to enlarge his legal practice and argue cases before the U.S. Supreme Court. Lincoln remained on the frontier to practice law. As he gained experience in the law, he also honed his political skills and versed himself in world affairs. At the core of his political philosophy was his understanding of the unique model of self-government for the world that was embodied in American freedom. For example, in the early 1850s Lincoln supported Hungary's efforts to achieve its independence from Austria.[7] Hungarians a century later paid tribute to Lincoln's moral support by having its new generation of freedom fighters recite the Gettysburg Address over Free Hungarian Radio at the end of the 1956 Hungarian uprising against Soviet domination.[8] Closer to home, during his single congressional term Lincoln condemned not only "filibustering expeditions" in Latin America as international law violations but also President James Polk's position in the United States–Mexican War of 1846–1848.[9]

Lincoln's democratic leadership was recognized by leaders from other countries. Benito Juárez seemed to intuitively understand the situation confronting Lincoln during the American Civil War. Others throughout Latin America appreciated Lincoln's behavior. South America became the first and only other continent outside of North America to name two of its cities after him, precursors to a host of other tributes to him, from schools to stamps to streets to statues.[10] Lincoln understood that the world watched to see if America's great experiment in democratic government would survive the bloody civil war. They saw that not only did it survive but that it also eventually inspired democratic movements throughout the world.

At the beginning of his presidency, Lincoln's priority was to preserve the union. He realized that a critical element in the preservation of the union was preventing foreign governments from recognizing the Confederacy. Draw-ing on his legal and political skills, Lincoln framed the conflict between the North and South as a domestic insurrection within the domain of America's sovereignty rather than as a rebellion that could open the door to European involvement under international law.

Lincoln's first major decision was whether to acquiesce to demands from Confederate leaders that the federal garrison at Fort Sumter, located in South Carolina's Charleston harbor, already under siege and running out of supplies, surrender and turn the fort over to them. The international implications were significant. Surrender of Fort Sumter would imply de facto if not de jure recognition of the Confederacy under customary international law. On March 15, following the early advice of Winfield Scott, the general in chief of the U.S. Army, a majority of the cabinet, led by Secretary Seward, recommended the fort's surrender. Acting without authorization from his superior, Seward inappropriately informed Confederate commissioners that the federal contingent at the fort would withdraw.

By the end of March, in contrast to his cabinet's rush to surrender, Lin-coln had reached the opposite conclusion. His decision had two results: it reminded his secretary of state that his role was subordinate to the president and, more importantly, it laid responsibility for starting the war directly at the feet of firebrand Confederates, which served to unite the North.[11] By the time Lincoln reached his conclusion, the fickle cabinet majority had aban-doned its March 15 stance in favor of Lincoln's more deliberate policy. On April 6, 1861, Lincoln notified the governor of South Carolina that he was sending food only for the federal troops, without additional men, weapons, or ammunition. Lincoln's action put the onus for starting a war back on the Confederates, whose artillery surrounded the harbor. When the rebels opened fire on the supply ships on April 12, it provided clear evidence to the world that Confederate aggression started the war. The international issues confronting Lincoln would soon become more complex.

The Blockade. The first major question of the Lincoln administration involving immediate international law issues concerned whether to institute a blockade or mere closure of the Southern seaports. The cabinet continued to be divided over the issue. Navy secretary Gideon Welles advocated only closure of the seaports of the seceded areas to international commerce. He did not think a blockade was justified in international law. If the ports were closed and a foreign merchant ship disregarded the closure, then the ship would be subject to seizure and its officers could face prosecution for violating the customs laws of the United States. The major drawback of this approach was that under international law the United States could only enforce its customs laws within its territory and waters extending three miles off the coast. This presented the possibility of a foreign steam-powered merchant ship entering and escaping a closed port before a U.S. revenue cutter or warship could intercept it. Once beyond the three-mile limit the merchant ship would be back on the high seas, making it immune from the enforcement of U.S. customs laws. An attempt to enforce the closure of a port by stopping British and French merchant ships in international waters would have been a violation of international law and an invitation to war.

In contrast, declaring a blockade of the Southern coast would allow the U.S. Navy to stop neutral merchant ships on the high seas, inspect their papers and cargoes, and then seize any ship that appeared bound to or from a blockaded port. Additionally, the declaration of a naval blockade was a war measure in international law. It would admit to other nations that the United States was engaged in a civil war rather than dealing with a few citizens who refused to pay taxes. Moreover, it conceded that the insurgents exercised control over the blockaded ports and coasts. This, in effect, recognized the Confederacy as a belligerent by the U.S. government, permitting Britain, France, and other neutral powers to do the same. While short of acknowledging the independence of the insurgents, it did accord them with certain rights and privileges, such as buying goods and obtaining loans, and often was a step toward recognizing full independence.

Given these two options, Lincoln chose a naval blockade as the more effective measure from a military viewpoint, even though it accorded a limited measure of international legitimacy to the enemy. Secretary of State Seward and Attorney General Bates supported the president's decision. The decision engendered further controversy since Lincoln issued the blockade proclamation while Congress was out of session; he considered it as part of his implied presidential war power. With hardly more than fifty ships, Secretary Welles immediately implemented the blockade of ten major Southern ports along the 3,500 miles of coastline. Congress subsequently ratified Lincoln's emergency action, and in 1863 the U.S. Supreme Court upheld his action in a 5–4 decision (the Prize Cases). As expected, Great Britain declared neutrality, becoming the main source of military supplies for the Confederacy without having to go to war. Lincoln, however, personally never accepted the view that the Confederacy constituted a legal belligerent, for he believed secession was not constitutionally possible.

The Trent Affair. This incident became the most serious diplomatic crisis to arise during the Civil War, threatening to bring the British to war against the United States. It began on November 8, 1861, when Captain Charles Wilkes of the USS *San Jacinto,* acting without orders, seized two Confederate envoys and their secretaries who were aboard the *Trent,* which was bound for England and France. Wilkes removed the men, then released the *Trent* to continue on its voyage. He argued that international law allowed the seizure of a neutral merchant ship carrying enemy dispatches and that the envoys were the equivalent of enemy dispatches because of the information and instructions they carried in their minds. Only Gideon Welles commended Wilkes.

The problem with Wilkes's position was that it in fact violated customary international law. His action would have been legal only if he had placed a prize crew aboard the *Trent* and sailed it to the nearest U.S. district court to adjudicate whether the ship had been taken lawfully as a prize of a war. If the court agreed with Wilkes's envoys-as-dispatches rationale, then the ship would have been sold at auction and the proceeds divided between the U.S. government and the crew of the *San Jacinto.*

Ironically, this course of action, which would have been more costly to the British owners of the *Trent* than Wilkes's action, would have placed the British government in a weaker legal position. The British government traditionally had taken an expansive view of the rights and powers of a blockading fleet and may have eventually conceded that the Union had the right to retain the Confederate envoys had proper procedures been followed.

American public opinion supported the seizure of the Confederate envoys, but Attorney General Bates argued privately that it violated international laws. Lincoln wanted to avoid both war with England and the appearance of backing down, so initially he favored arbitration by a neutral power. His position was consistent with the lessons he had learned from his domestic law practice years earlier that led him to favor negotiated settlements.[12] Lincoln's minister to the Court of Saint James, Charles Francis Adams, provided a solution to Secretary of State Seward by convincing him that in giving up the envoys the United States would be supporting its traditional view of freedom of the seas. The president and the British government found this resolution acceptable by the end of December 1861.

International Arbitration. After the Civil War, the United States settled the famous *Alabama Claims* through arbitration, a centuries-old process whose modern usage began with this settlement. By late 1870, the British and American governments agreed to set up a joint high commission to resolve the issues. Signed on May 8, 1871, the Treaty of Washington included a procedure for resolving the *Alabama Claims.* In a sense, Lincoln's international legacy from the *Trent* affair prevailed. President Ulysses Grant's secretary of state, Hamilton Fish, persuaded him to appoint Charles Francis Adams as the American member of the five-nation international Tribune of Arbitration convened in Geneva in December 1871. The next fall the tribunal awarded the United States $15 million compensation for direct damages, which the British promptly paid.[13]

The Emancipation Proclamation. By mid-1862, Lincoln was redefining the scope of presidential authority consistent with his expanding view of it. He signed the Republican legislation that helped to emancipate not only the South but also the entire nation. This effectively enlarged the middle class by means of three of the most important pieces of legislation ever to pass the Congress: the Land Grant College Act, the Homestead Act, and the Pacific Railway Act. He signed this trio of transforming measures in 1862, overturning the precedent of his Democratic predecessor, who had declined to approve them. Enactment of these laws positioned the federal government to play a major role in higher education, agricultural policy, and economic development. Through these legislative measures, the Republican Party and its president were effectively emancipating an entire social class.

Lincoln next tackled slavery by issuing the Emancipation Proclamation as a presidential war measure. As noted earlier, William Whiting, who served in Stanton's War Department, was author of *The War Powers of the President,* which had argued that as commander in chief the president had the power to emancipate slaves in the South. By early summer 1862, Lincoln had drafted such a proclamation.

In his public letter of August 26, 1863, written to his old friend James C. Conkling, Lincoln explicitly linked the proclamation to his understanding of the international law of war:

You dislike the emancipation proclamation; and, perhaps would have it retracted. You say it is unconstitutional—I think differently. I think the constitution invests its commander-in-chief, with the law of war, in time of war. The most that can be said, if so much, is, that slaves are property. Is there—has there ever been—any question that by the law of war, property, both of enemies and friends, may be taken when needed? And is it not needed whenever it helps us, or hurts the enemy? Armies, the world over, destroy enemies' property when they can not use it; and even destroy their own to keep it from the enemy. Civilized belligerents do all in their power to help themselves or hurt the enemy, except a few things as barbarous or cruel. Among the exceptions are the massacre of vanquished foes, and non-combatants, male and female.[14]

As often noted, the proclamation was limited to areas where the federal government lacked control, but it sent an unambiguous message to slaves, the Confederate government, and the world: that the Civil War now had dual purposes. It was being fought not only to preserve the nation but also to end slavery. Lincoln heeded Seward's advice to wait until after a Union military victory to issue the Emancipation Proclamation. Appropriately, that victory at Antietam occurred on Constitution Day in 1862. On September 22, Lincoln issued the preliminary Emancipation Proclamation that authorized enlistment of black troops immediately. Issuance of the final Emancipation Proclamation came on January 1, 1863, underscoring the symbolism of new beginnings.

The document itself contained narrowly constructed language, designed to pass the constitutional test that would inevitably come, and British leaders of the day dismissed it outright. However, the spirit of the Emancipation Proclamation resonated with individuals around the world. Lincoln had aligned the United States with freedom, undercutting any hope that Europe's ruling elite would recognize the Confederacy.[15] At once, Lincoln managed to reconcile America's Constitution—the nation's practices—with the Declaration of Independence—its promises. The world's great experiment in democracy was put solidly on the side of human rights in international law. Lincoln would soon make yet another presidential decision that would return the United States to the forefront of international law.

The Lieber Code. Respect for Lincoln's legal skill as a self-taught lawyer increases with appreciation of an often overlooked fact: his administration pioneered humanitarian protections during armed conflict. Lincoln personally sought insights and perspectives from others, and his administration similarly consulted academics. This practice is best illustrated by the outcome of his administration's collaboration with Francis Lieber (1800–1872), which produced the administration's most enduring legacy in international law. Lieber, a German immigrant who arrived in the United States in 1827, was the most important political scientist between the time of James Madison and the late nineteenth century. After teaching in 1835 at South Carolina College in Charleston, ironically the home of Fort Sumter, he moved to Columbia College in New York in 1857. In June 1861 he presented Lincoln with an honorary L.L.D. degree on behalf of Columbia College. He then developed ties with Attorney General Bates. He became an unofficial adviser for Bates as well as Senator Charles Sumner, and the Union army.[16] But Lieber's greatest influence was on Henry W. Halleck, the general who eventually became general in chief of the Union army and who was also the author of a volume on international law that dealt primarily with the laws of war. By late 1862, Halleck had appointed Lieber to a special board created by the War Department to review the rules of war. The only civilian board member, Lieber was assigned to draft a code of rules of land warfare. By May 1863 the revised draft was issued with Lincoln's approval as General Orders No. 100 and entitled "Instructions for the Government of Armies of the United States in the Field." Though Lincoln did not draft the Code, Lieber had made it consistent with Lincoln's jurisprudence by incorporating in it the philosophy of the Emancipation Proclamation and the natural law found in the Declaration of Independence. It was the first code of law of land warfare contained in international law. It became the basis for the revised code of laws of war at The Hague Conventions of 1899 and 1907 as well as the later Geneva Conventions of 1929 and 1949.

Lieber's motivation for this work was in part personal since he had three sons in the Civil War, two in the Union army and one in the Confederate. His oldest son, the Confederate, was killed at the battle of Williamsburg; another son lost an arm from a battle injury.[17] The development of a humanitarian code of war conduct under Lincoln's authority solidified the sixteenth president's reputation as the modern model of the classical magnanimous leader.[18] The concern of the Great Emancipator extended to those who fought in armed conflicts.

St. Albans Raid of 1864. Issues related to aspects of international law continued throughout the Civil War. On October 18, 1864, twenty Confederates robbed three banks in St. Albans, a town of five thousand located in northern Vermont, twenty-five miles south of the Canadian border. After killing several residents and attempting to burn St. Albans, they returned to their base in Canada. General John A. Dix, a New York Democrat and commander of the Military District of the East, authorized Union troops in Burlington, Vermont, to pursue the criminals and destroy them, even if forced to enter British Canada to accomplish their mission. Canadian authorities captured a dozen of the raiders, but they were released by a Canadian magistrate. Ignoring Canadian sovereignty, Dix then authorized the troops to capture the wanted men in Canada and bring them back to the United States for trial. Lincoln, who by 1864 had come to value Seward's advice, countermanded General Dix's order to pursue the Confederate band in Canada, then braced for negative editorials in newspapers that favored Dix's aggressive actions.[19] In doing so, the Lincoln administration had again averted another potential military conflict with the British.

Conclusions

An often overlooked facet of Lincoln's leadership was his skill at seamlessly incorporating his understanding of both the law and politics into his executive behavior. An examination of his de facto role as an international lawyer reveals complete integration of Lincoln's lawyer-president strengths. Despite being self-taught using Blackstone, Lincoln's consummate political acumen is demonstrated by the way he handled both the South and the sympathetic European elitists who identified more with the South than the North. His self-confidence, along with his intuitive understanding of human nature, allowed him to engage others whose greater experience and expertise in international law transcended his own frontier background. This unique combination of strengths accounted for President Lincoln's handling of domestic as well as international relations with aplomb that surprised not only the average American but also international leaders, who, at least initially, looked askance at the frontier president with credentials and manners inferior to their own.

Lincoln's adept political maneuvering led to the firebrands in the South beginning the Civil War. Using similar techniques, he let his cabinet debate international legal issues while he consulted with others, especially Senator Sumner, as a check on the cabinet's recommendations. His cabinet came to recognize the wisdom of Lincoln's approach and then emulated it by seeking outside advice, especially from Francis Lieber.

Lincoln's blockade of the South's ports rather than closure amounted to a secondary blockade against the European powers' impulse to recognize the Confederacy, with which they sympathized. Lincoln accomplished his immediate war goals while he sought competent Union military leaders for the battlefield. In the process, he emerged as the Great Emancipator and his administration set a precedent in international humanitarian law during armed conflict that later became the basis for the twentieth-century Hague and Geneva conventions. Lincoln's "perfect pitch" in resolving the pervasive constitutional issues of the Civil War has led at least one legal scholar to rank Lincoln among the greatest lawyers in American history, second only to John Marshall.[20] After examining his considerable success in the field of international law, Lincoln could easily be ranked also as the greatest international lawyer ever to serve as president of the United States.

Notes

1. For example, specialized reference works contain no references to either international law or Francis Lieber, the political scientist who contributed the most to the Lincoln administration in this area. See Mark E. Neely Jr., *The Abraham Lincoln Encyclopedia* (New York: McGraw-Hill, 1982), and Paul Finkelman and Martin Hershock, eds., *The Political Lincoln: An Encyclopedia* (Washington, D.C.: CQ Press, 2009).

2. Thomas M. Green and William D. Pederson, "The Behavior of Lawyer-Presidents," in *The "Barberian" Presidency,* ed. William D. Pederson, 153–67 (New York: Lang, 1989).

3. Jay Monaghan, *Diplomat in Carpet Slippers* (Indianapolis: Bobbs-Merrill, 1945), 121.

4. Michael Dobbs, *One Minute to Midnight* (New York: Knopf, 2008), 14, 340.

5. Doris Kearns Goodwin, *Team of Rivals* (New York: Simon and Schuster, 2005), 213.

6. Ibid, 342.

7. Roy P. Basler, ed., *Collected Works of Abraham Lincoln* (New Brunswick, N.J.: Rutgers Univ. Press, 1953), 2:115; Richard Carwardine, "Abraham Lincoln in the United States and the World," *BBC Knowledge,* February 2009, 33.

8. Harry V. Jaffa, *A New Birth of Freedom* (Lanham, Md.: Rowman and Littlefield, 2000), 78.

9. Robert E. May, "A Different Destiny," *Lincoln Lore* (fall 2007): 15.

10. William D. Pederson, "Lincoln's Legacy in Mexico, Central America, and the Caribbean," German Historical Institute, Washington, D.C., October 6, 2007.

11. James M. McPherson, *Abraham Lincoln* (New York: Oxford Univ. Press, 2009), 31–33.

12. Brian Dirck, *Lincoln the Lawyer* (Urbana: Univ. of Illinois Press, 2007), 160–61.

13. Dean B. Mahin, *One War at a Time* (Washington, D.C.: Brassey's, 1999), 315.

14. William E. Gienapp, ed., *This Fiery Trial* (New York: Oxford Univ. Press, 2002), 177.

15. Mahin, *One War at a Time*, 286–300.

16. Frank Freidel, *Francis Lieber* (Baton Rouge: Louisiana State Univ. Press, 1947), 307–9.

17. Ibid., 324–32.

18. William D. Pederson, "Amnesty and Presidential Behavior," in *The "Barberian" Presidency,* ed. William D. Pederson, 113–27 (New York: Peter Lang, 1989).

19. Mahin, *One War at a Time*, 246–60.

20. Bernard Schwartz, *A Book of Legal Lists* (New York: Oxford Univ. Press, 1997), 221–23.

Contributors

Roger Billings came to the Salmon P. Chase College of Law of Northern Kentucky University in 1972 after working seven years for a New York City publishing company, Charles Scribner's Sons. He received his A.B. from Wabash College and his J.D. from the University of Akron. He has written four books for practitioners, *Prepaid Legal Services*; *Handling Automobile Warranty and Repossession Cases*; *Floor Planning, Financing and Leasing in the Automobile Industry*; and *Handling Business Transactions in the Common Market and Eastern Europe*. Since 2004, when he was designated Fulbright Distinguished Professor at the University of Salzburg, Austria, he has returned each year to Salzburg as a visiting professor teaching international trade law. Professor Billings writes articles and speaks about Abraham Lincoln, specializing in Lincoln's legal career.

Brian Dirck is professor of history at Anderson University in Anderson, Indiana. He received his Ph.D. in American history from the University of Kansas, specializing in American legal and constitutional history and the Civil War era. He has written numerous books and articles on Abraham Lincoln and the Civil War, most recently *Lincoln the Lawyer,* which was awarded the Benjamin Barondess Award from the New York Civil War Roundtable for the best book on Lincoln in 2007. He is currently working on a study of Lincoln and race, to be published sometime in 2011.

Billie J. Ellis Jr. is a partner in the law firm of Locke Lord Bissell & Liddell LLP in the firm's Dallas, Texas, office. His practice consists of real estate, private equity, and finance. He has chaired various state and national bar committee groups. He is a frequent writer and speaker on Abraham Lincoln and his legal career. Mr. Ellis is currently working on a course for law students on the history of the American law firm. He received his undergraduate degree in history at the University of Texas at Austin, his M.B.A. at Southern Methodist University, and his J.D. from the University of Houston Law Center.

William T. Ellis received his master's degree in theological studies, concentrating in religion, ethics, and politics, at Harvard Divinity School in 2010. He received his B.A. from Kenyon College in 2005, *cum laude,* with department honors in philosophy. He is now studying law at the University of Texas at Austin.

Harold Holzer, who served nine years as cochairman of the Abraham Lincoln Bicentennial Commission, is the author, coauthor, or editor of thirty-six books on Lincoln and the political culture of the Civil War. He has also lectured widely, written some 440 articles in popular and scholarly journals, published dozens of monographs, and contributed chapters to dozens of additional books. Among his awards are four Barondess/Lincoln honors, a second-place Lincoln Prize, and awards of distinction from Lincoln groups throughout the nation. In 2008 he won the National Humanities Medal from the president of the United States. Holzer, who lives in Rye, New York, currently serves as vice chair of the Lincoln Forum.

John A. Lupton is the director of history programs with the Illinois Supreme Court Historic Preservation Commission. Previously, he worked for nearly twenty years on the Lincoln Legal Papers and Papers of Abraham Lincoln projects. Lupton received his bachelor's degree in history from Southern Illinois University at Carbondale and his master's degree in history from the University of Illinois, Springfield. He has published dozens of articles and chapters on Lincoln's law practice and antebellum legal history and was an assistant editor in the publication of *The Papers of Abraham Lincoln: Legal Documents and Cases* in 2008 and of *The Law Practice of Abraham Lincoln: Complete Documentary Edition* in 2000 on DVD and in 2008 on the Internet. Lupton also specializes in Lincoln's handwriting and has appeared in several television programs to authenticate Lincoln documents.

Mackubin Thomas Owens is an associate dean of academics and professor of national security affairs at the U.S. Naval War College in Newport, Rhode Island, and editor of *Orbis,* the journal of the Foreign Policy Research Institute (FPRI) in Philadelphia. He is a Marine Corps infantry veteran of Vietnam, where he served in 1968–1969. He is the author of a 2009 FPRI monograph on Lincoln as war president, titled "Abraham Lincoln: Leadership and Democratic Statesmanship in Wartime."

William D. Pederson is the American Studies Endowed Chair and director of the International Lincoln Center at Louisiana State University in Shreveport. He is the editor and author of many books on the American presidency and hosts the Center's triennial presidential conference series and annual Abraham Lincoln lecture series.

Christopher A. Schnell earned his master of arts degree in public history from the University of Illinois at Springfield in 1993. Schnell spent the next seventeen years working for the Lincoln Legal Papers and its successor project, the Papers of Abraham Lincoln, the final eleven as an assistant editor. During his tenure, Schnell helped to publish *The Law Practice of Abraham Lincoln: Complete Documentary Edition*, DVD-ROM (2000), and *The Papers of Abraham Lincoln: Legal Documents and Cases* (2008). He also published and presented several papers about Lincoln's law practice. Schnell is currently a student in the American history Ph.D. program at Saint Louis University.

Mark E. Steiner is professor of law at South Texas College of Law, where he teaches American legal history, consumer transactions, torts, and Internet legal research. Steiner is the author of *An Honest Calling: The Law Practice of Abraham Lincoln,* which was named among the "Best of the Best" for 2007 by the Association of American University Presses and given a superior achievement award by the Illinois Historical Society. He received both his Ph.D. in history and his J.D. from the University of Houston. In 2005, he taught at National Taiwan University as a Fulbright Scholar. In spring 2011, he will teach as a Fulbright Scholar at the University of Latvia. He is a former associate editor of the Lincoln Legal Papers.

Frank J. Williams is the retired chief justice of the Supreme Court of Rhode Island. He is the author or editor of over fourteen books, he has contributed chapters to several others, and has lectured on the subject throughout the country. At the same time, he has amassed an unsurpassed private library and archive that ranks among the nation's largest and finest Lincoln collections. In 2000, the chief justice was appointed to the U.S. Abraham Lincoln Bicentennial Commission created by Congress to commemorate the two hundredth birthday of Abraham Lincoln in 2009. Since 1996, Chief Justice Williams has served as founding chairman of the Lincoln Forum, a national assembly of Lincoln and Civil War devotees. For nine years he served as president of the Abraham Lincoln Association and for fourteen years as president of the Lincoln Group of Boston. He is currently at work on an annotated bibliography of all the Lincoln titles published since 1865. His book of essays, *Judging Lincoln*, was published by Southern Illinois University Press in 2002. He, with Harold Holzer and Edna Greene Medford, has written *The Emancipation Proclamation: Three Views, Social, Political, Iconographic*, just published by Louisiana State University Press. His *Lincoln Lessons*, with William D. Pederson (SIU Press, 2010), received an Award of Excellence from the Illinois State Historical Society. He also serves as literary editor of the *Lincoln Herald*, where his "Lincolniana" appears.

Index